# Coves of Departure

# Coves of Departure

Field Notes from the Sea of Cortez

*John Seibert Farnsworth*

Comstock Publishing Associates
*an imprint of*
Cornell University Press
Ithaca and London

First published 2018 by Cornell University Press

Printed in the United States of America

Library of Congress Cataloging-in-Publication Data

Names: Farnsworth, John Seibert, author.
Title: Coves of departure : field notes from the Sea of Cortez / John Seibert Farnsworth.
Description: Ithaca [New York] : Comstock Publishing Associates, an imprint of Cornell University Press, 2018. | Includes bibliographical references.
Identifiers: LCCN 2018021682 (print) | LCCN 2018022083 (ebook) | ISBN 9781501730191 (pdf) | ISBN 9781501730207 (epub/mobi) | ISBN 9781501730184 | ISBN 9781501730184 (pbk. ; alk. paper)
Subjects: LCSH: Natural history—Mexico—Baja California (Peninsula) | Natural history—Mexico—California, Gulf of. | Farnsworth, John Seibert—Travel—Mexico—Baja California (Peninsula) | Farnsworth, John Seibert—Travel—Mexico—California, Gulf of. | Baja California (Mexico : Peninsula)—Description and travel. | California, Gulf of (Mexico)—Description and travel.
Classification: LCC QH107 (ebook) | LCC QH107 .F37 2018 (print) | DDC 508.72/23—dc23
LC record available at https://lccn.loc.gov/2018021682

Dedicated to Carol

Were it not for my field notes I should probably find it difficult to avoid confusing one island with another, one bay with another, and even one expedition with another.

**Joseph Wood Krutch,** *The Forgotten Peninsula: A Naturalist in Baja California,* 1961

# Contents

Acknowledgments xi

Headwinds 1

1. Vernal Equinox 9

2. Night Life 21

3. Transect in the Sierra de la Laguna 31

4. To the Island 43

First Interlude: August in Bahía de los Angeles 59

5. Same Beach, Different Expedition 97

6. Sea Sparkle 107

7. Red Sky at Morning 117

Second Interlude: June in the Sierra San Pedro Mártir 131

Essay: The Cove of Departure 161

8. Death and Poetry in the Sand Dunes 175

Tailwind 187

Bibliography 191

# Acknowledgments

This book would have been significantly less interesting were it not for the critique and mentoring provided by Kathleen Jamie, Fellow of the Royal Society of Literature.

With apologies for lumping you all together as Dr. Awesome, as well as for leaving out some of the best stories about you, I gratefully acknowledge the companionship and collaboration of those colleagues who served as naturalists on my various expeditions: Patrick Archie, Christopher Beatty, Elizabeth Dahlhoff, Roger Luckenbach, Michelle Marvier, and David McMahon. Effusive thanks are due as well to the teaching assistants whose hard work afforded me the leisure to attend to my field notes: Andrew Connor, Cynthia Dick, Meridith Hollowell, Kelly Ferron, Annette Ochoa, Erin Chadwell, Aven Satre-Meloy, Claire Ryan, Mary Heil, and Colleen Henn. *Reconozco la orientación y la amistad de mis guías y cuidadores Manuel (Manuelito) Rodriquez, Christian (Garambullo) Zalvado, Aracely Rojas, Mario del Angel Alfaro, y Rogelio Vazquez Peña.*

A special course release was provided by the dean of the Santa Clara University College of Arts and Sciences, Atom Yee, to provide time for the revision process so crucial to good writing. My stay at the California Condor Field Research Station was underwritten by a grant from the Santander Foundation. Other institutional support came from the University of Stirling, Estación del Mar Cortés of Glendale Community College, and the San Diego Zoo Global Wildlife Conservancy's California Condor Field Research Station. I also commend and recommend the services of my outfitter, Baja Outdoor Activities of La Paz, BCS.

I am grateful to the naturalists from whom I have learned so much about Baja's ecology: Roger Luckenbach, Steve Webster, Greg Meyer, Guy Van Cleave, and Mike Wallace. I thank those who afforded me the chance to teach in Baja, especially Dennis Gordon, the former director of international programs at Santa Clara University, and the various chairs of the Department of Environmental Studies and Sciences at SCU: Iris Stewart-Frey, Leslie Gray, Lisa Kealhofer, and Michelle Marvier, with apologies for any headaches I may have caused over the years. Correspondingly, I thank my former ENVS 142, Writing Natural History, students—all 160 of them—for their perspective and energy as we explored Baja landscapes, both literary and littoral, together.

I am grateful for the guidance and wisdom of my editor, Kitty Liu, who, were such an entity to exist, would be enshrined in the Natural History Hall of Fame. I am equally grateful for the ministrations and exhortations of my agent, Regina Ryan. Thanks also to senior production editor Susan Specter and copy editor Marie Flaherty-Jones, both of whom impress with their patience, poise, and professionalism.

Finally, I am grateful to Carol, the love of my life, with whom I have shared many fine adventures in Baja, but who, during the composition of this book, graciously allowed me to wander wifeless through the wilderness for more than a hundred long, lonely days south of the border. Thank you for the many ways in which you inspire and support my writing.

*Gracias a todos. ¡Muy amable!*

*Coves of Departure*

# Headwinds

Natural history is a verb.

THOMAS LOWE FLEISCHNER, "Our Deepest Affinity," 2017

We struggled with headwinds today, kayaking into a northerly breeze, slogging windward one cove at a time. The group wasn't staying together as well as I'd hoped. Headwinds are where physical aptitude counts, and a few of my duckies have yet to develop windward muscle. Those out front would have to stop and wait in the lee of every successive point, hiding from El Norte behind another outcropping of wind-sculpted basalt. The lead students noticed that every time they pulled into a lee, there would be a great blue heron foraging, tall and stately, inevitably fleeing as we encroached.

Herons make an impression. These intense birds have never been happy about sharing a planet with humans, and they articulate a series of resonant *hrawnks* whenever they curse our species, swearing expertly with a Pleistocene accent. When we talked about the herons later, finally encamped on a friendly beach, the pattern of finding one in the lee of each point made sense, given this organism's style of stalk-hunting. During windy days they would logically be more successful on the side of an outcropping where the water was less disturbed, than on the windward side, where wind chop and spume would diminish visibility.

These are the things you can't learn from field guides.

Each student has been assigned five organisms on which they must become experts. A fish, a bird, a variety of cactus, a lizard perhaps, maybe even a marine mammal. They are to study these organisms before the trip, teaching each other about them, and then they're to find them once we get to Baja. When my budding naturalists observe their designated *amigos* for the first time in the field, they're to watch for the sort of things that didn't show up in field guides.

One of the students, a junior anthropology major on the verge of becoming a type-A naturalist, had found four of her five assigned organisms prior to our current encampment, and it seemed that she wanted to be the first to befriend all five. In the part of my brain I keep to myself, I call this "Amigo Bingo." There is always someone, or perhaps some two, who wants to win the undeclared competition. This student has been frustrated, however, in her pursuit of the blue-gray gnatcatcher. So, after paddling twelve kilometers into a moderate headwind, and then setting up camp, she prevailed on me and two classmates to accompany her back into the buttonwood mangroves to search for the missing bird.

A small perching songbird that seems to move incessantly, the blue-gray gnatcatcher flits from branch to branch in thick underbrush, making it a tough bird for the uninitiated to identify. In the shadows of the foliage, it can be difficult to distinguish a blue so pale, at least for my color-blind eyes, if you've only seen this bird in field guides where the blue-gray plumage is so easy to see.

Our mission becomes all the more complex when we discover, the moment we leave the coarse sand at the back of the beach, *Crotalus enyo,* the Baja California rattlesnake.

Thicker than my thumb but slightly less stout than my big toe, it was not a particularly large snake, maybe seventy-five centimeters long. For this species, that's a full-grown specimen. Perfectly coiled on a knee-high rock, perched there like the scitalis from a medieval bestiary, it blocked our path without paying us the courtesy of a warning rattle. When we shooed it away into the brush I counted eight rattles, neatly stacked one on top of the other, but my count may have been hasty.

It would be difficult enough to pursue a blue-gray gnatcatcher were your eyes not constantly downcast, sweeping the trail for snakes—not that there's much of a trail here in the first place, just a few narrow paths where you can squeeze between the thorns if you're careful. I search for our quarry with ears only. The field guide claims that it makes a thin, wheezy *zeewt*. Our lead student had played a recording of this vocalization to the class a month ago, and I remind her now to hunt with her ears.

We listen, duly, and nature plays with us. Instead of a gnatcatcher, we hear the evenly spaced toots of the northern pygmy-owl. It sounds like a toy, something you may have played with in the bathtub as a kid. We didn't study this bird in class, so with a low voice I tell my companions that the pygmy-owl is the only diurnal strigiform commonly found in this neighborhood. It's likely to fly off if we come close, so watch for false eyespots in its nape as it flies away.

I want them to see this—a tiny daytime owl with eyes in the back of its head.

We cannot find the owl even though we are close. The terrain is too steep, our path is too brambly, and memories of the rattlesnake are too fresh. When the call for vegetable choppers goes out, my companion, a member of tonight's dinner crew, turns back to camp compliantly, accompanied by her classmates.

I remain on station, summoning the patience required to attend to a landscape where things proceed at south-of-the-border gait. I've long understood that natural history is only one part patience, augmented by equal parts attentiveness and stubbornness. This is where the casual observer need not apply.

A friend of mine, a colleague, insists that natural history is a verb. He may be right, but language somehow fails us in this endeavor. Where botanists can botanize, naturalists cannot . . . naturalize. Naturecate? Instead, we have to tune up the senses, consciously, one by one, in a process that parallels mindfulness.

I smell the creosote, and the sand on the beach upwind of me. I taste low tide, even this far from the water. I watch how light distorts in the heat, especially near the canyon walls above me. I see how it reflects off the mantle of a perched raven. I hear how wind resonates differently through cactus spines as it does through the mouse-ear leaves of a green-barked palo verde. I feel the sun on my shoulders, feeling it through my shirt, knowing that the owl feels this same energy through its feathers.

There's a conscious decision to attend to this landscape in ways that force it to give up its secrets. *Where is that owl?*

*The owl has vanished*, the desert replies.

I continue to listen anyway.

Finally, I hear the gnatcatcher's wheezy *zeewt*.

I do not look for the bird itself, searching instead for movement of any sort. This is what I should have done from the beginning. I pick up the movement almost instantly. Indeed, I know it to be a gnatcatcher just from this movement, and I realized that I'd found it even before I was able to discriminate the blue-gray coloration, or the bird's erect tail, or such field marks as the black forehead that tells me it's an adult male in breeding plumage.

I call down to the camp that I've got one and then I use my binoculars to track it from tree to tree until the student returns. The gnatcatcher never stays on any one branch for more than a few seconds, a behavior typical of small insectivores.

When my type-A naturalist finally arrives, I point out the appropriate tree, a tall, slender, white-trunked palo blanco up a steep side canyon, and instruct her to look for movement rather than for the bird itself. Using this technique, she finds it almost as quickly as I had, although with considerably more delight in the discovery.

The adult world underappreciates delight. Lacking the celebratory religiosity of joy, it tends to be a more fleeting phenomenon, somehow less trustworthy. In defense of delight I argue that it goes hand-in-hand with discovery, and I observe it often folds appreciation and gratitude into the discovery process. I've searched my thesaurus for a better word for discovery-delight, something less sentimental, perhaps less twee, but I don't think the word I want exists in English. Spanish lets me down almost equally, adding little more than a syllable: *deleite*.

I came up short of delight when discovering the gnatcatcher. What appreciation I experienced almost entirely derived from being able to apply my knowledge of this organism's voice and foraging behavior to the practical task of locating it. Actually observing the bird, however, was not as delightful as it should have been, it being a widespread bird I have identified numerous times in the past, both in its summer and winter ranges. For my part, I was less invested in observing the gnatcatcher, and more concerned about not losing it before the student returned on site. The student's discovery of this bird rated much higher on the discovery-delight scale, not only because locating this particular organism completed an assigned task, but also because it was the first time she'd ever been introduced formally to *Polioptila caerulea*.

I am enough of a romantic that I don't want my world to be one where familiarity breeds contempt, mollifies delight, or for that matter curtails appreciation.

A few days ago we identified our first black-headed grosbeak. To the best of my recollection, this was the first member of its tribe that I've seen in Baja. I cracked open a field guide to check its winter range, and the first word in the range section was "common."

Should we allow our discoveries to be spoiled by such words? If a bird is common, should we be any less appreciative of its bicolored bill, its orange rump and breast, or the white patches glowing on its wings?

I observe the transitory nature of delight with my students. They are clearly elated when spotting their first magnificent frigatebird when adding *Fregata magnificens* to their species list, and they take appropriate pride in being able to differentiate between adult and juvenile plumage, as well as being able to describe the sexual dimorphism of adults. After a few days on the island, however, the magnificent frigatebird is no longer magnificent, it's just another frigging bird that they can no longer add to their frigging field notes. Rapture takes a hit when the magnificent becomes mundane.

This is not just about birds, of course. The first time my students witness a mobula ray leaping clear of the water they hurrah as with a single voice. For the next few days they sing out each time they observe the aerobatic spectacle. After the better part of a week, however, they just keep paddling, unwilling to interrupt the progress of the voyage for a single mobula. Unless a dozen are jumping at once, as they so often do, why bother attending to a single?

This morning, while I was writing about a hermit crab one of the students had befriended, two large falcons, *Falco mexicanus*, came screeching over the ridge, the pursuer making its staccato *chi-chi-chi-chi-chi* threat, the pursued screaming bloody murder, wings beating furiously. Almost directly overhead they locked talons, each falcon shrieking at this point as they plummeted toward our beach, no longer flying, but falling instead.

Spiraling clumsily around each other, feathers askew, the combatants fell from the harsh sunlight above the ridge into the canyon's early-morning shade, losing about two thirds of their altitude before releasing each other. The *chi-chi-chi-chi-chi* threat resumed immediately, each bird laboring to regain altitude and speed, the pursuer never more than a meter behind. When they disappeared over the ridge, it appeared the chase would continue for miles.

Two paragraphs ago, I made the conscious decision to reference these falcons by the scientific name, *Falco mexicanus*, rather than by their common name, "prairie falcon." Is it possible that enjoyment of this narrative has been augmented for some readers by supposing that these were exotic creatures? Would critical appreciation have been diminished by knowing that these were the common falcons that spend the summer months escaping the Baja heat by perching on the telephone lines that border Kansas wheat fields?

How do we preserve our delight if we presume that the common is less appreciable than the exotic?

That question seemed to answer itself a few hours after I penned it, when we went diving at the sea lion colony at Los Islotes, a site too famous for its own good. I've snorkeled here at least a dozen times, and was therefore not expecting the momentary bliss that accompanies a novel experience. This was fine, of course, since teachers experience bliss vicariously whenever their students make discoveries. This holds true even when anthropology majors are involved.

Even though it was Tuesday, Los Islotes was crowded. Spring break in Baja. I led our group to an end of the rocky islets less frequented by the tour boats, but before we could get there I spotted a shiny-new snorkel that had been dropped in ten meters of water, a depth beyond the range of most novice snorkelers. Intent on the snorkel's rescue, I took a breath, jackknifed, and had nearly reached it when a juvenile sea lion zoomed past, beating me to the snorkel and grasping it in its mouth the way a dog grasps a bone. The pup swam away a few meters, just beyond my reach, spat the snorkel out, and then re-gripped it by the end—in other words it now held the snorkel's mouthpiece in its mouth. Mimicking me thus, it swam off.

I suppose I will never know for certain whether the sea lion was consciously trying to mimic human practice or was just haphazardly playing "Snatch the Snorkel." I prefer believing the first alternative, perhaps because it appeals to my sense of whimsy, a sense that would have been all the more delighted had I been resting at the surface the moment a sea lion popped its head out of the water with a snorkel held properly in its mouth. Regardless, the novelty of the experience added to my pleasure, this having been the first time I'd seen a sea lion snorkel.

I trace my recent travels thus: perturbed herons >>> nonrattling rattle-snake >>> elusive gnatcatcher >>> fierce falcon fight >>> snorkeling sea lion. But for every organism/event to which I pay attention, there are many others I fail to note. One of my favorite writing exercises, back in the classroom, is to ask students to spend five minutes writing about the things they failed to observe on their way to class that morning. I probably get more detail from this question than had I asked them to take notes while they walked toward our seminar room.

It is possible, I suppose, that my students and I would enjoy these trips immensely were we simply to paddle our way around this archipelago rather than attempting to study our way around it as well. What would suffer, I fear, is the quality of attention we pay to the various elements of natural history we encounter. Had the blue-gray gnatcatcher not been assigned, it would most likely not have been seen. We would still notice the charismatic megafauna, like the humpbacks that sometimes breach directly in front of our kayaks, and we would delight in that, but how deep would such appreciation run?

I don't like the word "seaweed" because "weed" seems judgmental, and because college professors are allowed to be snippy about such things. A better term would be "macroalgae," were it not so pretentious. The locals here in the Sea of Cortez call their free-floating macroalgae "sargasso," as do I, my organismal vocabulary in Spanish far exceeding my mastery of Spanish verbs. My students prefer to use the genus name, *Sargassum*, intentionally mispronouncing it so that it rhymes with "orgasm." The student who has been assigned to study sargassum can undoubtedly tell you that it's holopelagic, which means that it can reproduce without ever needing to attach to the sea floor. In the past, I've had an entire class claim to be holopelagic.

For some naturalists, understanding the physiology of vegetative holopelagic reproduction might be the cool thing. For me, however, the cool thing about sargasso is that patches of it, floating on the surface, often hide juvenile Pacific seahorses, *Hippocampus ingens*, with their horse-like heads, their monkey-like prehensile tails, and their kangaroo-like pouches. You'll never find them, however, unless you're actively looking for them. Masters of camouflage, they are able to match their color perfectly with the sargasso's greenish brown. They blend in so well that thousands of sea kayakers have paddled through sargasso down here in Baja without ever spotting one. For most of these people, sargassum is just a seaweed, a weed floating in saltwater, something that wraps around your paddle when you're not paying attention.

This book is about paying attention in an ecosystem where heightened attention becomes its own reward.

# 1

# *Vernal Equinox*

The design of a book is the pattern of reality controlled
and shaped by the mind of the writer. This is completely understood
about poetry or fiction, but is too seldom realized about books of fact.
And yet the impulse which drives a man to poetry will send another man
into the tide pools and force him to try to report what he finds there.

JOHN STEINBECK, *The Log from the Sea of Cortez,* 1951

Vernal jocularity washes through the cabin as I pass out the prompts for field notes. Almost everyone here in the back of the plane is of college age, tanned and expectant. Despite the fact that winter will not end for another three hours, no hint of pallor remains on these faces. Mercifully, only half of these spring breakers are my students. A few of the revelers not affiliated with my expedition, or for that matter my university, want assignments anyway, or so they claim. I notice, without appearing to take note, that my students are the only ones not drinking.

"Is that our island?"

Our island. We haven't set foot on it yet, and the imperial impulse has already kicked in. What is it about islands that makes us all want to play Prospero? I peer out the tiny window; down below lies Isla Angel de la Guarda, looking far more topographical in real life than it does on the map tacked to the wall of my office. No, this is not our island. Our island is colossal, indeed, but not quite this Brobdingnagian.[1]

---

1. According to Jonathan Swift's *Gulliver's Travels,* we would have had to voyage north coastwise from San Francisco to reach the Brobdingnag peninsula. Although our flight departed San Francisco, there can be no doubt that we have been heading south—the morning sun streams through the port windows.

I lean closer to the window. The island seems to be peering up at me from twin granitic peaks, locking me in a stare-down. I've looked down on these crags before, but the island has never seemed this arid, this devoid of a guardian angel. Hostile, almost. No vegetation is visible from our ten-kilometer-plus altitude; to my color-blind eyes there is not even a suggestion of green. All is the inexplicable color of rock and sand, but not white sand, not the sort of sand tourists prefer. In fact, I don't see any real beaches, at least not the type you'd want to land a kayak on. No mangrove lagoons either—we're still north of where mangals thrive here in the Sea of Cortez.

I search for signs of life, of the boojum or cacti I know must be down there, but from this altitude I'd need binoculars to see anything that size. Although a professorial sense of decorum prohibits wearing binoculars inside an Airbus A320, I'll make up for this soon. I've come home from past expeditions with binocular-strap tan lines.

As the plane moves south my gaze is drawn to the island's alluvial fans, which coalesce in a way that suggests the work of the violent *chubascos* of the tropical Pacific. It took power to carve this island, not mere time. We can see the naked beds of the ephemeral streams that feed the alluvial fans, empty now as they almost always are. I know from my reading that there are no springs on this island, only a few *tinajas*—water tanks carved into the rock—that might hold water for a few weeks after a rain. With no springs, there are no large terrestrial mammals to keep the island's guardian angel company, no coyotes or bighorn sheep or even jackrabbits. Certainly no humans. Not even my old friend *babisuri*, the ring-tailed thief who will no doubt be trying to steal the food where we camp this evening, can survive on this island.

The middle student I'm leaning over asks whether I've visited this island, and I shake my head, mumbling that I've traveled up and down its western coast, looking for sperm whales, but that I've never set foot on it. This island is not on my bucket list: not enough flora, not enough fauna, and the same Köppen climate classification as the Sahara Desert.

I feel an uncommon apprehension building within me as the island passes from view. The desert that has revealed itself below is not the desert I've been romanticizing for the past ten weeks while teaching this class. Although that desert was harsh, this one is harsher still. It seems to have asked me, *"Why would someone bring students down here?"*

As I return to my seat, I tell the students on the starboard side of the airplane to be on the lookout for Isla Espíritu Santo. Our island. I'm hoping to take a long look at it myself, hoping that it still appears as hospitable as it appeared the last time I flew over it.

Today is the vernal equinox. I have not missed the spring equinox in Baja since 2007. I don't do as well with the other holy days, having attended the winter solstice down here a mere four times, the summer solstice only once, and having never been on this side of the border for the autumnal equinox, a time when I'm inevitably grading papers back home.

I didn't start flying down here until I started bringing students during the breaks. Prior to that, we would always drive the Transpeninsular Highway—a sedentary torture back in the highway's early days, when even the potholes had potholes. You could always tell the fellow Americans without needing to read license plates: we were the ones with the surfboards, kayaks, gas cans, and water jugs strapped to our roof racks. We carried extra spare tires and beer coolers and guitars and gas lanterns and massive first aid kits stocked with every possible treatment for diarrhea.

It's easier to fly. These days I always book the same flight on the same airline. We leave on Thursday of finals week, and if some of my students still have exams to take, I proctor them on the plane. A couple years ago, as I write this, I sat in the middle seat; the student to my left struggled with inorganic chemistry while the student to my right grappled with mechanical engineering. Neither scholar wanted to hear how hard it had been to transit Baja in the old days.

Those two kids have gone on and graduated now. One of them just sent me an email from Antarctica, where he runs a remote submarine through a hole in the ice. The other just got married, and works as the membership coordinator for a bicycle coalition. I somehow tend not to lose track of former Baja students as readily as I lose track of others.

The plane lands, we collect our gear, we clear customs. Anticipations of trouble are not rewarded, this despite the fact that I carry my carbon-fiber kayak paddles in a cheap plastic rifle case, the only affordable luggage I've been able to find. The rifle case has never been trouble entering Mexico, but has always been trouble returning home. Should my homeland ever be invaded by hordes of sunburned college professors wielding kayak paddles, they're ready.

The Transportation Security Administration, back in the country I just left, could learn a great deal from Mexican customs. Down here, you push a button that randomly generates either a red or green light. When it glows red they search you, when it glows green you walk through. In both countries the work of customs officials largely depends on luck. The Mexican system admits this reality with disarming honesty.

Years ago we helped friends—he was a Brit, she was not—sail their boat down from San Francisco to Ensenada, in the northern part of Baja. The boat was lovely and new, but its larder lacked depth. We stopped in Morro Bay after the first couple days, and I hiked many miles to a grocery store to purchase my favorite brand of just-add-water pancake mix. The discovery that breakfast can actually be tasty is a life-changing experience for anyone who grew up in the United Kingdom. When our friends finally sailed their boat around to La Paz, they sent open-ended plane tickets, along with the dire information that they'd been unable to purchase just-add-water pancake mix anywhere in Mexico.

Friend that I am, I packed a five-kilo bag of my favorite pancake mix in my dive bag, nestling it protectively between fins.

My wife, who always packs lighter than me, got the green light and scurried ahead into our friends' open arms. I got the red light, of course, and was directed to open my dive bag.

I zipped it open and gasped audibly when a cloud of fine white powder wafted up. Visions of Mexican prison danced in my head as I realized I did not know how to say "pancake" in Spanish. The best I could do was to stammer, *"¿Como se dice* 'pancake' *en español?"*

The agent smiled, replied, *"Panqueque,"* and then indicated that I was free to enter the country.

Mexico comes flooding back to me once I'm clear of the airport. We roll down the windows in the vans, and as we head north toward the Tropic of Cancer, the beach to our right and the desert to our left, I begin to remember all the parts I love: how the turkey vultures roost in the massive cardon cactus, wings outstretched in an impressive droop, thermoregulating while facing the sun in what appears as an act of worship; how the cardon themselves, some of them weighing twenty-five tons, form forests of their own, the largest specimens towering so tall you'd swear they are guilty of hubris about their reputation as the loftiest cactus in the world. How the mesquite functions as a nurse plant to juvenile cardons, and how the cacti ultimately repay this hospitality by killing those who nurse them, although it may take close to a century to do so.

Every year is different along this stretch. The lomboy brilloso, a drought-deciduous plant that straddles the border between shrub and tree and is endemic to Baja California Sur, tells the story of when it last rained, and how much. On dry years, there are only branches. When it's been wet, ovate leaves the size of a coyote's ear glisten for months as a testament to the glories of rainfall. The palo adan—literally, Adam's stick—which is much more treelike here in the cape region than farther north in the Vizcaino desert, similarly tells tales of the weather, appearing fuzzy and green with its mouse-ear-sized leaves when there's enough water for a tree to splurge on leaves. In the dry years, all one tends to see of palo adan are his thorns.

Some years, sticks. Some years, leaves on sticks. Some years, leaves and flowers as well. I always wish for the latter, of course, even though I recognize the naïveté of wishing the desert would be perpetually green. If it rained enough to answer everyone's prayers, this desert would be replaced by a thousand golf courses. The dry years give the wet years their glory, and the scarcity of the wet years lends them their special character. Still, as I grow attached to the students who will accompany me on each expedition, I can't help wishing for each class that they'll see this place lush and enticing.

We turn off the highway down the bouncy road to Santiago, only we don't bounce. I'm dumbfounded, for the road's been paved. At first I resent this encroachment of civilization, but I remind myself of something Joseph Wood Krutch wrote over fifty years ago, when castigating the "selfish point of view" of naturalists who would like to see Baja remain primitive. He reminded us, "Baja is not a park or a museum and has not been set aside as a wilderness area. The good of its own population comes first" (270).

Founded as a mission in 1723 on the site of an enormous palm oasis, the Misión de Santiago el Apóstol was subsequently abandoned after a series of Pericú rebellions. I wonder what the indigenous Pericú would have thought about all this asphalt. Perhaps they would tell us that there's nothing timeless about a place. The mountains erode, the indigenes get television, fisheries collapse, and the climate warms. Then they pave the roads.

The palm oasis is still here, thank the gods. The forest of native blue fan palms stretches for more than a kilometer, showing no signs of diminution from when I saw it last. The palm fans are harvested to thatch *palapa* roofs, but the harvest is restricted to the full moon by local custom because of a belief that the fans last longer when the sap has risen. At that point, *palmeros* will cut a *carga* of 250 fans, for which they might earn the equivalent of fifty US dollars if the leaves are of the highest quality. Not an easy way to make a living.

We stop in the town plaza to switch our gear to the outfitter's vans, for the airport shuttles will take us no farther. My teaching assistant, who made this trip with us last year and will function as camp director this year, instructs her peers to get into their hiking clothes, fill up their water bottles, and make certain they have a bathing suit. Hiking boots and broad-brimmed hats are mandatory. Burritos are distributed; sunblock is slathered.

Beyond this point, all the roads up into the mountains are sand.

It takes a few hours for Baja to blow away the stink of the jet. And it will take a few hours more for my various senses to get back in tune with this dulcet landscape. I rig the lanyard to my glasses, knowing that I will not remove it until we return to the airport in ten days. An oriole flashes by, sparkling with a yellow that doesn't exist in higher latitudes, and I drape my binoculars around my neck, unwilling to miss another bird just because I'm riding in a van.

Everything now is a reawakening. Baja has its own smells, and they are not merely the smells of desert flora. Hot basalt, mesquite, and the distant sea all lend their scents to the mix. A touch of citrus, perhaps, mixed with the lingering aroma of the local *tortillaria*. Fragrances the color of agave. Were you to blindfold me and transport me here, my nose would tell me where I am, and I would feel, after two breaths, a sense of not being lost. Every time I leave Baja, I know I will return, and every time I return, I go through this same reconnection, this same feeling of unlostness in a foreign, exotic locale.

Every year since the US Department of State issued its travel warning due to the violence of the Mexican drug cartels, the university has wanted me to take this program elsewhere. They've even offered to pay my expenses to spend a summer in Costa Rica so that I can learn its natural history. But I resist, and resist, and resist. I tell those who manage the university's risks that this program would not work elsewhere. It's not just the kayaking, and the hiking, and the nature—it's the reconnection.

We see our first tarantula hawk—a huge spider wasp that lays its eggs inside tarantulas—within a hundred meters of leaving the van. One of the students gave a brief report on this critter back in the classroom, showing us a particularly violent YouTube video of a fight between a female tarantula hawk and its prey. What never comes through via YouTube, however, is the beauty of the creature itself. The body is a blue-black that seems blacker than black, contrasting with wings the color of rust, only brighter. The student who made the in-class presentation recites a few details of the tarantula hawk's natural history, including widely held speculation that the sting resulting from the female's seven-millimeter-long stinger is the most painful sting in the insect world. We can see the stinger through our binoculars, and it seems particularly lethal thus magnified.

What the student hasn't told us is that the tarantula hawk, being nectarivorous, sometimes consumes spoiled, fermenting fruit that can intoxicate it to the point where flight becomes difficult. I've observed this phenomenon, and I've seen an inebriated spider wasp fly directly into the trunk of a venerable Brandegee's fig. Not pretty.

If, as a penalty for my sins, I come back as a tarantula hawk, I'd prefer to come back as a male. They leave all the tarantula hunting to the females, instead feeding placidly on the flowers of mesquite trees whenever they're not imbibing spoiled fruit. In their spare time, male tarantula hawks engage in an activity called "hill-topping," where they sit in solitude atop tall plants, watching for receptive females to pass by. Life is good, I'm told, for hill-toppers.

We've come to our first waterfall. It's actually a series of large cascades, each one approximately ten meters from crest to pool. The upper fall has worn a smooth, rounded groove into the rock from which it tumbles, and has carved out a fairly deep pool. Strangely, the water in the pool is cooler than the rock-warmed water cascading down. I know from a previous visit that the cascade itself will feel like a warm shower to those treading in the pool, a "shower" with a flow rate of three hundred liters per minute.

A flame skimmer dragonfly, its wings looking like fire itself in the sunlight, skitters about the pool, ovipositing, and I point out that what she's doing is laying her eggs in various spots within the pool so that the resulting naiads, once they hatch, don't eat each other. Only a few of my scholars are listening, the rest are frantically shucking off their clothes. One of the guides has leaped from the flame skimmer's pool over the lower waterfall into the creek below. My naturalists-in-training transform instantly into daredevils.

A student in a yellow bikini is the first to jump, prompting all four male students to scramble up the rocks after her, eager to defend the honor of their gender. In their baggy board shorts, they jump. They splash. They celebrate their bravado.

The original jumper climbs, barefoot, back to the top of the waterfall. There's something purposeful in the way she climbs, but I miss it because I'm thinking that I would never have been able to climb that confidently in wet feet, not even when I was her age. When she reaches the top, after a momentary adjustment she leans forward and then flips.

Flips!

Her intent, apparently, was to pull off a single rotation and enter the water feetfirst. But she overrotated, pulling off a one-and-a-quarter flip that culminated in the most spectacular belly flop I've ever witnessed. Ever. Her classmates immediately swim to her rescue. Magnanimously, she accepts assistance that she doesn't really require, thus releasing the other students of any obligation to attempt flips of their own.

The pool clears, and the other students take their turns jumping, usually in twos or threes, perhaps grouping up in order to reinforce the resolve to leap. Within a few minutes, the only ones remaining at the upper pool are the flame skimmer, me, and Dr. Awesome.

I am honored to introduce my esteemed colleague, Dr. Awesome, the expedition naturalist. This dear scientist, who morphs into someone else every year or two, is sometimes a female and at other times a male. Regardless of gender, discipline, or specialty, the students consistently comment in the course evaluations that "Dr. XYZ is awesome." Hence the name. This person has alternately been a field ecologist–entomologist, an evolutionary biologist with expertise in marine biology, an agroecologist, a physiologist, a combination ornithologist and herpetologist, and even a conservation biologist. All but one are younger than me; all are awesome humans; and, for the sake of accuracy, one was still working on his doctorate when he teamed up with me. I beg the reader's forbearance for conflating them, just as I beg forgiveness from my colleagues for dragging them into this narrative. I have learned a great deal from each of them, and if I get any of the science right in this book, the credit is theirs.

(Having already diverged, I might also mention the makeup of the overall expedition. I take sixteen students each year, not counting the TA, all undergraduates studying at the upper-division level. As is the national trend for more adventurous study abroad programs, this one attracts far more females than males. This year's twelve-to-four ratio is the least gender-balanced group I've ever taken abroad. We have used the same two Mexican kayak guides year after year, and they are fabulous—they were an amazing team until one of them went off to grad school. You will no doubt meet them soon.)

We follow the creek back down from the waterfall. At one point we must cross a large floodplain of boulders, hopping more than hiking, slow going because I have to look down at every footfall, a process I'm finding difficult with my new progressive lenses. I stumble, finally, but the blame lies more with my old boots than my new glasses. The injury to my pride is greater than the damage to my skin; one never wants to falter in front of undergraduates, let alone collapse.

I had wavered about purchasing new hiking boots prior to this expedition, but this is only the third trip to Baja for these slippery boots, counting a somewhat more relaxed trip without students this past Christmas. Although they're comfortable, I've never liked these particular boots—I've never been able to trust them entirely. Back in my dormitory I had ultimately lectured myself about sustainability, and decided to try to wear these boots out a bit more before investing in a more capable pair.

If it's difficult to determine when a given pair of boots have made their last expedition, it will be much more difficult to tell when I have made mine. Back when I was still in my fifties I informed my department chair that I wanted to keep this up at least until I turned sixty, but that milestone came and went without reinforcements being summoned. The Department of Environmental Studies and Sciences could not care less, apparently, about how many pairs of boots I wear out trekking through Baja.

I wave off the guide who wants to bandage my knee, and after hobbling a step or two, summon my resolve to make it back to the van without limping. The resolution holds; what I lack in grace I can more than make up for in stubbornness.

Perhaps this is why Baja and I get along so well. Desert is the ecology of stubbornness. For example, during today's hike we passed by hundreds of rock figs, *Ficus palmeri*, growing out of the granitic cliffs that line the walls of canyon we ascended. Beautiful, thick-trunked, fruit-bearing trees with white roots that grasp the rocks like the tentacles of an enormous, ancient cephalopod. You'll never see one growing out of a nice patch of dirt, or even sand. They root in the rock itself, a niche for which no ficus need compete. These trees command so much respect, and provide such marvelous shade, that the locals have never developed a market for their lumber.

It would take a particularly heartless individual to cut down a tree stubborn enough to flourish in these rocks.

⊀

We set up camp in a mango plantation. Leaf litter from the mango trees is ankle deep, and we warn the students that rattlesnakes hide amid the leaves. Mango leaves are particularly large, at least the size of a burro's ear, and stiff. It wouldn't take many mango leaves to conceal one of the sneakier snakes. The campfire area and the kitchen have been raked, along with several clearings where we can pitch our tents. We camped here the previous year and enjoyed it, but will not stay here in the future because I'll find a better location next Christmas.

There is just enough light when we arrive for the students to set up their tents without having to use their headlamps. We have new tents this year that we've brought down with us, planning to leave them with the outfitter at the conclusion of the expedition. Symbiosis evolves at all levels.

A Baja California *rancho* tends to be significantly more wild than the farms back home in Alta California.[2] One is more likely to find predators here, for

2. *Baja* best translates "lower," while *alta* best translates "upper." "Alta California," as referenced from the Mexican perspective, includes both northern and southern California of the United States, the entirety of which was Mexican territory circa 1823–48.

example. And one is less likely to find barns, tractors, or running water. Indeed, the only electricity in this particular *rancho* runs from two solar panels supported by a rickety *cabaña* woven of palo de arco sticks. This is an old Baja craft, weaving such things as sheds and furniture from sticks the diameter of your index finger without ever using fasteners such as screws or nails. Here in the cape region, no self-respecting *rancho* is without a live arch of palo de arco delineating its entranceway, with bright-yellow trumpet-shaped flowers blooming year-round.

From the solar array atop the *cabaña,* the sun's energy flows through extremely thin wires to the mango trees over the open kitchen area, terminating in LED lights that barely seem worth the effort. Regardless, I compliment the *ranchero* on this new addition to his kitchen, and he is pleased that I've noticed.

"We burn less Coleman fuel now," he tells me. "This is a good thing."

He wants to teach the students how to make their own adobe tomorrow morning. I tell him that we won't have time, but the eavesdropping students clamor that they want to learn. In no uncertain terms I let them know that I don't want their adobe-making time to come out of their writing time. Tomorrow's hike will be longer than today's, especially if people want time to swim. We compromise, ultimately, and the students agree to wake up a bit earlier than we'd planned in order to give themselves the extra time. Symbiosis again.

After a short, somewhat graphic lecture on how to use the composting toilet, we set about the task of assembling dinner. It will turn out to be no less messy a process than tomorrow's adobe session.

The consumption of pizza is a weekly event for most US college students, and yet few have a clue as to how to build one from scratch. I see eyebrows arching when we mention such things as dry yeast and olive oil, and there is momentary hesitation when they learn that they'll have to mix this all with their fingers. They participate anyway, because there's no alternative for those who wish to dine. It's an absolute mess as flecks of dough suddenly find their way into hair and onto T-shirts. But it's fun, and we're hungry, and there are far worse ways to celebrate the equinox.

On this expedition we do as much as we can from scratch. The guide announces happy hour and asks whether anyone wants a piña colada. All hands are raised. The guide pulls out a pineapple, a coconut, and a bottle of rum.

"Who wants to make it?"

Fewer hands this time.

They'll learn.

The wood-fired adobe oven is a perfect half sphere that comes as high as my navel. The mud-colored, unfinished exterior surface has a rough texture with bits of straw sticking out everywhere. It was built within the last year, and a few small handprints of the builders are still discernible. School children? We can't fit all the pizzas into the oven at once. The first few come out a bit too crisp, the second batch is amazing, and the last group is just a tad doughy, but the dinner is absolutely perfect nonetheless. After dishes, I pull the black light out of my pack and introduce the students to the scorpions.

The outer layer of the cuticle that forms the scorpion's exoskeleton contains a protein that fluoresces when exposed to ultraviolet. I'm told that the color is a bright blue green, but I've also been told it's an electric yellow green. It always fascinates me when naturalists who are not color-blind diverge in their descriptions of hue. Regardless, a few minutes running around with a black light persuades the students that they should shake out their hiking shoes in the morning before stepping into them.

One of the students has been assigned the scorpion as one of her designated *amigos*, which means that she's prepared to enlighten us on a bit of this genus's natural history once we encounter it. She chooses to describe the scorpion's mating habits, where the male grabs the female with his pedipalps (which is what naturalists call the pinchers) and then steers her to a smooth surface, where he extrudes a glandular secretion on which he deposits his spermatophore so that it sticks up like a stalk. He backs the female up so that the spermatophore makes physical contact with her gonophore, at which point fertilization occurs. Then, if the female feels like it, she eats the male.

I can't help but wonder whether one of the male students would have described this aspect of arachnid behavior more romantically. In other venues I've heard the part where the male "steers" the female referred to as a "dance," a complex mating ritual commonly called, in French, *promenade à deux*.

A reverent campfire is going, and I tell the students to enjoy it while they can because we are not permitted to build fires once we reach the island. They already know this, having been thoroughly indoctrinated via Facebook by the members of last year's expedition.

A few students begin to scratch notes in their journals, a few others discover that the stars here are more amazing than any stars they've ever seen, and one of the students borrows a guitar from the *ranchero*. When he begins to strum, I am overcome with fatigue, and I barely have enough stamina left to brush my teeth before crawling into my tent.

The guitar plays a tune perfect for a *promenade à deux*, and I feel myself drifting off to sleep before I can complete the stretching exercises for my lower back. My last thought, before surrendering to my dreams, was that I should have instructed the females not to devour the males.

# 2

## *Night Life*

Each night by a campfire, my pen swells field notes into a gnarly
bulge. Everything is of such great importance, it is well worth the trouble
to note it. At first, I become a list maker, naming plants, trees, fish,
mountains, and coves in English, then in Spanish. Soon the names stop
and the notes become mostly questions. Then the notes stop and I try
to feel rather than think my way through. I try to distill this land.

ELLEN MELOY, *Eating Stone*, 2005

Despite my exhaustion, sleep comes fitfully the first night. A ringtail has discovered our camp, and doesn't seem to understand that the faculty tents are
off limits to any creature without an advanced degree.

*Bassariscus astutus* is a case study in how we misname fauna. In English,
we commonly call this diminutive omnivore the "ring-tailed cat," perhaps because it's almost the size of a skinny house cat, albeit a somewhat short-legged
cat. Other English common names include "civet cat," and "miner's cat," this
last term having come from the practice of miners domesticating ringtails and
keeping them in their cabins to control rodents. Spanish common names can
be equally misleading; for example: *sal coyote* (salt coyote) or *mico de noche*
(monkey of the night.) The one Spanish common name I can't argue with is
*babisuri*, a word for which there is no translation, and which seems to have
captured this creature's magic.

Anyone schooled in taxonomy would be quick to point out that the ringtail
is not properly called a cat, if by "cat" you mean something feline. This is why
we prefer "scientific" names, right? But the Latinate phrase *Bassariscus astutus* translates, literally, as "clever little fox," and neither is the ringtail canine.

Rather, it is a procyonid, from the Greek meaning "before the dog," which makes it a member of the same taxonomic family as the raccoon.

Of course, Carl Linnaeus originally put the raccoon in the genus *Ursus*, making it a bear.

Were you to hold a ring-tailed cat in one hand and a raccoon in the other—and good luck with that—the first thing you might discover is that both procyonids share the same dentition, which is to say that their teeth are arranged in the same bite pattern. Other physical similarities would include the ringed tail, erect ears atop a triangular face, and whiskers.

The ringtail is more buff colored than the raccoon, at least to my eyes. Other than coloration, babisuri has two distinct differences from its gray cousins. First, it can rotate its hind limbs 180 degrees, which facilitates vertical headfirst descents while the animal holds on with its rear paws. Second, like the majority of the felines to whom it's not related, it has retractile claws that can be sheathed when not needed.

I generally hold babisuri in high regard, especially when it stays away from my tent. I'll never forget one morning on the island when a student reported that, from the cozy confines of her sleeping bag, separated from a ringtail by no more than a layer of mosquito mesh, she'd watched babisuri chew its way through her daypack to swipe a snack she'd squirreled away. Now that's a nature lover!

The ringtail moves away from my tent and I fall back to sleep briefly. Before too long, however, I am awakened again by the sound of dishes rattling on the table where we set them out to dry. I get up, reluctantly, to make certain that the ringtail isn't taking advantage of our inexperience so early in this expedition. There's no breeze, and I mistakenly judge it to be warm enough that I don't bother pulling on a sweater or trousers. I insert my bare right foot into my boot without shaking it out, remembering this precaution half a moment too late. Fortunately, there was no scorpion in the boot, nor is there one in the left boot, which I shake out prophylactically like a seasoned pro. By the time I make it to the cooking area I realize that I'll be chilled within a few minutes. Baja is reminding me that, no matter how far up I get in the mountains, I'm never really far from the sea.

Babisuri has found our cooking area, and it has already scavenged whatever was available. Probably just pizza dough. It sits there, in the moonlight, cleaning itself by first licking its forelimbs and then wiping its face, very much the same way a feline cleans up after a meal. Watching, I suddenly realize how the misnomer "cat" may have originated.

I don't know why some animals seem so cute while others fail in this regard. Perhaps the diminutive size? I certainly wouldn't be thinking in terms of cute if I met up with a version of this animal that outweighed me. The fluffy tail helps tip the cuteness scale, although foxes have fluffy tails and I don't generally think of them as "cute." Otherwise, the ringtail's eyes are distinctly expressive, the sort of puffy, globular eyes a Disney animator might create for an animal about to befriend a princess.

I watch for a full minute, and when I yawn I begin to wonder whether babisuri is ignoring me. How can it not know I'm here? I've read, somewhere, that miners used to cut a hole in a wooden dynamite box and place it by the stove in order to provide ringtails a warm place to sleep during the day. That's all it took, apparently, to domesticate these animals. As I stand there, I wonder whether this specimen has been domesticated by our host.

Probably not. The moment comes when I can watch no longer; my need for slumber becomes more urgent than my interest in procyonid grooming behavior, so I turn on my headlamp, hoping to scare it away. Babisuri's eyes glow ferociously, and it stares at me for a few moments, as if to assert territorial imperative. This is its country, not mine. When I take an imperial step forward, however, babisuri scurries away.

I'm happy to turn the headlamp out again, the better to preserve my night vision. If a silver lining fringes the cloud of my color blindness, it's the superior night vision I enjoy, although my nocturnal ability is nothing compared to that of a ringtail. I look skyward before heading back to my tent. The gibbous moon having just cleared the horizon, the stars are nowhere near as spectacular as they were the first time I headed off to bed. There are no clouds, of course, which is why the night has cooled off so rapidly.

I step into the clearing where the campfire's embers no longer glow, look up at the stars, attempt to locate Mars, and am astonished when Regulus blinks off for a moment. At least I think it was Regulus. Then I notice that other stars are blinking as well—not flickering but actually turning off for brief moments. I watch this curious phenomenon for the better part of a minute until I notice a black streak cross the moon and realize that what's occluding these heavenly bodies, at least from my perspective, are bats. Lots of bats.

Bats are the bugaboo of the casual naturalist. Right now I have no way of knowing whether I'm observing *Tadarida brasiliensis*, the Mexican free-tailed bat, *Macrotus californicus*, the California leaf-nosed bat, or some other denizen of the night. And there's really nothing I can do to get me closer to identifying these animals, even just to genus.

Bat identification wasn't always this uncertain for Baja naturalists. In 1964, George Lindsay, chronicling that year's proceedings of the California Academy of Sciences' Sea of Cortez Expedition, wrote: "As usual, bats appeared and were hunted just at dusk. They are difficult targets for 22-caliber pistols. A fusillade of pistol shots, punctuated by an occasional blast of a shotgun, netted a big brown bat, *Eptesicus fuscus*, and two representatives of *Pipistrellus hesperus*, new records for the island" (233).

I'm probably seeing Mexican free-tails. There's a cave not far from here that used to house a population of 20 million of these bats, a population that diminished 95 percent due to human incursion, not only in the form of tourism but also as the result of guano mining. Unfortunately, bat shit makes great fertilizer. The good news is that the cave was recently purchased by an environmental group; the bad news is that I'm not going to tell where it is, regardless. Those bats need to be left alone for a few decades; I don't even take students there. However, in exchange for the reader's kind forbearance, I will tell a crazy-but-true tale about the Mexican free-tailed bat at the end of this chapter.

Free-tailed bats have a mouselike tail that protrudes beyond their flight membranes, and it's from this protrusion that they take their names. Try as I might in the moonlight, I can't see well enough to tell whether the tail is there. They do seem to have the long, pointy wings characteristic of these bats. I ponder the animals as long as I can stand to, but a shiver turns me back toward my tent.

I use an ultralight down bag on these expeditions, one that compresses to the size of a coconut. When I return to it I discover its warmth to be inadequate, and I have to mummy myself, hood drawn tight, to warm up enough to sleep. Attempting to kick-start my lousy Spanish, I whisper, "*Tengo frio*," literally I *have* cold, rather than I *am* cold. South of the border, coldness functions as a commodity rather than an existential state. Here in Mexico, were I to say that I *am* cold, "*Soy frio*," the locals would understand me to suffer from sexual frigidity. This is not a condition one would want to advertise in Baja.

I fall asleep thinking what a shame it is that I can't save this chill for tomorrow afternoon.

In the compressed time of restless sleep, it seems that no sooner do I succumb to my dreams than I'm awakened by the braying of a feral donkey nearby, an animal that sounds as if it has just come face to face with something more ferocious than a ringtail.

The burro was the preferred mode of travel in these parts until quite recently. Horses were less able to navigate the rocky terrain, were less able to browse the desert flora, and were far more susceptible to thirst. Then, gradually, as both roads and economy improved, the pickup truck became the connection between *rancho* and *pueblo*, and the burros were quite literally sent packing. They've thrived, of course, out in the desert on their own, browsing much of the vegetation formerly consumed by desert bighorns.

The braying continues, and I check my dive watch, its luminous dial barely glowing this long after sundown. It's 4:30 a.m., precisely the same time I met the students to pick up the airport shuttle the previous morning. I had been planning to sleep in until sunrise this morning, expecting to meet the dawn fresh and relaxed. Instead, I grab my pocket notebook, find my glasses and headlamp, and begin scribbling invective about burros.

Two expeditions of note took place in Baja in 1905–6. The first, a biological survey organized by the US Department of Agriculture, traversed the entire peninsula under the direction of Edward W. Nelson, the chief of the Bureau of Biological Survey. Nelson opted to travel on horseback, a decision that was to limit his journey severely. He wrote:

It is true, however, that we found conditions exceedingly hard for our stock, and it was only by exercising the most judicious care in stopping at frequent intervals where the scanty forage appeared most favorable, in order that the animals might rest and recuperate, that the trip was practicable. All of our animals were forced to depend on such forage as they could find, since the sparsely inhabited character of the country rendered it impossible to supply them with grain or other cultivated feed of any kind, except to a small extent at long intervals. (14)

The other 1905–6 expedition, privately financed, involved a San Francisco lawyer, Arthur Walbridge North, an explorer-hunter cast in the Teddy Roosevelt mold, who traveled the peninsula via burro, getting as far as La Paz before receiving news of a devastating earthquake that had destroyed his hometown. North was a big fan of burros:

For a time I fretted constantly over the slow advance of my burros and chafed because, not daring to assume that the San Francisco banks had weathered the storm, I could not, by recourse to my check book, purchase horses. But when the caminos were at their worst and grazing scant I realized that the horse has his limitations and the burro his advantages. For the humbler beast no sierra trail is too fearful, no provender too poor; browsing on cacti he can exist without water; he survives or avoids the eating of poisonous herbs; he outlasts all other beasts of the sierra caminos. Though his pace is deadly slow, it is steady, continuous; it goes on, on, monotonously on perhaps, but ever on, unswervingly on, on, cutting away and wearing down distance until the goal is attained. And yet when one is in a hurry this perfect mountaineer, this faithful, slow moving, unhastening servant rarely receives his due. (226)

Given a choice between horse and burro, I will always opt for a sea kayak. My single experience packing with burros, at a scout ranch where I worked as a merit badge counselor during my college years, convinced me that it was easier to carry the weight myself than to rely on any form of conveyance with a four-legged conflict of interest. My resolve to resist this form of trekking in Baja was confirmed a few years back when, in a used bookstore down in San Jose del Cabo, I purchased a book written by an Englishman, Graham Macintosh, who followed a north-to-south route from Tecate to Loreto in 1997 with a burro named *Misión*. The narrative plodded along the way you'd expect when a man spends six months alone with a burro, and I've never had the intellectual stamina to finish it.

⤙

I catch a few scattered moments of sleep, constantly reawakened by the burro. The braying ceases the moment sunlight hits my tent, and is replaced instantly by the undulating drone of hundreds of bees. Maybe thousands. All humming the same basic note, they sound conspiratorial, as if there's great meaning behind the volume they are able to produce as a group.

I'm only vaguely aware of birdsong at the moment. Dawn happens fast in lower latitudes, and although this tent is constructed almost entirely of mesh, the interior temperature rises quickly in direct sunlight, dissipating what little chill I was able to store. *¡Tengo calor!* I unzip my sleeping bag and the zipper complains loudly, as if to protest being pressed into service this time of day. Having added my own noise to the din, I begin to listen more deeply, harkening for the descending spiral trill of my old friend, the canyon wren. There do not appear to be any around presently. Instead, what avian noise I'm hearing mostly is the white-winged dove.

*Hooo-cooooo-hoo-hooo.*

Listening in English, we claim that these birds ask, "Who-cooks-for-you?"

White-winged doves are referred to as *la plaga* (the plague) by Mexican farmers because of their habit of aggregating in large flocks, reportedly as large as a thousand birds, and descending on fields of sunflowers or grains to eat the seeds. An entire harvest can be lost in the span of an hour. In defense of *Zenaida asiatica*, it should be pointed out that these doves are important pollinators of the cardon cactus, and the entire desert ecosystem would be impoverished by the loss of this bird.

I listen once more for the canyon wren, and then decide to make do with the doves' coos for the moment because these birds are telling me that I'm not far from the Tropic of Cancer, and right now that's a good place to be.

Doves, apparently, were a breakfast staple for North's expedition. While I don't share his culinary preferences, I respect his prebreakfast attention to the writing process:

> After dressing myself, performing my ablutions and rolling my blankets away in a dunnage bag, I would proceed to transfer the preceding day's entries from pocket notebook to journal. Soon Praemundi would appear with the burros, and while he put the pack-saddles on Cabrillo and Vapor, Jesús and I would saddle our riding animals. Then sitting together, cross-legged by the fire, we would eat a plain breakfast of broiled doves or "cottontail" rabbit, stewed prunes, boiled rice, hard-tack, or flour and water *tortillias*, and wild honey. My mozos drank strong coffee, water sufficed for me. (226)

*"Who cooks for you?"* There are no mozos in this camp to prepare the breakfast, which this morning will feature mangos and melons sliced by collegians. There are guides, however, one of whom insists on making the coffee each morning. For years now I've been maintaining I could do a better job, but he doesn't seem to trust a Californian to make proper Mexican coffee.

During last year's expedition I learned a neat trick: if the students see me sitting on the edge of camp scribbling in my notebook, they're far more apt to pull their journals out and summon the muse.

Our guide has already dumped the ground coffee into the boiling water, and the sludge has begun to form. He greets me in our customary Spanglish.

"Good morning, Juanito, *como dormiste?*" (How did you sleep?)

"Better than *el burro*, Garambullo."

Garambullo is not his given name—it's an old joke. On a hot, windless day several expeditions ago, he scolded me for having my life jacket unzipped. When I ignored him, he affected the best British accent a Mexican kayak guide can manage, and commanded, "Young man, zip up your life jacket."

I'm twice his age, of course, a situation that demanded a retort. In the heat of that moment I could not remember *viejo*, the Spanish for "old man," but I could remember *Garambullo*, the Spanish name for a fuzzy, columnar cactus, *Cephalocereus senilis*, commonly known in English as "Old Man Cactus." (The species name, *senilis*, also means "old man" in Latin. The plant gets this appellation from its coat of fuzzy, white hairs that protect it from the sun.)

As I obediently zipped up my life jacket, I replied, *"¡Sí, Garambullo!"*

The appellation stuck, and many of the other local guides use it to this day.

Garambullo pours the intense coffee through a formerly white filtering sock that appears to be the same sock he brought on this expedition last year. As he filters directly into my mug he assures me in Spanish that I'm going to like the brew this morning. In return I assure him in English that I'll try to keep an open mind. I examine the bag, a dark roast from Oaxaca, noting that regardless of the region in which it is grown, all Mexican coffee I've ever encountered describes itself as "dark."

"*¿Va a escribir esta mañana?*"

I sip the coffee—it's as strong as ever—before replying good-naturedly that I am indeed planning to write this morning if the coffee doesn't kill me first.

My friend smiles so broadly that it seems he'll crack his pierced eyebrow, which currently sports what appears to be a cactus thorn. He smiles because he knows that I would never compliment his coffee this early in an expedition, not even when my sleep was sabotaged by an abandoned burro bemoaning its fall from grace. A single night's sleep deprivation is not yet serious enough for me to appreciate Mexican coffee.

I wander off to find a writing perch, ending up on a well-worn log over by the remnants of last night's campfire. Although it's not particularly comfortable, it's obviously a sitting log rather than a burning log, and I'm glad to see that it has survived another campfire. I check for scorpions before plopping down.

I'm a morning writer for the most part, a member of a different genus from most other animals in this camp. As a general rule college kids think of writing as a nocturnal activity. Writing becomes synonymous with "homework," something that gets done once it's too dark to skateboard. Employing an elaborate system of due dates, the educators of this world have trained our students to become nocturnal binge writers, their productivity being directly related to the proximity of deadlines. These patterns are so deeply engrained in the American childhood experience that I no longer rail against counterproductive writing habits in my lectures. What good would it do? But here, inside the ring of tents, in the relative cool of a Baja morning, I can only hope that a few expeditioners will observe this strange behavior of mine and decide to experiment with it.

A student approaches finally, hair disheveled, coffee in one hand, notebook in the other, and whispers, "I forgot what today's prompt is."

I counsel that it's too early to worry about prompts. She cocks her head, rakes back her hair with her fingers, and looks at me as if I've just espoused heresy. Do I really expect an upper-division student from Our Fine University to write without academic prodding, or at least a formal learning outcome?

Ignoring the implicit question, I suggest, "Try exercising your powers of observation."

She alights on the log beside me, sets her coffee down in the dirt at her feet, and begins to look around. I tell her to close her eyes. She does.

"What do you hear?"

"Birds."

"Those are white-winged doves. They're common in the tropics."

"Cool."

"Tell me what they're saying."

Although the question begged to be answered metaphorically, she replies mimetically: "*Hooo-cooooo-hoo-hooo.*"

"Good. Now describe their conversation in your journal."

"Can I open my eyes?"

"Yeah. Open your eyes."

She opens her eyes, begins to write, and the morning unfolds its beauty.

### Big Numbers: A True Tale of the Mexican Free-Tailed Bat, as Promised

Mexican free-tailed bats, hereafter called "free tails," form the densest clusters of mammals in the world, huddling upside down at a density of up to eighteen hundred adults per square meter. Pups, which roost in crèches apart from their mothers, can hang together at a density of five thousand individuals per square meter. Mothers visit their pups once daily to nurse them. Each time a mother visits the crèche, she must locate her pup via olfactory and vocal clues. Pups recognize their mothers and will move toward them to suckle, but instances of milk theft do occur from time to time. Despite what seems like a chaotic system, the advantages of this alloparental nursing arrangement override its costs, and lead to a high survival rate at the point of weaning.[1]

In particularly large caves, free-tails can cover a thousand square meters of the cave's roof, and populations exceeding a million bats per cave are not uncommon. They are migratory, and sometimes form maternal colonies of over 100 million animals. In central Texas alone, free tails are thought to consume nine hundred thousand kilograms of insects each night during the roosting period.

1. See Gary F. McCracken and Mary K. Gustin, "Nursing Behavior in Mexican Free-tailed Bat Maternal Colonies," *Ethology* 89, no. 4 (January 1991): 305–21.

During the Second World War, $2 million was invested in "Project X-ray," a program to develop bat bombs. This weapon would be dropped by parachute from an altitude of one and a half kilometers, and at three hundred meters each bomb would release 1,040 free-tails to which timed incendiary devices were attached. These devices utilized napalm. The bats would be given time to disperse throughout a range of sixty kilometers, in hopes that they would roost under the eves or in the attics of Japanese buildings, which, because they were constructed of wood and paper, would ignite readily when the napalm went off.

The plan was to send a squadron of ten B-24 bombers from Alaska, each one carrying one hundred of the bombs, ultimately releasing 1,040,000 napalm-bearing free-tails throughout the area surrounding Osaka Bay.

I'm not making this up.

The program suffered a few setbacks, including a disaster where free-tails burned down an army airfield base in Carlsbad, New Mexico. Project X-ray was cancelled in 1945 due to its slow development, the bat bomb having been overtaken by the atomic bomb developed through the Manhattan Project, a device that promised to end the war more expeditiously.

Unfortunately, the Mexican free-tailed bat has not fared particularly well since the species' discharge from the military. Part of the problem is that they crowd into large caves such as Carlsbad Cavern in New Mexico, where their population has dropped from 8.7 million to half a million, and Eagle Creek Cave in Arizona, where their population has dropped from 25 million to thirty thousand. In other caves, especially where guano-mining operations have bored through cave roofs, free-tails have been eliminated entirely.

Free-tailed bats rely on fat reserves during migration. These reserves make them particularly vulnerable to the bioaccumulation of pesticides. Organochloride pesticides are especially problematic because they are fat-soluble, and can be passed via mother's milk when pups are being nursed. It doesn't help that the pups migrate soon after being weaned, and that there's naturally a high mortality from the stress of this early migration.

While there is not consensus as to whether human disturbance of caves is a greater problem for the Mexican free-tailed bat than pesticide use, it is clear that the combined effects of these two stressors are taking a toll on the species.

Free-tailed bats can occupy a wide range of habitats, from sea level to an elevation of three thousand meters, from desert to pine-oak forests, including pinyon-juniper woodlands. Their range extends from Oregon all the way to Argentina. With their long, narrow wings they can cover fifty kilometers in a single night's feeding. They have a low incidence of rabies, are one of the most populous mammals in the Americas, and are the bat featured on the Bacardi rum label.

# 3

# *Transect in the Sierra de la Laguna*

I am still a learner, not a teacher, feeding somewhat omnivorously,
browsing both stalk and leaves; but I shall perhaps be enabled to speak
with the more precision and authority by and by—if philosophy and
sentiment are not buried under a multitude of details.

HENRY DAVID THOREAU, letter to Harrison Blake, 1856

The wild is never distant in Baja, not even in town.

One winter morning, down in La Paz when the grand Los Arcos hotel was
still open, I awoke to the sight of a scorpion on the wall opposite my bed. Easily
as long as my little finger, with appendages the color of ripe cantaloupe, to my
bleary morning eyes the tail appeared to be barred. I snatched up my binoculars to inspect it more "closely" while maintaining a respectful distance, but it
scrambled behind a crooked oil painting of an appropriate desert scene before
I could identify it with confidence.

I dressed quickly and then, with a kiss, awakened Carol, my wife, warning
her not to straighten the painting. She sat up in bed, began to braid her long
blond hair, and told me that she wanted to get in a quick jog before breakfast.
She promised to catch up with me before I'd finished a second cup of coffee.
I grabbed my notebook and a favorite ballpoint and then made my way in
shorts, sandals, and a lightweight hoodie to a café just off the *malecon*, the
beachfront walkway, my binoculars around my neck.

La Paz wakes up slowly for a town its size, especially in December. The
crowing of downtown roosters lacks intensity, and the dogs, many of whom
bark all night, celebrate daybreak with a nap. Fishermen are in no great hurry

to wet their nets, and the taxi drivers seem content to wait for business to come to them. Whoever decided to name this town La Paz—*the Peace*—described how it comports itself just after daybreak.

I take a seat at an outdoor table facing the water. Almost alone in the café, I immerse myself in my writing, daubing ink neatly on the pages of a notebook too small for my sentences. Slow, dusty observations are interrupted periodically by *pangas* putting out in the harbor, each one manned by two sunbaked fishermen, the narrow, open boats piled with nets. Elegant terns, *Thalasseus elegans*, dive for fish, dart-like, within a hundred meters of my table, just far enough away that I can't tell what sort of fish they are catching even after I resort to binoculars.

Finally, just after my coffee is refilled for the second time, my rumination is interrupted by the commotion surrounding my wife's arrival. As soon as she enters the courtyard, a pale yellow Scott's oriole, female, alights on her shoulder. Carol stops walking, her hair still wet from the shower, and a waitress hurries toward her to shoo away the bird. With an open hand I gesture for the waitress to stay back. I order my wife's tea, hot—*"Té, caliente, por favor"*—and Carol continues to her place at the table, the bird still on her shoulder. She sits down gingerly, not wanting to frighten her passenger.

I make a perch of my forefinger and then slowly, gently press it upward under the bird's breast. The oriole responds as if we'd been pet and master for many years, stepping up onto my finger and gripping this new perch tightly.

The oriole's beak is open, slightly, as if it wants to sing its flutelike song, but there is not sufficient magic in the moment for it to do so. The bird seems distressed, at the very least apprehensive, but not at all inclined to fly away. Carol asks softly whether I think it is sick, and I shrug that I have no idea.

The bird continues to perch on my finger for the minute or two it takes the waitress to bring a cup of tea for Carol. The moment the cup is placed on the table the bird takes flight, ending our encounter. I ask the waitress whether this was a regular occurrence in the café, and she responds that birds would scavenge for crumbs on the floor, always, but they'd never had one land on the shoulder of a *cliente*.

And so it is with the wild in Baja—one has to be careful not to disrupt the magic.

I traditionally hand the program's reigns over to Dr. Awesome on the second day, and then stand back to watch science unfold. It's always an adventure to enter someone else's passion.

In this particular year, Dr. Awesome led us on a three-biome transect through the Sierra de la Laguna. It began high up in a thorn forest, a biotic community too few people ever experience. If you imagine what a tropical rainforest might look like moments before it turned into a desert, you'd have yourself a thorn forest. Thick and yet arid, leafy and yet prickly, genetically diverse and yet highly patterned, a thorn forest is a great place to hike if you can find a trail. Lose the trail and you're well advised to backtrack until you find it.

The students have been instructed to ignore their writing prompt until we reach the riparian zone, so they're attending solely to science at the moment, looking for what Dr. Awesome calls "patterns of convergent evolution between divergent organisms." Their attention is drawn to waxy leaves, nodular roots, and sessile inflorescences. I'm more attentive to the thorns myself; every vascular plant in this forest seems to have been designed to puncture mammals, especially bipedal academicians 1.9 meters tall. This trail was cut by someone substantially shorter than that, and my broad-brimmed hat is constantly being impaled by thorns on low-lying branches. I find myself wishing I'd brought a pith helmet along. (I'm eccentric enough to own one, but not quite quirky enough to wear it in the presence of students.)

My self-assigned job this morning is to make certain the duckies stay hydrated. They're all carrying at least two liters of water, but this is going to be a hot hike, and in this terrain if they wait until they're thirsty before drinking, the penalty will be dehydration. Today's official motto is: "Drink before you're thirsty!"

This transect is all about water. The thorn forest exists because we're in a relatively wet zone that receives an average twenty-eight centimeters of water per year. That may not sound like a lot if you're from somewhere like Cleveland, which annually gets ninety-two centimeters of rain plus another hundred centimeters of snowfall, but here in Baja, twenty-eight centimeters is a tremendously moist environment. Today doesn't feel moist, however. It's hot. And it's dry. I'm wearing long trousers—the only ones not wearing shorts are the guides and the faculty—and carrying extra water. Thank goodness we're going downhill.

My first-ever job was teaching hiking merit badge at a scout ranch back home in Colorado. I would lead five ten-mile hikes and one twenty-mile hike every week, without variance, all summer long, for which I received a stipend of thirty-five dollars per week and all I could eat. Well, I could eat a lot back then, and I thought it was the world's best job even though I had to wear gartered knee socks. Green. While a few of my fellow counselors grumbled that we only made five dollars per day, I figured that I was actually being paid fifty cents per mile, most days, which seemed like a pretty good deal to hike through groves of ponderosa pine.

So here I am, more than three decades later, leading an expedition of college students through some of the most exotic terrain on the continent, and what do I fantasize about? Getting my old job back at Peaceful Valley Scout Ranch.

I've fallen behind a bit during my reveries, but one of the students is waiting for me. When I catch up she asks a question we'd covered in class: how to tell the difference between two columnar cacti, pitaya dulce and pitaya agria. She remembers that *dulce* means "sweet" and *agria* means "sour," but can't remember how to tell the two cacti apart. I reply that pitaya agria doesn't fit its genus name, *Stenocereus*, which comes from the Greek *steno*, which means "straight."

"Oh."

From the brevity of the response I deduce that Greek etymology might not have been the most helpful mnemonic for this particular student. Contrite, I suggest, "Or you can remember that a common English name for pitaya dulce is 'organ pipe cactus.' Even though I don't teach it, the name is fairly descriptive of how pitaya dulce looks if you squint."

"So then why don't you teach it?"

Speaking softly enough so that my voice doesn't reach the group ahead of us, I report that if I teach English common names, my scientist friends tend to get edgy, but that if I teach the Spanish common names they let me get away with it.

"Oh."

Things were never this complicated back at the scout ranch.

We hike together a while in silence, and find a tall pitaya dulce, one with at least twenty twice-my-height branches coming off a central trunk, the branches looking very much like organ pipes when we squint. With our eyes wide open the branches appear to have vertical ribs striped with parallel rows of thorns clustered in starburst patterns. I search for flowers, but it's too early in the season, which is a shame because it's one of the coolest flowers ever to have evolved. I tell my hiking partner about it anyway, describing the large, fragrant, deeply tubular white flower that attracts its primary pollinator, the hawk moth. Unfortunately, it's hard to get undergraduates excited about flowers not yet in bloom, and there's never a hawk moth around when you need one.

Moving along, we don't have to search far to find pitaya agria. It's hard to tell whether we're looking at one plant or several because of how pitaya agria sprawls, inevitably becoming a bramble of serpentine, thick-as-your-arm branches that seem to want to grow in every direction. This thicket is a good ten meters across, and is completely impenetrable. I examine the radial spines, shaped like tiny daggers, but don't comment on them lest I skew the botanizing that's supposed to be taking place. I am about to mention that the juice from pitaya agria's fruit makes a nice margarita, but I'm interrupted by my hiking partner, who has looked the plant up in her field guide.

"It's called galloping cactus."

"Really? I've never heard that."

She doesn't believe me, of course, opining that anyone who can remember *Stenocereus gummosos* could certainly remember "galloping cactus." This proves the point, I suppose, that my colleagues constantly make, that sooner or later common names will get a fellow like me in trouble. In this case, where I'm apparently in trouble for not knowing a common name that I've never before heard, the point seems well taken.

We resume our hike. The head guide, Manuelito, waits for us, and when we catch up to him I ask whether he's ever heard the common name "galloping cactus."

"*Por supuesto*," he replies with a knowing nod. He then translates himself for the student's sake, "Of course."

There being nothing more to say on this particular topic, we continue the transect, soon catching up to the main group.

During the season when the pitaya was ripe, the aboriginal people of Baja would subsist on it exclusively, and were said to experience a general euphoria as a result. When the Jesuit missionaries first came to Baja, they were appalled to discover that at the end of the pitaya season the natives would pick through their dried feces to reharvest undigested seeds, which they'd grind into a meal from which they made a type of *pozole*. The Jesuits forbade the practice. Manuelito, a trove of indigenous lore, loves telling this story, especially since we come from a Jesuit university. He also tells us that if you crush up pitaya branches and throw them into the water, it will stupefy the fish, bringing them to the surface without poisoning them.

One of the guys wants to try this, of course, to test the scientific validity of the claim, but I discourage any thought of conducting the experiment. There will be no environmentally destructive science on my expeditions.

Padre Norberto Ducrue, writing in 1765, tells the story of one of his brother Jesuits discovering the second harvest:

When Padre Francisco Maria Piccolo made a certain exploration at the time when the missions were just being established, at one *rancheria* the people gave him as a gift or honorary present some of the flour from these seeds (something which we call the second harvest of the *pitaha-*

*yas*). The Padre, not knowing what it was, and in order to give the natives the pleasure of seeing him eat the gift which they had given him, ate all or part of the flour. What he had eaten later came to be recognized by the Padres, and whenever any of them met with Padre Piccolo the story of the event provided an occasion for amusement and laughter. (88)

We continue the transect. Thorn forest gives way to a more standard sub-tropical coastal desert ecology, and I miss the shade. There is nothing particularly leafy here, and any semblance of an overhead canopy has disappeared. We no longer need to follow a trail to get from point A to point B because the plants have spread out, many of them poisoning their turf so that other species cannot cross roots with them. The soil itself seems less alive, and certainly less familiar with water. I can feel the heat radiating upward, collecting under the brim of my hat. While the brim still shades my face, the shade itself is no longer cool.

The guides are uncharacteristically impatient at this point, eager to lead us to the gorgeous riparian zone ahead, but we faculty are digging in our heels. We want the students to realize that this is more than just a dry spot in the hike. We're in a different biome now, and we want them to notice how the soil has changed, and the biological density, and even the biodiversity itself. This is where transects get really cool, but it's also where this one gets really hot. I let my biologist partner do the explaining, and return to my primary function of reminding the students to hydrate.

One can do one's job too well, I suppose. At the hottest part of the hike, which just happens to be the area with the least vegetation behind which to hide, female students suddenly and urgently need to pee. Appropriate arrangements are made, and after warning the departing naturalists to watch for rattlesnakes, I pull out my notebook and jot down a recommendation for next year's trip. *Pee earlier on the transect.* I will not realize how goofy this sounds until I review my notes in order to make programmatic adjustments six months from now.

While wandering away from the trail in order to attend to my own bladder, I spot a crested caracara, sitting atop a majestic cardon cactus, looking directly down at me. White neck and throat, orange-red face, black crested head, yellow legs. Long yellow legs. I've read that the facial skin, which is devoid of feathers, will turn yellow when the bird feels threatened. This bird is not advertising any stress whatsoever, and it occurs to me that I've never seen one this far from a highway. The eyes look red to me, but I learn later that the eyes of adults are an orange brown. I notice a bulge in the caracara's crop; this bird has had a recent meal. I presume, optimistically, that it ate something it killed—a lizard, perhaps, or even a small mammal—for these birds will also eat carrion, which is why I usually see them in proximity to highways. I sniff the air, but I don't smell carrion, I only smell heat.

There's no way I could dislike *Caracara cheriway*, although its former scientific name, *Polyborus plancus*, connoted a less-likeable organism. The "borus" in the genus name translates "gluttonous"; polyborus implies that it eats just about everything. The species name, "plancus," refers to its flat feet. Although it has talons, unlike vultures, the flat talons affixed to its long legs allow it to sprint quite gracefully. I'm told it can outrun a man, but not a roadrunner.[1] And there you have it: *Polyborus plancus*, the flat-footed omni-glutton. Such an ignoble name for such a noble falcon, thank goodness they finally changed it.

The slowest-flying member of the falcon family, topping out at about eighteen meters per second,[2] the caracara is better adapted to hunt on the ground. Unlike most members of the family, who prefer the taste of fowl, this falcon is not particularly fussy about its protein source. And yet it has a regal dignity that rivals that of the golden eagle. This dignity positively radiates from my *amigo* atop the cardon, framed between two peaks in the distance, its jaunty cap proclaiming its fearlessness. I recall that William Beebe, writing about his 1936 expedition to Baja aboard the schooner *Zaca*, described the caracara as the master of Baja birds because he'd seen caracara drive ravens and vultures away from a kill (185).

The bird watches me piss, and it unsettles me to be taking such a casual approach to bird-watching. I glance down at the stream of urine and notice, just in time, that it isn't soaking into the parched soil, but instead is running toward my boot. I back away, and when I glance back up to the top of the cardon, the caracara has vanished. Serves me right.

I associate two animals with Beebe. In addition to the caracara, I also think of him in terms of whale sharks. The sixth chapter of *Zaca Venture*, the book Beebe wrote about his Baja expedition, is called "Whale-Sharking." Herein the author narrates the attempt to collect a whale shark specimen that they estimated, from photographs, to be forty two feet long.[3]

> When we came alongside the fish was only about three feet below the surface. We waited until he was almost awash, when both men made a beautiful pole-vaulting dive, with the harpoon between them. They struck hard and then leaped into the air and let their whole weight bear

---

1. For the record, it should be stated that, unlike in the cartoons, in real life a coyote can outsprint a roadrunner on the open road, but not through dense scrub.

2. As a point of comparison, the peregrine falcon has been clocked at 108 meters per second.

3. I've seen the photograph, and would suggest that Beebe was a bit too optimistic about the shark's length.

down, driving the harpoon home. At the same moment I fired the revolver straight down into the creature's head, making at least two direct hits. (163)

They were never able to kill this spectacular animal. When they finally pulled the whale shark up to the *Zaca*, it tore off the harpoon "as if it were a pin," and swam away.

I sometimes have to defend Beebe in class, lest the students apply today's standards for scientific collecting to an earlier age. He was willing to sacrifice aquatic specimens for scientific research in 1938 because of his conviction of "the superabundance of life" (his term) in Baja waters. He wrote of a day where, during several hours of trolling, they spotted more than fifty turtles at the surface. He reports that almost 20 million tuna were caught along the coast every year, "and yet the fishermen told me that they can detect no diminution in their numbers."

Those days have changed. During our expedition this year, in a full week of paddling we will see two sea turtles.

I would probably be less concerned by the Baja I visit these days were I not to spend so much time in dusty volumes studying the region's historical ecology. I recently acquired an original copy of the report of the Townsend expedition, which visited the Sea of Cortez aboard the US Bureau of Fisheries steamer *USFC Albatross* in 1889 and 1911. At one point in the annals of the second expedition, Townsend referenced an extraordinary sighting of green turtles that had congregated to lay eggs during the first expedition. He wrote:

When the "Albatross" visited San Bartolome on April 11, 1889, a very remarkable catch of green turtles was made. The U.S.S. "Ranger" was there at the same time and a seining party was made up consisting of members of the crew of that vessel and of the "Albatross." In a single haul of a seine 600 feet long we brought to shore 162 green turtles, many of large size. Probably half as many more escaped from the seine before it could be beached; there being a continual loss of turtles crawling over the cork lines during the entire time we were hauling it. The great bulk of this catch was, of course, liberated, although both vessels took on board all that could be used. There are doubtless other bays around the Peninsula which are frequented by turtles at the egg laying season and where large numbers might be obtained by seining. (445)

Townsend's Baja, and even Beebe's Baja, are places I will never know. I find myself wondering whether, a century from now, some academic interested in

Baja historical ecology will pick up this book and fret that she will never experience the abundance of Farnsworth's Baja. Let's hope not.

We reach, finally, the riparian zone, and the students abandon their observations of convergent evolution. It's cool here, lush, and it's as if someone just rang the recess bell, for they are good enough naturalists to know there's water below. Swimmable water. The pace picks up, notebooks are jammed into back pockets, and the faculty are left behind. It's all good—*todos bien*—because we know that we'll be able to reengage our students at the first swimming hole. We'll eat lunch there, have them do a bit of journaling, and then let them in on the secret that there's actually a better swimming hole half a kilometer downstream.

When I finally remove my boots and dip my feet into the water, I am reminded of an essay written by John Nichols, "The Holiness of Water." I try to remember his closing sentence: "Consciousness and soul owe their incredible being to every drop of moisture that ever fell from a cloud and awakened a spadefoot toad, called forth a mosquito, or birthed a dragonfly."

There are dragonflies here aplenty. And damselflies. It is a blessing to share their holy water.

I watch the students cavort, pleased at how quickly they find one of their designated *amigos*, a cape water snake, *Nerodia valida celano*, hiding unsuccessfully in the in-water vegetation. Although it's endemic to this area, it's not particularly exotic, looking like a garter snake that some vandal spray-painted black. The discovery draws me into the water.

Back in the classroom I had described this snake as "harmless," which may have been a mistake. One of my best students, eager to show her designated *amigo* to her classmates, chases it into a gentle cascade, attempting its capture in waist-deep water. She grabs it inexpertly, and it bites her in the tender web between thumb and index finger, causing her somewhat instinctively to fling the snake backward over her shoulder, where it lands on one of her best professors. The poor thing bounces off my sternum as if this were part of its daily routine, and then swims away without suffering further mayhem.

I'm happy to report that the student only bled for a few minutes, and that she's currently well on her way toward earning a PhD. Strangely enough, it won't be in herpetology.

Attention shifts from snakes to damselflies, which are particularly lustrous here in the direct sunlight. Numerous pairs are coupling, and the question is raised as to why different color damselflies are copulating with each other. In the process of focusing on this question, the expeditioners shift from snake-hunter mode into a more reverential mode. Their sudden attentiveness sparkles with intellectual curiosity.

On my long-range list of things to do I plan to invent a religion that focuses entirely on reverence rather than faith. Aesthetics will trump philosophical propositions, and ideas will ultimately be evaluated by their ability to stimulate awe. (Or, at the very least, appreciation.) In this new religion we will studiously avoid asking each other what we believe, and will focus instead on what we revere. When we do that, we will have finally developed a sect that unites rather than divides, a church in which a few pews are reserved for naturalists.

In my new religion, more of us will be able to identify the damselflies inhabiting this lovely stream, distinguishing between *Hetaerina americana*, the American rubyspot, and *Argia vivida*, the vivid dancer, regardless of whether we've learned the Latin. Despite their similar structural phenotypes, it's not at all difficult—for those who are blessed with normal color vision—to discriminate between these species. The field guides report that the male vivid dancers are an electric blue, while females are tan. The male American rubyspots have a red metallic thorax and head, while the females have orange and green highlights. Both species of damselfly prefer spring-fed streams in arid areas, and are in turn fascinating to watch as the males defend their temporary territories, domains that will change on a day-to-day basis.

After consulting the appropriate field guide, it is decided that what at first appeared to be trans-genera mating weirdness was in actuality sexual dimorphism at work. Dancers were copulating with dancers, and rubyspots were copulating with rubyspots. All was as it should be in the world of odonate courtship.

After a leisurely lunch the time comes for a bit of journaling. Today's writing prompt is two words long: "Describe water." Every year this one turns out to be a religious exercise.

Even midstream, the rocks are radiating heat by the time the expeditioners have had their fill of riparian writing. I wet my shirt before donning it, wrap a wet bandana around my neck, cowboy style, and then fill my hat with cool creek water before placing it on my head. The students follow suit, some getting everything wet except their hiking shoes. All will be dry by the time we get to the rim of the canyon carved by this creek.

Very little botanizing takes place on the uphill trek back to the *ranchero* where we'd parked our vans. As students run out of water, we distribute the extra that the guides and I have been carrying. There will not be enough, ultimately, and we will outhike our water supply by at least a kilometer. Students with more are encouraged to share with students who need more, but the intense heat of the afternoon seems to dry us from the inside out. Once we're back in the shade of the thornscrub I encourage the students to drink what they've got, there will be plenty of water for everyone once we make it to the vans. Better yet, there's a cooler full of *cerveza* on ice. These will be the best beers most of these kids will ever taste.

Energy is low by the time we get back to camp. Dinner is a bit desultory, even though spirits remain high. I huddle with the guides, the TA, and Dr. Awesome, and we decide to cut out the sunrise bird hike that we'd been planning. We don't want to wear these kids out before we get them to the island.

Manuelito has a surprise, one he was not planning to unveil until we got to the island tomorrow. He pulls out a long, wedge-shaped dry bag, and from it withdraws a travel guitar. It's a funky little thing, and seems funkier still when Manuelito explains that he's discovered that he can paddle with it between his legs and still do a roll, even in a loaded kayak. We pass it around, admiring it as if it contained all the entertainment potential of Hollywood, Nashville, and Las Vegas combined. I'm kicking myself for not bringing a travel guitar of my own, a situation I will remedy next year, once I've purchased one.

Students gather. Some are assigned water bottles, some are assigned pots. A few scour the nearby landscape for drumsticks, and are distracted by the discovery of a tarantula hiding under a cactus rib not far from where I've pitched my tent. It's huge, bigger than the palm of your hand, entirely black, hairy, and appears unusually well-groomed for a creature in this environment, looking more like something you'd purchase in a toy store than encounter in the desert. We provisionally identify it as a Mexican black velvet tarantula, but we haven't got an appropriate field guide with which to confirm this or with which to discover the proper scientific name.[4] This has always been part of the frustration of these expeditions: even when we carry a dozen field guides, we never seem to have the right one on hand, perhaps because many of the field guides we'd love to carry have not yet been written.

The few nonmusicians in the group light candles.

Manuelito plays, and we all join in. Some of the duckies know the Spanish to a few of his songs. One of the fellows begins bebopping base harmonies to the music, using nonsense syllables that make more and more sense as the performance matures. At one point, Manuelito hands me the guitar, and I sing a version of "Wild Thing" dedicated to Dr. Awesome.

It was glorious, and it was entirely Baja.

We would think ourselves silly were we to put together such entertainment back at the university, especially if sober. Here in the desert, however, where everything making noise has significance, our concert takes on an arid resonance that makes it work. Even though we've been here such a short time, we have already earned the right to be enchanted by simple activity.

---

4. *Brachypelma vagans.*

What I know, and the students have not yet learned, is that it will only get better from here on. A day from now, a few pelicans fishing in a cove will be all it takes to engross us during breakfast. A day later, hermit crabs along the tide line will command the attention of our more engaged naturalists for the better part of an hour. By the end of next week, a kettle[5] of frigatebirds climbing a thermal will be enough to spellbind the entire expedition.

5. In ornithology, "kettle" is a collective term used to describe a group of birds—usually raptors, but sometimes gulls or frigatebirds—riding a thermal together in a circular fashion. The origins of the term are controversial.

# 4

# To the Island

We had read what books were available about the Gulf and they
were few and in many cases confused. . . . A few naturalists
with specialties had gone into the Gulf and, in the way of
specialists, had seen nothing they hadn't wanted to.

JOHN STEINBECK, *The Log from the Sea of Cortez*, 1951

We make a quick stop in La Paz on our way out to the island, just long enough
to get the students fitted into wetsuits and snorkel gear.

La Paz had its own nineteenth-century pirate, an Englishman named
Cromwell whose buried treasure was never found. According to the story, the
locals had a difficult time pronouncing his name, and "Cromwell" became
"Coromuel." As pirates go, Cromwell was something of a minor leaguer; his
biggest claim to fame is that a local weather phenomenon, the Coromuel
breeze, is named after him.

The Coromuel is a spring phenomenon for the most part, generated when
cool marine air from the Pacific is drawn over the peninsula into La Paz after
the warmer air over the Sea of Cortez heats up. As a general rule, the Coromuel
begins around sundown, blows all night, and dies around a little before noon.
The people of La Paz love the Coromuel because it keeps them cool, except
for in July and August, when there's not enough of a temperature differential
to fuel it. Knowledgeable kayakers appreciate the Coromuel as well, because it
has better manners than El Norte, the spiteful, despotic northerly blowhard
that, although properly considered a winter phenomenon, can still make us
miserable in these early days of spring.

After we leave La Paz, wind will dominate our lives. Tailwinds will become a source of cheer, and headwinds may do more than dishearten.

An eight-kilometer deep-water channel runs between two named points that juxtapose nicely in Spanish. At the northern tip of the La Paz peninsula, Punta Arranca Cabellos translates literally as "the point where people pull out their hair." At the southern tip of Isla Espíritu Santo lies Punta Dispensa, which demarcates the theological point where one is exempted from religious duties. Depending on the winds, this channel can be too rough to transit via panga. When it's flat, we zip across it effortlessly; when it's choppy, the slog seems to take forever.

Of the dozens of times I've crossed this channel, only thrice have I crossed via sea kayak, and each of those times I was returning from the island, crossing from north to south, the prevailing wind at my back. That's theoretical wind, of course: two of these crossings were begun after allowing the Coromuel to die, which entails departing at the hottest part of the day. The heat can be intense if there's no wind in the middle of the channel; sometimes the better paddlers will do Eskimo rolls just to cool off.

Other than for the heat, what I remember most about paddling the San Lorenzo Channel are encounters with *Execoetus volitans*.

Properly called the "tropical two-wing flying fish," *Execoetus volitans* can be every bit as entertaining in a pelagic environment as whales or dolphins. I realize how preposterous that might sound, even as I write it, but I write from the kayaker's perspective, not that of a shipboard naturalist. The closer one is to the water, the greater the surprise when a fish erupts from the surface only a meter or two from one's bow, and then "flies" forward forty or fifty meters, sometimes more, before vanishing into a wave. Now imagine several flying fish erupting at the same time or, on a good day, even a dozen.

There's never warning. Even when you expect them in the middle of the San Lorenzo Channel, there's always mutual astonishment when it happens, as if panicked chickadees have just erupted from the depths. Flying fish operate on pure terror, which is a good thing because they require tremendous speed when they launch themselves out of the water. They never really fly—they leap, they glide, and then they splash down, rarely attaining a height of more than a meter. They wiggle their deeply forked caudal fins side to side as they launch, and continue finning the entire time they are airborne, as if they imagine themselves still to be immersed in liquid. They do not flap their "wings" (elongated pectoral fins) to gain altitude, they merely extend the pectoral fins to prolong their glide. They want to get as far away as possible from whatever frightened them out of the water in the first place.

Once, after spending a week on the island with my fast-paddling nephews, halfway across the channel we arranged our flotilla in the flying fish formation, seven boats side by side, as close together as we could get without banging paddles. We had perfect December conditions—wind at the back and a gentle swell to push the kayaks along smartly. Moving at the quickest pace we could sustain while keeping the formation together, we herded flying fish before us, inciting scores of fish to leap ahead at any given moment. It was dizzying: the only thing missing was a kayak band playing Wagner's "Ride of the Valkyries."

I've only been able to examine *Execoetus volitans* close-up a few times, usually first thing in the morning after sailing through the night in tropical waters. It's a common experience to find flying fish on deck, and I've heard that some sailors actually collect them each morning and fry them up. While I've never been quite this hungry, a dead fish on the deck is always an opportunity to engage in natural history. Their two-tone coloration is common to fish who dwell at the surface: silver white on the bottom to make it more difficult to be seen by swimming predators looking up, and a deep, dark blue-black on the top to make it more difficult to be seen by airborne predators looking down.

The students still being greenhorn kayakers, we never paddle across the channel in this direction, opting instead to cross in two large pangas provided by our outfitter. While this affords a less intimate experience of the sea, we still see the occasional flying fish during the crossing. They seem even more frantic when fleeing from a powerboat. Who can blame them?

As we approach the southern tip of the island I spot numerous species of charismatic avifauna that students should be identifying, everything from boobies to frigatebirds, but I don't point these *amigos* out because the time has come for the class to discover the flora and fauna on their own. We don't want them becoming dependent on faculty eyesight. As we draw nearer and nearer, the students are far too preoccupied with the island's resplendence and general magnificence to waste attention on birds. One of the students has appointed herself to be my "seeing-eye" companion for colors, and she reports that the island is "very pinkish." I don't bother to remind her that the island's palette is the result of how the clastic rock has integrated volcanic ash; for now it's sufficient to enjoy the island's pinkness and temporarily forgo the geology we learned back in the classroom.

I wait and wait, but we round Punta Dispensa without anyone noticing what's overhead. We're missing birds so magnificent that the word "magnificent" is actually part of their names. The winged creatures here are clearly more aware of us than we are of them; the white-headed juvenile frigatebird directly above us keeps up with the panga effortlessly, without even needing to flap its wings.

Once, during some alone time on the southeastern tip of the island, watching a mixed kettle of turkey vultures and magnificent frigatebirds circling the updraft created by a knoll, I began to wonder which species would go the longest without flapping. Establishing a somewhat informal method for this observation, I decided to begin by singling out whichever bird first flapped its wings and then timing it to determine how long it took before it again flapped. Then I would repeat the experiment with the other avian tribe, and whichever species' champion held the longest delta between flaps would be deemed the victor. So I watched, and watched, and watched some more for what had to be an hour before abandoning the experiment because not a single bird in the kettle had flapped.

Frigatebirds have a similar wingspan of a bald eagle but are approximately flour times lighter. Picture a dark bird with a two-meter wingspan that only weighs a kilo. Long wings, a long forked tail, a long bill, and not much else. They are designed to soar, not to flap, and can reportedly soar through the night at great altitude. They specialize in catching flying fish, swooping low over the water and then snatching up a fish when it leaps into the air. This seems to be a particularly risky activity if you believe the field guide that claims that the magnificent frigatebird is unable to take off again once it lands in the water, and will ultimately drown. I've personally seen a frigatebird land in water and take off repeatedly, as did students in expedition 7, which suggests that field guides need as much ground-thruthing as other literature.

Years ago I found myself wondering whether I'd ever witnessed a magnificent frigatebird feed by surface skimming. I'd seen them engage in their classic kleptoparasitic behavior many times, stealing food from boobies as they returned to their nesting colony to feed their booby chicks, but I found myself more interested in how often frigatebirds actually collected their own prey. Having made a point to look for skimming, I observed two or three birds actually catching fish that way during every hour of that day's paddle. They swoop down to the water's level, glide across the water so low that they couldn't possibly flap their wings, and then open the lower mandible so that it delicately skims the water's surface. When they catch something, the head twists down quickly, the entire bill in the water for a brief moment, and then they snap up, again without flapping, with a fish hooked to the end of the bill. I observed, further, that they were able to snatch fish, and these were not flying fish, from the water's surface without getting anything more than their bills wet, which probably explains why they've evolved such a long, hooked bill in the first place.

This exercise taught me something important about how I go about observing natural history: I'd never seen this particular feeding behavior until

I specifically looked for it, even though it had presumably been happening in my presence for years. How much else was I missing during my paddles?

As reflected in this chapter's epigraph, Steinbeck would complain that I was only seeing what I was searching for and nothing else. Point well taken. A couple years ago one of the students asked when we'd start seeing boobies, and I replied that I'd been seeing boobies for several days. She laughed, thinking that in jest I'd referenced mammalian anatomy, but I assured her that two species of avian boobies had been circling about for the last few days. Within a few minutes, fortunately, she spotted her first brown booby and thus corroborated that I'd been observing the correct organisms. Sometimes you just have to look up.

Our kayaks are already out on the island. Waiting. We've been anticipating landing on the first beach, which for us is at Playa Dispensa, for twelve weeks if not longer. Now we finally get sand between our toes.

I touch the island. Old friends. While I'm happy for my island time to begin, Island Day no. 1 is always my least favorite day of the expedition. Logistics consume the greater part of the day, and the process of expediting seems to crowd out Baja itself.

This would be a good time for me to let the guides and the TA run things. Without my help it will take better than two hours to pack the boats, make lunch, orient the students, and finally begin paddling—with my help it will take better than three. I'm tempted to grab the binoculars and head over the hill for some gratuitous bird watching, but I never do. Some year, I keep promising myself, I will. Instead, I grab a paddle and one of the smaller single kayaks, wade out into chest-deep water, and then invite the students, one by one, to come out and practice a wet exit. It's a fairly simple exercise where they capsize so that they're completely upside down, reach their hands up and out of the water so that they can bang on the hull three times, grab their spray skirt by what kayakers call the "oh shit strap," pull the strap forward with enough energy to release the skirt, and then swim to the surface. The university prefers that they complete this exercise without drowning.

The first ducky to venture out is the kid who'd attempted the flip at the waterfall two days earlier. It appears that she's to be the DBP—designated brave person—for the remainder of the trip, and she's already got some nasty bruises as a result of her exploits. While she mounts the boat and adjusts her skirt, I ask whether the bruises are the result of her flip, and she responds, brightly, "Some of them."

I don't inquire further, but she gives me a tour of her bruises anyway. They are numerous and multicolored, and each one appears to be a badge of honor. I beg her not to add to the collection during the week ahead, and she responds, again brightly, "OK."

There are cheers on the beach when the first successful wet exit is executed, but then we get down to the business of cranking out repeat performances. Our DBP returns to the beach to begin manufacturing lunch, and the TA is putting a crew together to fill water bladders. One by one the remainder of the expeditionary force performs the drill, during which time I have the opportunity to ask each one how the writing is coming along so far. Most of them complain that there's too much to do, and I admonish each scholar not to become distracted by classmates. "Pay attention to the island," I advise. Then we capsize the boat. Always the sermon before the baptism.

My role evolves as the program matures, and this is a good thing. During the first few expeditions I tended to focus somewhat single-mindedly on bringing as many students home as I'd taken abroad. I try to fixate less on survival each year. Instead, I've begun to perceive my role as not all that different from that of the students: to observe and to write while focusing on our collective learning. In doing this, I keep in mind something said by my former PhD supervisor, Scottish poet Kathleen Jamie, in a profile in *The Guardian*:

> When we were young, we were told that poetry is about voice, about finding a voice and speaking with this voice, but the older I get I think it's not about voice, it's about listening and the art of listening, listening with attention. I don't just mean with the ear; bringing the quality of attention to the world. The writers I like best are those who attend.

*Bringing the quality of attention to the world.*

Having completed the final wet exit, I emerge from the water and realize that I have not been paying attention to my own body. I should be shivering at this point, having spent at least an hour chest-deep in the vernal Sea of Cortez without the benefit of my wetsuit, but I'm not feeling the least bit cold. The moment I step foot on the beach, Garambullo cries, "Lunch," but it is not until I hear this command that I realize how famished I am. Or how thirsty. One of the fellows brings me a cold beer and helps me carry the kayak back up the beach. The coolers, unfortunately, will be going back with the pangas in another hour, and these will be our last cold cervezas until we get to La Paz in a week. My fingers are pruned from all the time in the water, so I ask the student to open the beer for me. When I take the first swig I actually shiver; now that my body is warming up it finally realizes that it was cold.

*Bringing the quality of attention to the world.*

I eat quickly. The students have already packed all our communal supplies into the boats, and I am suddenly the expedition slacker. Watching these guides over the years, I've noticed that they can get all the expedition business done—whether setting up or breaking camp, while at the same time bandaging blisters or extracting thorns—and somehow, magically, get their own gear packed or unpacked ahead of everyone else. I crave a bit of the magic for myself, but I'm resigned to the fact that my own tent, once we arrive on the next beach a few hours from now, will probably be the last one erected. I can only hope it's up before dark.

I find my trusty old yak on the beach, the same boat I use every year. The white surface has dulled a bit since I last saw it, but the boat still looks like it will float. The outfitter has had a name painted on the bow of each boat. The doubles are named after whales, the singles after birds. My boat, which was supposed to be called "Osprey," suffers permanent transposition. *Opsrey.* None of the outfitter's staff noticed the error until I pointed it out the first time I was assigned to this boat. Nothing worse than assigning your only misspelled boat to a writing instructor.

I drag my gear to the boat's rear hatch. The forward compartment has already been packed with breakfast supplies. I'm always the breakfast boat, and I don't know whether the guides instruct students to pack breakfasts in my boat because they are light, or because I'm always the first one up in the morning. Either way, it works.

Before beginning to pack, I look westward toward the Baja peninsula, some thirty-two kilometers distant, and become aware for the first time this trip of the water's luminosity. Even to my color blind eyes it seems somehow special, and calls to mind Steinbeck's description of the hue: *Below the Mexican border the water changes color; it takes on a deep ultramarine blue—a washtub bluing blue, intense and seeming to penetrate deep into the water; the fishermen call it "tuna water"* (36).

I finally give the TA the okay to assign boats, and the students pack their gear into the aft compartments. There's not enough room, of course, so I show them a few tricks, like strapping their snorkel gear to the top of the hatch, and folding their wetsuits to use as seat cushions.

The pangas depart, finally, and we are on our own. Manuelito yells from the other end of the beach, "*¿Listo, Juanito?*"

He wants to know whether I'm ready, and I reply—"*¡Nací listo!*"—that I was born ready. I turn to face my charges, and with full professorial comportment

I announce that the most sacrosanct rule of expeditionary sea kayaking is never to get into a boat without peeing first. The rule receives full compliance.

And thus, another circumnavigation of Isla Espíritu Santo is attempted.

ᐳ

As reported in *The Log of the Sea of Cortez*, what Steinbeck appreciated most about Isla Espíritu Santo was that it provided his expedition with its first opportunity to turn over boulders during their collecting excursions. He wrote, "The boulders on this beach were almost perfect turning-over size—heavy enough to protect the animals under them from grinding by the waves, and light enough to be lifted." Amazing. Here's an island that covers ninety-five square kilometers, not counting the seven distinct islets that fringe it, and Baja's master narrator has little more to say about it than to compliment the convenient size of its boulders.

Steinbeck could have written about the alternating layers of black lava and pink volcanic ash that comprise the island, or about how the elements have sculpted the softer layers into sedimentary ribbons that appear to have been gnawed on by time itself. He might have noted the fourteen distinct bays that fringe the western side, eight of which support populations of mangrove. He might even have described the sound of the waves sloshing through the sea caves on the east side, or the ospreys' piercing calls as they soar the six-hundred-meter-high cliffs above those caves. At the very least, he could have reported what it's like to stroll along the spectacular white-sand beaches, one of which is almost four kilometers long.

No. He wanted us to know how perfect the boulders were for flipping.

ᐳ

The first boat off the beach is mine. My class comes to me in ones and twos, and while we wait for the tardies I counsel those at hand on how to adjust their foot pegs while under way, or how to flip their rudders into the water, or maybe that they're carrying their paddles upside down. They're at their ragtag worst at the moment, but a few days from now they'll appear to have grown up in sea kayaks. Over the course of the afternoon I'll coach them, here and there, to improve on bad paddling techniques before they become habitual. Posture. A loose grip on the paddle shaft. The angle of the blades. Using the torso muscles rather than relying on arm strength. Some students will master the stroke quickly, others will never experience it. The university loves them dearly either way.

We paddle. Eighty kilometers to go, I think to myself, before we return to this beach, coming back in boats that weigh half as much as they do now.

They're singing already, in one of the doubles. I should have guessed that this would be a euphonious group, given how well they worked together back in the classroom. It seems so far away now, that other world from which we've come.

We traverse a low point and then make for the first clump of mangroves we see. This is awful timing—asking rookie paddlers to navigate mangroves with the boats at their absolute heaviest—but this first mangrove lagoon is the most spectacular one on the entire island, and it would be even more awful to miss it.

Steinbeck hated mangroves. He wrote:

> As the tide came up we moved upward in the intertidal toward the mangrove trees, and the foul smell of them reached us. They were in bloom, and the sharp sweet smell of their flowers, combined with the filthy odor of the mud about their roots, was sickening. But they are fascinating to look into. . . . We suppose it is the combination of foul odor and the impenetrable quality of the mangrove roots which gives one a feeling of dislike for these salt-water-eating bushes. (100)

*The Log of the Sea of Cortez* was reviewed in the same issue of the *New York Times* that announced the bombing of Pearl Harbor, at a time when there was almost no realization of the tremendous ecosystem services provided by mangroves, especially in terms of serving as a nursery for many species. A 2008 study from the US National Academy of Sciences estimates that the economic median value of the fisheries supported by one hectare of mangrove fringe in Baja is $37,000.[1] Even now, people who object to the overfishing of Baja waters are only marginally aware that mangrove deforestation is a major cause of fishery decline.

The tide is ebbing, and the students in the doubles are having a hard time turning up against it into the tight channel. I get out of my boat to help them turn their bows, and there seems to be general surprise to see me shuffling in knee-deep water. One says, "I didn't realize it was so shallow," and I suppress the urge to respond, "If you look down, you'll be able to see the bottom."

Back in my yak, I follow the slowest double. They are having such difficulty maneuvering the ever-narrowing channel that they don't seem to be taking note of the mangroves. The grove is so thick, at this point, that eyesight can't

1. Octavio Aburto-Oropeza et al., "Mangroves in the Gulf of California Increase Fishery Yields," *Proceedings of the National Academy of Sciences of the United States of America* 105, no. 30 (July 2008): 10456–59.

penetrate it for more than a couple meters. I note the complete absence of birdsong, and then note that I can barely hear the students ahead of us. All is dense. The water here is turbid, and we can only see that part of the root systems that emerges above the tide line. It would be oppressive to have to paddle through mangroves day after day.

We catch up to the main group just as Dr. Awesome is pointing out the pneumatophores (gas tubes) being uncovered by the dropping tide. The students are reminded that the soil in which the mangroves grow is anaerobic. I suspect that even if the students had forgotten this point from the lecture given several weeks ago, they'd be able to discern the anaerobic quality of the soil from its characteristic odor.

A propagule floats by, looking for all the world like a giant green bean floating vertically. I snatch it up and toss it to my colleague, who catches it expertly, dangling it in front of the class to remind them that mangroves are viviparous. The students are all looking for propagules of their own now, and I realize for the zillionth time that this is why we bring them into the field. Reproduction via viviparity means so much more when you're floating with the propagules than when you're reading it off a PowerPoint slide

"Are you going to want to snorkel today, Juanito?"

Our Mexican guides are so polite I feel sorry for them having to work with people like me. I interpret the question to mean that they want to move along, and I understand their uncharacteristic impatience. We've got a few kilometers of slow paddling ahead of us, and they've still got to instruct this group how to beach the boats, how to set up camp, and how to make dinner. And they know me well enough to realize that I'm probably going to want to take the students snorkeling once we make camp.

"Let's see how long it takes to find a beach," I reply. In other words, yes, it's time to blast out of these mangroves.

This is the problem with Baja as a classroom. There isn't a day when I don't want the class to snorkel, but I want them to take a daily nature hike as well, and of course we have to average at least four hours paddling daily if we want to make it around this island. And then there's my insistence that the students get plenty of time to write in their journals. None of this would be at all difficult if cooking, eating, and sleeping didn't consume so much time, here on a desert island.

We blast.

Steinbeck's experience of Baja was far less frantic than my own, and I hope one day to experience it his way:

One thing had impressed us deeply on this little voyage: the great world dropped away very quickly. We lost the fear and fierceness and contagion

of war and economic uncertainty. The matters of great importance we
had left were not important. There must be an infective quality in these
things. We had lost the virus, or it had been eaten by the anti-bodies of
quiet. Our pace had slowed greatly; the hundred thousand small reac-
tions of our daily world were reduced to very few. When the boat was
moving we sat by the hour watching the pale, burned mountains slip
by. A playful swordfish, jumping and spinning, absorbed us completely.
There was time to observe the tremendous minutiae of the sea. (173)

I have no such time for observation of minutiae, and blame it on the quarter
system at the university where I teach. I experience Baja ten days here, two
weeks there, and if I've been a really good boy, maybe three weeks for Christmas. I scribble frantic notes while I'm in the field, often not taking the time
to remove the binoculars from around my neck before I begin to write. I have
little doubt that when my students return to campus after this expedition, they
will find the resumption of classes to be somewhat relaxing.

They're singing again, two of the doubles this time, as if oblivious to how
hard we've been pushing them today. I decide, as a reward for their sweetness,
that we don't really have to snorkel this afternoon. Or maybe I'll just swim
alone, and permit the students to work on their tans. A mini spring break.

We form a diamond when we paddle. One of the guides takes the point,
another takes the rear. One of the faculty takes the right flank, the other takes
the left. The goal is to keep all the boats within earshot of each other, but on
some of these expeditions it's a futile effort. This group, however, is sticking
together, and I have to wonder what's up with that.

Less than three hours after we left the first beach, we hit the second. This
will be our shortest day on the water, mercifully, except for the lay day. Our TA
forms two teams, one of which carries the boats up above the tide line, the other
of which sets up the shade. A breeze has come up, and I work with the shade
team to dig pits for sand anchors. I scan the encampment while I dig, and
notice that all guides and faculty are wearing shirts, but that all of the students
are shirtless. And then I notice, while a subgroup sets up the kitchen area, that
some of the students are pulling snorkel gear out of their boats.

"I guess we're snorkeling," I mutter to no one in particular, realizing that
I'd never mentioned the possibility of free time. The student I'm working with
replies, "Yeah. That's next."

The TA, working so hard to run the camp, has failed to read my mind.
Within fifteen minutes we're gathered downbeach from the kayaks. There's a
moment of hilarity when one of the students gets into her wetsuit backward,
not remembering that her rental suit was designed with the zipper in the rear.

This in itself was not particularly funny until her tentmate said, "Uh, I think the boobs are supposed to go in the front."

Once everyone is successfully zipped up, they turn to me for a moment of guidance. I encourage them to forget about natural history for once and to focus, instead, on the Zen of propelling their bodies through the water.

"Turn by dipping your shoulders, not by using your hands, because flailing hands frighten fish, and we're here to see fish. Any questions?"

"Yeah."

I wait.

"What about sharks?"

I remind them that the local shark fishery, the collapse of which was a theme of one of their in-class presentations, is still collapsed. There had been significant moral indignation expressed during our discussion, especially after we were shown a short, graphic video depicting the makings of shark-fin soup by harvesting fins from live sharks. But even an environmental science major tends to feel more sympathy for sharks in the classroom than when standing on the beach in a wetsuit. I assure them that a group as large and as ugly as ours is certain to scare any sharks away, and that they should be more concerned about stingrays.

The water sparkles, reminding us that the sun is already on its way down. We do the stingray shuffle until we're deep enough to don our flippers.

I hear a strange cooing emanating from the snorkels of the first few students to immerse their faces in the water, as if every last one of them is exclaiming, "Oh my God!" through a tube. We're into a huge school—and by "huge" I'm talking about several thousand fish—of Pacific flatiron herring, *Harengula thrissina*. The fishermen hereabouts call these herring *sardineta plumilla*, which translates roughly as "pen sardine." It's the type of fish that wouldn't even have a name if there were not so many of them.

The sand is so bright, here in the shallows, and the herring are so fast that it's difficult to focus on them. The school seems to be in absolute terror, sharing this cove with so many undergraduates, and there are fish swimming in every direction attempting to escape the monsters wearing rubber. One of the monsters grabs my shoulder and asks, "What are these, Juanito?"

So much for focusing on the Zen of propulsion. I ask her to describe the item she wants identified.

"These little fish."

"You'll have to do better than that."

She puts her face back in the water to collect impressions. After a few quick breaths through the snorkel she comes back with excellent field marks. "About fifteen centimeters. Large eyes with a black spot behind the gill cover. Lateral stripes, sort of, but not really. Silver. Shiny."

"Oh, *those* little fish. Those are Pacific flatiron herrings."

"Wow. They're fast."

"They have to be. The slow ones become pelican food."

Another shout comes from yet another student ignoring my instructions to focus on the Zen of snorkeling rather than natural history. "Hey Professor! I think I've got a stingray."

This class has been trained to call me by my first name, but they tend to revert to the honorific whenever they become excited. I swim over to where the alleged stingray awaits, noticing that as many students seem to be leaving the general area of the discovery as seem to be converging on it. The animal that is quite literally the center of the latter group's attention is semisubmerged in the sand, little more than a set of eyeballs glancing nervously about.

Rays have a way of fluttering when they settle into the bottom so that they kick up enough sand to camouflage them. This one has done that, and I can just make out where the tail ends, about forty centimeters away from the eyes. It seems too round to be a stingray, and I signal one of the students to back off a little bit. He does so clumsily, and almost instantly an explosion of sand erupts. From the cloud of sand something that looks like a dinner plate with a sturdy tail emerges, and I can see that the pectoral and dorsal fin structures overlap, giving it its characteristic roundness. More to the point, as it darts away I can make out the telltale pattern of concentric circles in the middle of its back. *Diplobatis ommata.*

I spit out my snorkel and report, "That wasn't a stingray."

"Really? What was it?"

"Bullseye electric ray. Did you notice the bull's-eye target in the dorsal area?"

I don't get an answer—a question instead: "Is it in our book?"

I understand the impulse that prompted this question. The field guide will provide the closer look that the student was unable to take, and the closer look is needed not just because the animal was camouflaged in its sand covering, but because the species was originally misidentified. This student never really saw an electric ray because he thought he was looking at a stingray. The book will provide a remedy, showing him vicariously what he was supposed to be seeing in the first place.

How did we ever learn without books?

Steinbeck and Ricketts took a library along on their expedition—at least that's what they called the steel-reinforced wooden case that contained the twenty large volumes they carried on the *Western Flyer*. They discovered, once aboard, that there was no room for the library, and subsequently had to rope it to the top of the deckhouse, covered with tarps. Steinbeck complained that it took ten minutes to retrieve a book, and then observed: "For many little errors like this, we have concluded that all collecting trips to fairly unknown regions should be made twice; once to make mistakes and once to correct them" (10).

Steinbeck should have known better, for an expedition never gets its library right, even when academic expeditions return to the same blessed island every year for the better part of a decade. This is no accident—there's something about the process of doing natural history that demands books, and this may well be a matter of precedent. Natural history and books were born at roughly the same time out of the same intellectual impulse.

Field guides were always a frustration during my years as a scuba instructor: I could never take books along underwater. I have a great electric ray story nonetheless, which I'm happy to tell even if it didn't take place in Baja.

I was teaching an Advanced Open Water Certification class off Del Monte Beach in Monterey, a gradual, shallow sandy bottom with little more than eel grass, which stood a meter up off the sand and flowed gently back and forth with the surge. I'd set up a few underwater courses to teach compass navigation skills. The last exercise of the morning was to run a triangular course from a starting buoy with three equilateral legs of fifty meters. On paper it's a fairly simple exercise: take off on any bearing for however many kicks it takes you to cover fifty meters, then turn 120 degrees and run on the new bearing for the same number of kicks, and then turn 120 degrees again and repeat. If you do it right, you end up back at the original starting point, but this is easier said than done.

One of my students, an attorney, couldn't get it right, so after I sent the other students back to the beach with the divemaster I ran the course above him to see what he was doing wrong. His mistake was somewhat mechanical, and I was able to correct it so that he could complete the exercise independently. Once this was done, I suggested he take a bearing back to the beach and navigate us through the surf zone. We descended, and my student was so intent on his compass and depth gauge that he almost ran into a medium-size (as big as a jumbo pizza) Pacific electric ray, waiting in prey on the sand. I stopped the student and made the danger signal, which is done by pointing a clasped fist at the source of danger. He mimicked my signal, pointing his own fist at the fish, which I interpreted as a question: "Is this fish dangerous?" I nodded my head in the affirmative, at which point he punched the fish.

To say that my student's body "jolted" would be an understatement. I immediately got him into a control position and took him to the surface, which was not a problem since we were in no more than three meters of water at that point. When I got him to the surface, he spat out his regulator and demanded to know why I had instructed him to punch that fish.

True story. This is why I no longer teach attorneys.

Each student is required to bring along a field guide, but they may select from among various guides depending on their particular interests. Some bring a plant guide, others bring bird guides, a few even bring a guide to reptiles and amphibians. Back on the beach, the scholars with Baja fish guides and with the field guide to subtidal marine invertebrates are extremely popular, and there's a great deal of sharing going on in order to get the scientific names right for the species catalog they're keeping for Dr. Awesome. I circulate among them, still in my wetsuit, pointing out that they can't list *Diplobatis ommata* unless they really saw it and were able to identify it. This frustrates a few of them, and they want my assurance that we'll see another one before the week is up.

If there's anything worse than encountering an electric ray, it's having a buddy encounter one while you're somewhere else examining an anemone. Although I'm sympathetic about missed opportunities, I make no guarantees.

Strangely, I manage to pitch my tent before some of them shed their wetsuits. The ones sitting at the high-tide line composing field notes with their wetsuits on and their tents down have just become naturalists.

# First Interlude

## August in Bahia de los Angeles

Few other bodies of water anywhere in the world so teem with fish as the Gulf of California. Look out onto Los Angeles Bay and you are sure to see pelicans and boobys diving into a ruffled patch of water which marks the spot where a huge swarm of small swimmers has risen to the surface to escape some large fish below, only to be devoured from above instead.

Joseph Wood Krutch, *The Forgotten Peninsula: A Naturalist in Baja California,* 1961

I arrived early for the final session of a monthlong raptor identification course, sat on a grassy knoll overlooking San Francisco Bay, and composed a splendid, almost Steinbeckian checklist of gear I wanted to take on my two-week writing retreat in Baja.

I would be traveling light: four field guides, a single pair of binoculars, two Meisterstück pens. No compact spotting scope. I decided that if I took six pairs of the high-tech, quick-drying undershorts I use on expeditions I would only have to do laundry twice during my stay at the field station in Bahia de los Angeles. Two long-sleeved shirts for days out on the pangas, two Hawaiian shirts for dinner, a couple T-shirts in which to write, and a sleeveless shirt to serve as pajamas. Check. A half liter of Doctor Bronner's Magic peppermint soap, enough to shampoo every other day and to wash clothing as needed. Camping pillow and a silk travel cocoon, since it would never get cold enough for a sleeping bag. A light windbreaker? Hmm. It was hard to imagine a second layer being necessary at any point. I added it to the list anyway, intuiting that I'd need it only if I didn't have it.

Class ended late, and I spent the night on my sailboat in Sausalito, planning to return to campus early the next morning to pack. Unfortunately, my splendid list, scribbled on the back of my raptor ID notes, was left on the sailboat.

It made no sense to invest three extra driving hours to retrieve a checklist that only took half an hour to compose. Besides, an old Baja pro like me shouldn't need a checklist. Right?

I was extra careful while packing. Dive gear. Lycra dive skin to protect against jellyfish stings. Sketchbook. Passport. Drawing pencils. Blank journals. Snacks for the long bus ride. The pesos that have been in my bureau since March. Sunglasses retainer. Primary broad-brimmed hat. Spare broad-brimmed hat. Extra sun lotion. Sport sandals for the boats, flip-flops for the beach. Travel guitar.

It felt silly to be heading to Baja without my kayak paddles. Or my students, for that matter. But this time I was accompanying someone else's class, there just to write and to observe the one season when smart people like me never visit Baja.

Summer.

I picked up Dr. Awesome early the next morning, drove to my sister's house in Southern California, played mandolin and guitar duets for a few hours, and then went to bed early, the alarm set for 3:00 a.m. since we had to meet the bus at 4:00. The alarm wasn't necessary, for I awoke at 2:30 a.m. to the sharp realization that I'd forgotten to pack my hiking boots.

So much for not needing checklists.

The first few hours on the bus are unimpressive. The border is sleepy, Tijuana is dusty, and the sprawl of Ensenada takes longer to get through than it ever had in the past. South of there, as far as El Rosario, we pass through a brown-gray landscape where towns constructed of cinderblock blend in with soft chaparral and coastal scrub. I wonder, lazily, what sort of first impression these students are forming of Baja, but most of them are asleep.

Things pick up as we climb up the spine of the peninsula toward Cataviña. I see the first spindly boojum, standing solitary like a giant upside-down taproot. Within a couple more kilometers the first giant cardon appears, looking thirsty. Although the landscape still seems brittle dry, it appears finally to have identity. This is desert. The sky's gray turns blue, the rock becomes distinct, and the horizon takes on significance. Around every corner an old friend greets me: ocotillo, garambullo, barrel cactus, ironwood, yuccas. Finally, elephant trees, enough appearing all at once to call them a grove. A herd?

The sun is setting by the time we arrive at the field station. A hot wind blows. It will blow all night, strong enough to blow the camp pillow off my cot when I get up to relieve myself, but not strong enough to blow sand around on the beach. Dr. Awesome and I are invited to store our gear in the wet lab for the next two weeks; the lights don't work but the outlets do, and a lamp should show up over the course of the next few days. Dr. Awesome seems surprised that we have not been invited to sleep in the faculty house where the two professors running this program are ensconced. I assure my colleague that the wet lab is fine for visiting scholars; one way or another, the heat will force us all to sleep on the beach.

I have offered to give a lecture on my research, and it has been scheduled for ten days hence. I will spend the mornings serving as a naturalist on one of the four pangas, and will spend the afternoons sketching the notes that follow.

## *Day 1*

I didn't wake up the first time, when the oystercatchers were celebrating first light. They serve as roosters for the field station, albeit unofficially. When I start forgetting birdcalls in my dotage, the oystercatcher's loudly whistled wheeps, announcing, *"Here I am now,"* will be the last to go. But this morning I was sleeping so deeply, now that the all-night blow had finally died, that the oystercatcher's proclamation failed to convince me to open an eye.

*"Here I am now."* Yes. Here I am. Now. On a beach fringing the bay of angels, Bahia de los Angeles, lying atop a home-built, canvas-on-wood Baja cot, covered only in silk, ignoring oystercatchers.

I'd made it halfway back to a dream state when I hear a sound the barely awake part of my brain wants to investigate. Ziiiiip. Ziiiiip. An old memory surfaces: *my brother and I throw our nearly exhausted sparklers into a high arc that descends into a Colorado lake. They make this same "ziiiiip" when they enter the water.*

Sparklers? Fourth of July?

I sit up in my cot, the sun not quite up on the horizon, my binoculars not quite within reach.

Ziiiiiiiiiiiip. Zip, zip zip.

A squadron of brown boobies, groggily estimated to comprise seventy birds, was diving a school of fish I can't yet see but that will turn out to have been grunions.

Zipzipzipzip. Sometimes as many as six boobies zipping simultaneously.

As I watch, a few brown pelicans join the frenzy, but pelicans don't zip.

Zip ziip plunge zip.

Were Olympic judges to appear on the beach, the boobies would earn the highest scores, for they enter the water without a splash, as if the Sea of Cortez had special openings between its ripples just for them. Their long, slender, pointed wings seem to hinge back completely at the point of entry, looking more like an arrow's fletchings than a bird's appendage.

Ziiiiip.

The time has come for the binoculars, before I've even donned my glasses this morning. But what I really need are optics that will slow down the motion, turn the ziip into a zoooop. Lacking that, I try to focus on individual birds to determine how long they submerge, and I notice that sometimes they seem to capture their prey from below, while surfacing. Were I a fish, I would complain of this—no bird should be able to prey on you from below.

I've always wanted to watch one of these feeding events from underwater, but I've not yet been in the right place at the right time, at least not for boobies. Cormorants, yes, lots of times, but not boobies.

I've set up a writing table under a six-post *palapa* built around a massive central pole, the entire structure assembled of former palm trees. My table faces the water and the merciful breeze coming off it. At any moment I can watch two or three zebra-tailed lizards, their color matching the sand beneath them. I enjoy watching them run, their muscular hind legs appearing to have been plagiarized from a bullfrog. Zebra-tails rise up as they run, and the faster they go the more space there is between torso and sand, so that their feet are barely making contact with earth. Here again I wish I had slow-motion real-time optics. (Are you listening, Carl Zeiss?) If I had these magical field glasses, I would be able to discern whether they are running on tiptoe. From here, with my old-fashioned Zeiss Victory 7x42 T* FLs, I cannot visually confirm that their feet are actually making contact with the planet.

Dr. Awesome, who is both a herpetologist and ornithologist and therefore knows everything, informs me that at a certain speed a zebra-tailed lizard's front legs will actually lift off the ground so that they run bipedally. I will spend the next two weeks watching for this without success.

I'm seeing mostly males from my writing table. They sprint, stop almost instantaneously while dropping their rear quarters to the ground, and then perform a few front-legged push-ups while inflating their bright-red throat pouches, the message clearly being one of sexual prowess. Were there any females around this morning, there would be no question as to which males were eager to make them happy.

I scan the beach for appreciative females, but the only female lizard I can locate is a gravid whiptail lizard, one not at all inspired by the posturing of the zebra-tails. She is everything that they are not: dark, thick-tailed, and sexually content. She moves as if she knows where she wants to end up, and she doesn't seem to care how much her dark coloration makes her stand out against the sand. I half expect a Harris's hawk to stoop down at any moment, but the only raptor in sight is a turkey vulture seeking carrion.

Wait, I'm wrong. North of here, no more than a hundred meters away, an osprey perches on a snag, facing the water. Its distinctive, masked countenance and eagle-like beak make it unnecessary to use binoculars to identify it, but the binoculars seem to add to its nobility. This bird could care less about lizards, gravid or otherwise. Do the lizards know this? Will they refuse to scurry for cover when the osprey takes flight, knowing it to be a strict piscivore? Something else to watch for the next few weeks.

We approach noon and the wind gets serious, right on schedule. For the first time this morning there are no lizards to be seen from my writing-table perch, and the boobies have vanished as well. I remain on station, a lifeguard with no swimmers in the water. I am free to watch the wind and listen to the growl of a distant panga. The wind plays with the pages of my notebook, making a two-handed process of writing. The osprey abandons me as well, but as it flies off a ketch with dark-brown sails heaves into view. This always happens to me at home: as the day gets worse for writing, it gets better for sailing.

Once again, Baja is all about the wind. But this is not El Norte, my nemesis of so many previous trips south of the border. This nameless breeze is distinctly local, not the result of some distant front recorded on a weather chart. No, this wind is homegrown, and it could brag that no meteorologist has quantified it empirically. It blows *from* here rather than to here, and it cares no more about the butterfly effect than an osprey cares about whiptail lizards. There will be moments when I will almost hate it, but I'll hate it more when it abandons us completely.

I acquaint myself with this wind the way only a sailor can, feeling its pressure on my skin and its direction in my hair. I take a full minute to taste it, smell it, listen to it, and to anticipate its transitions. It is not the same hot wind we experienced on our arrival, a wind that had flowed downhill from the escarpments above. This wind is about air rising somewhere nearby, and air from somewhere else taking its place. It is hot, yes, but a different kind of hot than the sundowner.

It is a different zephyr than I've ever felt in Baja.

Two reddish egrets fly wingtip to wingtip directly along the water's edge, something I've never before seen. I've always known these birds to be solitary—the grand loners of the egret world. This must be a summer thing, I tell myself, a behavior related to mating. But as far as I've heard, their breeding colonies are situated in tropical swamps or mangrove lagoons, not here, and they should have concluded that mating business in July.

Why are these two flying together?

My mentor, Kathleen Jamie, famously wrote, "Keep looking. That's what the keen-eyed naturalists say. Keep looking, even when there's nothing much to see. That way your eye learns what's common, so when the uncommon appears, your eye will tell you."

I find myself hoping that I have paid close enough attention to that which is common during the rest of the year to notice summer in such things as the local breeze or a pair of reddish egrets.

After lunch I experiment with the heat, which is turning out not to be as ferocious as I'd feared. It grows appreciably warmer the farther one treks from the beach, and the desert proper beyond the beach seems to intensify how the heat radiates. Out there the brim of my hat seems to trap the heat more than block it, but when I remove the hat I know instantly that this was not a good idea.

I tread gently in my sandals, craving hiking boots that would probably have been too hot.

Back at the field station the wispy palo adans are flowering, but I conclude that someone must have watered them. Out here there are no flowers, and where there are no flowers there are no insects to pollinate them. And where there are no insects, there are no birds. This realization stops me in my tracks. Surely there must be birds around, I think. But nothing moves, nothing chirps, nothing soars overhead. The cardon seem to be laughing at me, looking for birds on an August afternoon. *¡Gringo!*

I head back to the field station, almost as if fleeing a truculent desert bent on causing me harm. Here I finally see a California gnatcatcher and a Costa's hummingbird, and I feel relief. When I mention my observations to one of the host professors at dinner, he responds, "Yeah, the passerines all go to town during the summer. Rain could bring them back."

Back under the palapa I watch as a magnificent frigatebird attempts to steal a fish from one of its own kind, a first cousin, perhaps. Before I learned of kleptoparasitism, I might have observed this behavior and wondered whether some sort of play was taking place. The gymnastic turns of the bird being pursued are mirrored by its pursuer, making it easy to imagine this as a game of skill played between talented subadults. The binoculars, however, reveal that the only one with a juvenile's white head is the bird being chased.

The problem with an education, I've decided, is the point where "nature red in tooth and claw" replaces romantic notions of a benign natural world. Playful frigatebirds are far more magnificent than kleptoparasitic ones.

There are thirty students inhabiting this field station presently, and I rejoice that not one of them is mine. They're not sure what to make of me at this point, since I'm not one of the two faculty officially teaching this course, but this doesn't stop them from asking questions, especially when they can't figure out the name of a bush. I tell them that these are lomboy, but that some gringos call them "limber bush."

The students have been advised to take midafternoon siestas, and there are eight slumbering in the shade of my palapa at the moment. I've never been much for naps, so I've decided to use this time to sketch—an art in which I was once skilled but that I've neglected ever since being awarded my MFA. I make mistakes on this first sketch that I'd long ago learned not to make, but I'm finding the process restful, and the paper is as forgiving as it ever was. Unfortunately, I choose a schooner on a beam reach as my first subject, and it sails past before I can adequately describe its rigging. Tomorrow I'll cut my teeth on a still life in the hopes of working my way up to a frigatebird by the end of this retreat. Meanwhile, there are some marvelous whale vertebrae scattered about the field station, just begging to be sketched.

One of the older students asks me to confirm a bird she's identified as the Eurasian collared-dove, a species introduced in Florida that has only recently made it to the West Coast. To the best of my knowledge, they shouldn't be any closer than Hollywood at this point. I express skepticism, but look anyway, and am able to confirm three field marks: the black half collar at the nape of the neck, the dark-tipped wings, and the flash of white on its long tail feathers. I hasten to find Dr. Awesome, but by the time binoculars are retrieved, the bird has flown away. We track it down together, and my colleague confirms my confirmation. Baja officially has a new pigeon.

Gustav Eisen, a Swedish naturalist who collected specimens in Baja in 1894, was the first scholar I've been able to find who was concerned about introduced species. He wrote, "Immigrants are pouring in from all sides, but with them come unhappily foreign weeds and plants, and foreign animals, which are bound to, in a few years, considerably change the aspect of the flora and fauna of the country."

Indeed. I look back to where the Eurasian dove was perched, and note that there are now two foraging nearby. This is the second "new" species I've seen this trip, despite it being only my first full day in Baja. The first was a pair of green parrots I saw out the bus window while we rolled through Tres Pinos, a pair that seemed to belong here even less than the collared-doves.

## Day 2

The field station owns two pangas, and two local *pangeros* have been hired to provide additional boats. Dr. Awesome and I have been invited to serve as naturalists on the local boats while the two host professors drive the field station boats. I will spend the duration of this trip wishing I could drive my own boat, more certain of myself as a *pangero* than as a naturalist.

The panga is the most marvelously utilitarian boat ever invented. A long, open hull, fiberglass over wood, ours is eight meters long and only two meters wide, with high topsides and plenty of freeboard in the bow. It sports an ancient two-stroke Evinrude outboard, an engine that rated eighty-five horsepower back before Zedillo became president.

The seven students who pile into my boat are excited about the prospects of seeing a whale shark, but they are duly informed that whale sharking isn't on the agenda for today. Disappointment is palpable, and they want my reassurance that we'll swim with whale sharks before the program is over. When I suggest that they communicate their desires to the faculty running their program, I get looks of betrayal. These glances shift me into teacher mode, and I quickly but methodically assess their various degrees of intellectual curiosity. Some, clearly, are here to learn about natural history; others want only to be entertained by it.

While we head out to see what the Sea of Cortez has to offer, I observe to myself that it's too easy to be curmudgeonly with someone else's students.

There are storm petrels everywhere, two species, both of whom are black in color. Both species fly low over the water, never higher than a couple meters from the surface. Least storm petrels, *Oceanodroma microsoma*, seem to outnumber black storm petrels, *O. melania*, about four to one. Despite their size difference, I point out that the easiest way to distinguish between the two is that the black storm petrels swoop like swallows while the least storm petrels flutter like butterflies. Most students can perceive this right away, and based on the fact that this information is actually useful, a few seem ready to forgive their shipboard naturalist for not having a whale shark in his pocket.

They had a lecture yesterday on marine trophic levels, a lecture I didn't attend, so I ask them to identify the storm petrel's level. About half get it right, answering that these are secondary consumers since they feed on zooplankton rather than phytoplankton.

Our *pangero*, Pancho, spots a whale in the distance, and we zoom off as if storm petrels never really mattered in the first place. We get there right after the animal dives, and have to wait several minutes before we can identify it. In the interim one of the students wants me to guess what sort of whale it was, but I refuse to play along. Instead of a guess, this kid gets a minilecture about the importance of accuracy when engaging in natural history, and I have little doubt he'll chose another panga in which to ride tomorrow.

The whale surfaces, finally, and we identify it as a Bryde's whale, based on the dorsal fin being much like a fin-backed whale, only less obtuse, and on the smoky gray color. It's the least exciting of the whales we'll see over the course of the next two weeks, never lifting its tail flukes out of the water or letting us see the lateral ridge forward of the rostrum. Solitary, as well. I explain that Bryde's whales are probably the least known of all the *mysticeti*, the baleen whales. This is probably because they were confused with sei whales as late as the 1970s. Blah-blah.

I encourage the students to estimate the whale's size for their field notes, receiving an array of answers, none of which utilize the metric system. I point out that our panga is eight meters long, and suggest they use its relative size to measure the whale. We come up with eleven meters, which seems about right. When a student wants to know how big that is in feet, I insist that whales don't have feet. Blah-blah-blah.

We stay with the whale for about an hour, perhaps thirty soundings, and finally run off to a large, mixed-species raft of pelicans, black-vented shearwaters, boobies, Heerman gulls, and Brandt's cormorants. A feeding frenzy appears to have occurred somewhat recently.

Looking down through the birds into the clear water, we hit the jackpot, for a school of dorados still patrols below. This tells the story of the event we've just missed, that the dorados were driving prey up from below, and the resulting fish boils attracted all the diving birds in the vicinity.

While the dorado are clearly patrolling, there is nothing frenetic about their behavior. They seem to have eaten enough, just enough, to be nearly satiated. The birds above them seem a bit smug; they've consumed so much, it seems, that they're not interested in flying anytime soon.

The meter-long dorado are beautiful, robust, with tails and lateral stripes that iridesce when they swim near the surface, and wide golden flanks. We can make out their blunt heads and sharply concave caudal fins from the panga. Their other name, mahi-mahi, comes up in conversation, and I'm asked how dorado are rated on the Seafood Watch. The students seem surprised to discover that I haven't memorized the list.

In the lunch line back at the field station Dr. Awesome asks how the morning went on my boat, and I confess to my old friend that I'd been a bit snarky in my new role as shipboard naturalist. I make up for this, during the siesta period, by not retreating to my writing table under the palapa but rather by sitting on the picnic tables in the breezeway where we eat, where students have unfettered access. Dr. Awesome joins me, and we are soon surrounded by students seeking help with their field notes, like how to spell Bryde's—tricky since it's pronounced *Broo-duz*—or what was the name of that other storm petrel. I don't finish my own field notes until well after they depart for the afternoon lecture.

## Day 3

An electrical storm blew across the Vermilion Sea last night, east to west, and a swell was up outside the bay this morning. We ran into a few pods of common dolphins inside, but spotted an enormous herd heading outside, perhaps two kilometers away, thanks to Pancho's sharp eyes. We gave chase, of course, and everyone in my panga was immediately soaked.

I encouraged the students to try to estimate the number of dolphins in this herd, and the group consensus was five hundred. We will find out at our next stop that the other three pangas, each of which had an actual scientist aboard, independently conducted the same exercise. One boat guestimated a range of five hundred to a thousand dolphins, one boat was certain there were between one thousand and fifteen hundred dolphins, and the final panga's crew set the number at precisely two thousand. There were a lot of dolphins out there, by any measure.

We ran with the herd until a few of the students started feeling queasy, and then turned back toward calmer waters. Two or three dozen dolphins turned around with us, but escorted us less than a kilometer.

Running along the lee of the Midriff Islands, we headed north to Coronado Island, stopping in a cove that contains the northernmost mangal on the continent. We disembarked, ostensibly to observe mangrove natural history, the stop affording the queasier students a merciful reacquaintance with terra firma.

There were only red mangroves in this grove, the other species being unable to tolerate the "cold" this far from the equator. Mangroves seldom propagate higher than twenty-five degrees, north or south, but this mangal was at twenty-nine degrees north. The entire grove was stilted, none of the trees having grown higher than my navel. There wasn't a propagule to be seen anywhere, as if the mangroves had intuited the futility of attempting to propagate at this latitude. We spent half an hour chasing fiddler crabs and then moved on to the next cove north, locally called "Alejandra's Lagoon," for some of the most pleasant snorkeling I've ever enjoyed. Anywhere.

The outer parts of the cove were carpeted with stones ranging in size from a pelican's foot to a raven's wing: schist, quartz, some speckled granite, and basalt, but not too much basalt. The fish were mostly small, as if to match these stones. I was adopted by a large school of thumbnail-sized sergeant major hatchlings, their yellow dorsal areas highlighted by miniature black bars. I'm wearing bright yellow fins, a black Lycra skin with yellow side stripes, and a yellow mask, and I can't help wondering whether these hatchlings think I'm their mother.

Deep to shallow, deep again to shallow, belly snorkeling at its best. I ended my dive once I perceived that most of the students were eating on the beach, but on my way to lunch I noticed the remnants of a large rock seawall, no longer functional, into which someone had invested a great deal of work.

Bahia de los Angeles attends to its history, its volunteer-built Museo de Naturaleza y Cultura having been established long before the town had its own gas station. It was not difficult to find out how an abandoned seawall had come to be.

It turns out that one of the local citizens was concerned about the decline of local sea turtles, this locale having been a major player in Baja's sea turtle exports. The plan was to seal off the lagoon, creating a turtle sanctuary. The seawall was built and immature sea turtles were introduced into the lagoon, but once they grew to marketable size they were poached and sold for their meat.

Local wisdom is that a turtle refuge without an around-the-clock, on-site guardian is not really a refuge—it's a fattening pen for free turtles. Project abandoned.

After lunch I went back into Alejandra's Lagoon, mostly just to escape the heat. A brown pelican, juvenile, landed in the water about ten meters ahead of me, facing away. It did not seem to be aware of me, and it seemed terribly alone. I became aware that I've never really observed a resting pelican from below, and submerged quietly, breathing out in order to sink slowly. Three easy kicks and I was behind it, slightly below, feeling very much the voyeur.

The feet interested me most. Unlike ducks and gulls, whose webs connect three of their four toes, pelicans and their closest relatives—cormorants, boobies, and gannets—have totipalmate feet, meaning that all four toes are webbed. This juvenile's feet were huge, and they hung straight down, not paddling, completely relaxed. Unmoving. Immobile. I wanted to see the bird swim, but it just sat there while my air hunger increased. If only I'd taken a full breath before submerging! Finally, when I felt that I couldn't hold my breath any longer, I reached up and gently tickled the left foot.

The pelican blew out of the water like a . . . like a . . . well, like nothing I've ever seen from below. But that's not the point of this story. The point is that I tickled a pelican's totipalmate foot. Twenty years from now a fellow codger sitting across from me on a train will tell me that he once climbed Mount Everest, and with a polite smile I'll reply, "That's nice. I once tickled a pelican's foot while breath-hold diving in a failed turtle sanctuary in the Sea of Cortez."

We do plankton trawls on the way home, spend time with another Bryde's whale—or perhaps the same one?—and fail once again to spot a whale shark. When we return to the field station, the scientists, students in tow, head for the lab to discover what sorts of plankton they've collected. At this point I dutifully slink off to my makeshift writing studio on the beach, there to boast of pelican exploits, no need for microscopes or science in general. This writer keeps his binoculars on the writing table regardless, willing to allow nature to distract him if it so chooses.

After a respectable interval I walk over to the lab tables. Students diligently sketch the zooplankton revealed through their optics, all but ignoring the more microscopic phytoplankton. They draw copepods, larval crabs, ciliates, radiolarians—the usual. The sketches are not at all bad, even though I detect tentative lines here and there. But this is not art, it's science, and the point of the sketches is better to see what the optics reveal.

I don't loiter long, lest the muse abandon me completely. Back at the table, an osprey circles, and an unknown shorebird calls, begging me to take leave of my work to identify the culprit. But I resist. A Mexican dog trots down the beach, looking for nothing in particular. A pelican lands in shallow water, stretches its pouch, cranes its neck, and then stares at me accusingly.

## Day 4

According to Dr. Awesome we dove Punta Que Mal this morning, a name my colleague insisted on even though the navigational charts call it "Punta Don Juan." Regardless of appellation, it's a lush garden of sargassum still attached to the bottom, actively being grazed by gulf opaleyes. These chubs, cursed with the unglamorous name *Girella simplicidens*, are the plain-Janes of the tropical fish world, their bodies one of those drab, dark colors for which no crayon was ever manufactured. However, if you bother to look closely, you'll notice that they have bright-blue eyes that seem to have been lifted from a Thomas Hardy novel. One of these days, when I'm not so encumbered with prose, I will write a poem about drab chubs with gorgeous eyes, and I can only hope that people realize I'm writing about fish.

I was pleased to see so many mature hogfish, which have been in decline everywhere else I've been recently in the Sea of Cortez. These were my primary prey back in my spearfishing days, especially if ceviche was in the offing. In the deeper waters off to the west side of the point, I encountered plenty of larger fish, including two golden groupers that, while certainly not full-grown, were definitely not insubstantial.

Once again soon
I long to see
golden fish
out-spanning my arm.

One of the students called me over to a large boulder, pointed down toward a big warty thing a bit longer than his foot, and asked, "What is it?" When I said it was a brown sea cucumber, he asked, "So what is it?" It took me a while to realize that he wanted an answer along the lines of animal versus vegetable, since this critter represented something completely "other." I dove down, retrieved it, and placed it in his hand, instructing him to treat it gently, lest it eviscerate.

Full grown, *Isostichopus fuscus* reaches thirty centimeters. An animal, it has three rows of tube feet along the bottom, and spiked rows of warts that are smooth to the touch on the top. My field guide describes it as orange brown, with orange-red warts running along the surface laterally in rows.

Looking at the mouth now, the student asks what it eats. I reply that it's one of those detritivores that basically cleans up the bottom, adding that the animal is basically a long digestive track with a mouth on one end and an anus on the other.

By now, a school of almost a dozen students has gathered, and they pass the sea cucumber gently from one to the next as I warn that the poor thing will eviscerate its entire digestive track as a defense mechanism if it feels threatened. I dive down to retrieve a chocolate chip sea star, another detritivore they can pass around.

A chocolate chip sea star looks like the sort of echinoderm your grandmother would bake during the holidays, a brown-sugar shortbread cookie decorated generously with dark chocolate chips masquerading as defense mechanisms.

I enjoy putting marine organisms in a student's hands if it can be done without harming either organism. There is a certain fascination in touching the unfamiliar—the other—because touch conveys information that cannot be acquired visually. The sea cucumber's warts look thorny but feel soft. The sea star's spines look confectionary but feel hard—clearly not something you'd want to bite into had you developed a taste for the phylum *Echinodermata*.

Student engagement was palpable as the students passed these specimens around. As their relationship to these critters changed, via touch, their relationship to the marine ecosystem evolved as well. Here were two organisms that wouldn't have to be memorized for the quiz—they had not merely been seen. They had been handed along from one to the other, almost ritualistically, and "detritivore" was no longer a hard-to-spell word on a chalkboard.

There's another reason I want these students to care about the brown sea cucumber. In the early 1990s, when some of these students were already alive, Ecuador banned the export of sea cucumbers to the Asian food market, and Mexico followed suit. This caused a price spike in the Asian markets, which induced more Mexican fisherman to collect sea cucumbers than had done so before the ban. There was a time, back when I first came down to Bahia de los Angeles, when pangas would come back to port loaded to the brim with brown sea cucumbers. Predictably, the local fishery collapsed, and when I came to LA Bay a second time there were none to be seen. The fact that these students can actually handle a full-grown sea cucumber in the present moment is a story unto itself. While the population has not recovered, it can at least be said to be recovering.

We've fallen into a pattern where we rise early, put away our cots immediately, eat breakfast, gear up, and are heading for the boats by 7:30. We spend the entire morning out, scouring the Vermilion Sea for its secrets, sometimes eating lunch on a beach near good snorkeling. We return to the field station around 1:30–2:00, at which point the agenda calls for siestas. Few end up napping, however, and most of the students congregate in the shaded breezeway at long picnic tables, there to work on their field notes. The tables are piled high with field manuals, colored drawing pencils, water bottles, and snacks. Dr. Awesome and I have moved semipermanently to the tables with our own projects, enjoying a strange collegiality with students we'll never have to grade. It becomes a grand communal natural history session, everyone serving as a resource for everyone else. I help them with vocabulary, for the most part; they share their popcorn and their field guides, and help me describe the colors I cannot see.

This is a different sort of writing process for me—not only less solitary, but less focused as well. I'm enjoying the change, however, at least for now, and I'm finding it quite productive, much to my surprise, filling a good twenty-five pages of journal each day. Part of this productivity, no doubt, is that the students wander off to the afternoon lecture around 4:00, leaving me to scribble at a time when I've had my fill of distractions. However, I confess that I find their energy stimulating, and I'm hoping that some of it makes its way into my writing.

The students grow increasingly curious about my project here. A quick glance at the pages of my journal tells them that I'm not producing the sort of field notes that they have been tasked to develop, especially since I sketch in one Moleskine and write in another. Word has gotten out that I'm working on a book, apparently, because in the course of the past day they've begun to apologize before interrupting me.

One student, a future marine biologist, tells me that she can't imagine writing a book. The problem, clearly, is that she mystifies the process. I tell her that if she writes six pages a day, five days a week, she'll compose a book-length first draft within three months. The problem isn't the writing, it's having some-thing to say.

"So what are you writing about?" she asks.

"Right now," I tell her, "I'm writing about you."

My biggest distraction this afternoon comes after the students depart for their lecture. In the midst of all the quiet, a whale swims by maybe 350 meters from the beach. I don't have the binoculars at the writing table at that moment, a mistake I made consciously. Instead of running to get them, I content myself to listen for the breathing, two or three breaths every min-ute or so.

What a wondrous thing to be able to hear something wild breathe at this distance!

## Day 5

After dark last night a screen was set up under the stars and a fish-identification clinic was held, largely featuring photographs taken by one of the host faculty during the previous days' dives.

I was startled when the other host professor observed that groupers were difficult to approach and tended to shy away from humans. Really? When I started diving in the early 1970s, what impressed me most about groupers, other than their enormous size, was their approachability. A reasonably com-fortable diver could swim right up to a large grouper, even on scuba, and shoot it.

My colleague and I discussed this behavioral shift over coffee this morn-ing while being harassed by the sun's first rays. His expertise in evolutionary biology far surpasses my own, and when I asked whether the population of groupers could have selected for timidity in such a short time, he concurred that this had probably happened. In essence, when we shot all the easy prey, only the ones more inclined to flee were left behind to breed.

What a shame it's never been part of our morality not to prey on animals that haven't yet learned to fear us.

I didn't get a great amount of sleep last night, and I'm blaming the Perseid meteor shower, for it was a moonless night. Combine that with a desert sky and Baja's relatively low level of light pollution, and it becomes difficult to shut one's eyes.

(I note, with minor protest, that since I was here last, the municipality of Bahia de los Angeles has added streetlights, though they are few enough not to glare this far out of town. Still, it makes me pine for the days when the municipal generator shut down every evening at 9:00.)

The first time I slept out under the stars with my wife-to-be we were above timberline in the Colorado Rockies, struggling to stay awake while watching the Perseid shower. We served as the dividing line between a cohort of high-school students attending a summer camp I ran. The girls in their mummy bags slumbered shoulder to shoulder to Carol's south, the boys in their mummy bags slumbered shoulder to shoulder to my north. The kids fell asleep before we did, and I was the final camper awake. Spectacular. But last night's show was a close second.

Despite the late hour when I finally drifted off, I was awake at first light this morning, me and the oystercatchers. I stayed in my Baja cot, watching as the feebler stars dimmed out. I love the moment when only the constellations and a few planets are left behind. Just as the coyotes stopped yipping I heard the whoosh of a whale spouting, but it was not yet light enough to locate the column of mist.

As I lay there listening to the morning, I realized that I hadn't yet taken my guitar out of its case. I resolved that this would be the day it got back in tune.

We divide up into two groups today, and will only go out in two pangas, each searching for whale sharks. The youngest students charge the sign-up board and take all the spots in the first group, so I spend the two hours after breakfast writing, enjoying the relative quiet. The first group comes back, finally, with adrenaline-charged reports that they've just had the most amazing experiences of their young lives, et cetera. By the time the older folk get out on the water, however, the wind has picked up. We ended up seeing only one shark, twice dropping divers into the water in teams of three to swim with it, but the shark was moving too fast for either team to catch more than a passing glimpse. My team, the third and final team of the second group's second boat, never made it into the water. It was a pleasant morning, however, and we had lovely encounters with whales and dolphins on the way back to the field station. It was a delightful time once you got past the dearth of shark encounters.

The wind began to abate around 4:30, and it was decided to send the second group back out for another attempt. Once on site we spent at least forty-five minutes searching fruitlessly, but just as we were about to turn back we spotted a shark about nine meters long.

The host professor, who was driving the panga, suggested that this whale shark was moving too fast, but I told him I thought I could keep up with it. He shrugged, said I could give it a try, and I quickly donned my mask and fins, not having enough time to change into my dive skin. When we got close, I slipped into the water as soundlessly as possible, as did one of the students, a fifth-year senior majoring in marine biology.

This was not the first time I'd ever been in the water with a fish larger than myself—that honor went to a huge manta ray encountered during my honeymoon some thirty-six years prior. But it was the first time I'd ever left a boat to swim with a fish whose waterline exceeded the boat's.

Everyone who's ever watched the nature channel knows that a whale shark is a harmless, gentle giant. I've seen those shows as well. There are two realizations one makes on swimming up to one, however, for the first time: (1) *oh shit, this really is a shark*; (2) *oh shit, this shark is really, really big*. That and the fact that a big guy like me could swim down into the creature's gullet without choking it.

I begin to kick while noticing that in addition to its own natural spots the shark bore numerous perfectly round scars maybe five centimeters in diameter. These marks are where plugs of skin have been engorged by cookiecutter sharks, a phenomenon I know from having swum with spinner dolphins in Hawaii, where nearly every adult dolphin bears these scars.

As I break into the diving equivalent of a sprint, I notice that while most of these seem to be old scars, some look quite fresh, appearing more as craters than smooth scars. It creeps me out to think that there may be cookiecutters in the water at this moment; the whale shark's skin is ten centimeters thick, about four times thicker than my own, and I can't imagine losing a hunk of skin that size.

A remora not quite as big as my arm detaches from near the whale shark's mouth, but then quickly reattaches. I know that remoras have been documented attaching to scuba divers, but I think, strangely, that I'd rather deal with the remora than a cookiecutter shark. I force this strange thought out of my head, and my entire world reduces in size to me and the shark. I am determined to maintain my spot just behind its pectoral fin for as long as I can.

This shark is fast, and although I can keep pace with my high-tech split fins, I know I won't be able to do so for long. I already feel myself growing hot. Is it possible that I'm sweating? I'm certainly breathing hard at this point, and can feel my heart straining.

The shark turns a bit, as if to bear away, but I turn with it, concentrating on deep breaths followed by forceful exhalations. When the shark veers back toward me, I become aware that I am too close. Part of me wants to reach over and hitch a ride on the dorsal fin, but we've instructed the students not to do this, so I keep my arms in a streamlined position, thumbs to hips. I drop my left shoulder just a bit to distance myself a respectful two meters, a distance that I'm hoping will be far enough from the tail that I won't get swatted once this behemoth finally passes ahead.

I cannot accurately report how long the whale shark and I swam side by side. In some ways it seems only to have been a brief instant, in others it seemed longer than I should think possible given my age and deteriorated cardiovascular conditioning. At one point I lost myself, transcendentally, moving into a hanging-with-the-whale-shark groove. This proved to be my undoing, for the moment came when we both descended a centimeter too deep and I inhaled a breath of brine through the snorkel. Coughing violently, I lost my companion.

I turned back toward the panga, expecting it to have been following me. It was more than a hundred meters away, however, having stopped to pick up the student who'd entered the water with me and hadn't been able to keep up. Still coughing, I raised an arm to the sky, fist clenched, the diver signal for "Pick me up."

I vaulted back into the panga with a single kick, my muscles still surging with adrenaline. The shark I'd been diving with was joining its colleagues, which we could now see up ahead. The host professor instructed me to leave my fins on, but I knew at that point that I'd had enough for one day, content with the relationship I'd established with "my" shark.

It was fun watching the others dive. One of the older students, whose twenty-fifth birthday we'd be celebrating the following week, entered the water no more than a few meters from a shark and absolutely froze. I wondered whether he hadn't even seen the behemoth, but after the shark swam away, when we pulled him back aboard, I asked whether he'd gotten a good look at it. He responded, "Yes, I did . . . and it overwhelmed me." Another of our divers who also had a too-brief encounter reported that as soon as the shark approached her she'd begun to weep. Everyone in the boat understood that her tears had been prompted more by awe than by fear, not that those two emotions are always distinct from each other.

In thirty minutes' time we would encounter seven whale sharks. One swam under our boat, and another swam under one of our divers while she was attending to a different shark. Finally, one defecated spectacularly in front of one of our students before slapping its tail toward his head. We took this as a sign that it was time to return to the field station. The sun was beginning to set, and we were dangerously close to being late for dinner. The host professor assured me that at this particular field station, encounters with whale sharks are not an excuse for showing up late for meals.

After such a full day, neither students nor faculty felt up to the evening lecture, so it was replaced by a jam session in which I eagerly took part. We had three guitars, two fiddles, a mandolin, and a ukulele—just a banjo away from a proper hootenanny. We didn't run out of music until a half hour after mandatory lights out.

A long day.

## Day 6

At breakfast this morning I told the host professor that I'd be opting out of the morning dive in order to catch up with my writing, and he convinced me that this would be a bad day for a sabbatical. We were scheduled to dive Vantana Reef, renowned for soft corals and hearty fish.

I've always been a sucker for soft corals.

Within moments of descending on the reef I was glad of my colleague's counsel. The water was clear, the current benign, and the condition of the reef reminded me of Baja twenty years ago, back before spearfishing, overfishing in general, and excessive diving pressure.

I dove alone, remembering dives enjoyed before these students were born. I spent a good ten minutes hovering above a wary finescale triggerfish, *Balistes polylepis*, perhaps the largest I've ever seen, a fish whose longevity is undoubtedly a function of its fundamental distrust of humans. Laterally compressed, its dorsal and ventral fins are much farther apart than its pectoral fins, as if it had been squished between elevator doors. I am entranced to be watching a fish that is so obviously watching me, its eyeballs rotating in their sockets as it scans up and down from my fins to my mask. The fish would retreat whenever I encroached its ten-meter comfort zone, but it never swam entirely away, never retreated beyond the range of visibility, as if it wanted to keep me in sight just in case I was up to something dastardly.

A triggerfish propels itself by sculling its dorsal and anal fins alternately, keeping its tail stiff for the most part. This always seems comical to me, more appropriate for a Disney film than a granite reef, but it makes sense when one considers how the fish evolved to take refuge in narrow cracks through which its pursuers are unable to wiggle.

I finally concede the stare-down contest to the triggerfish, and move on to a lovely square corner of rock being defended from all comers by a mature sergeant major who has shed his native yellow stripes for bars of cerulean blue. He charges fish four times his size, seeming to base his aggression not so much on ferocity as on the absolute pleasure of being good at what he does.

After the dive the four pangas spread out as if looking for trouble, each boat determined to take the long route home. One boat radios that it found a whale shark in clear water, and the other three boats streak to its location. It turned out to be half the size of the ones we'd swam with previously. I took pity on this juvenile, pestered as it was by two remora and four pangas, and my boat departed to seek our own adventures. Our magnanimity was rewarded almost immediately, for we discovered a herd of common dolphins that had an unusual number of calves in its care. The only thing cuter than a dolphin is a baby dolphin; it was heartwarming to see the newborns being coddled by the adults. We would not tarry long with these dolphins, however, for off in the distance we spotted even larger cetaceans. Pilot whales! Half a kilometer away, traveling slowly, was a chorus line of at least seventy-five small whales, maybe more. We scooted away from the dolphins with even more abandon than we'd scooted away from the whale shark, with me screaming into the handheld radio that I'd struck the jackpot.

Pilot whales are the minivans of the Grand Order of Whales, their bulbous heads and stubby tails giving them the appearance of having been designed by an efficiency expert. These were short-finned pilot whales, *Globicephala macrorhynchus*, only about three times the length of the common dolphins we'd just abandoned. These were whales you could store in your garage.

The whales ignored us and yet seemed to tolerate us, sometimes coming within a body length of our panga. There seemed to be someplace definite they wanted to go, and yet they did not seem in a rush to get there. It occurred to me that here were cosmopolitan whales taking their summer vacations in Baja.

The marine radio crackled with warnings about being late for lunch if we didn't turn tail immediately, at which point the student serving as station manager stuck her submersible point-and-shoot camera elbow's length underwater, lucking into a perfectly pointed-and-shot portrait of a pilot whale's stubby tail. A fine conclusion to a perfect morning on the water, one I'd almost skipped in favor of getting some work done.

Reality hit us in stages as we returned to shore. A westerly breeze blew off the peninsula, feeling like a wall of solid heat a full kilometer from the beach. When we finally made it to the launch ramp the host professor's digital watch read 41 degrees Celsius, up from the low 30s out on the reef. It proved to be a difficult afternoon in which to write.

## *Day 7*

Focusing on birds today.

Turkey vulture
Osprey
Harris's hawk

Common raven
Gila woodpecker
Costa's hummingbird
Verdin
California gnatcatcher
Loggerhead shrike
White-winged dove
Eurasian collared-dove
American oystercatcher
Black turnstone
Sanderling
Red knot (!)
Willet
Wimbrel
Wilson's plover
Black-bellied plover
Heerman's gull
Yellow-footed gull
Sooty shearwater
Black-vented shearwater
Royal tern
Brandt's cormorant
Double-crested cormorant
Common loon
Brown pelican
Brown booby
Blue-footed booby
Least storm petrel
Black storm petrel
Magnificent frigatebird
Black-crowned night heron
Great blue heron
Snowy egret
Reddish egret

I've been here for a week now, and the closeness of the field station has begun to wear on me. We tend to concentrate in the shady breezeways in the afternoons, and a few of the younger students habitually make conversation even when they've got nothing more interesting to discuss than their tan lines. Two groups seem to have evolved, the scholars and the magpies. When the magpies begin planning a trip into town, it's all I can do to keep from offering to pay for ice cream if they agree to stay away until dinner.

Moments after they leave, a gnatcatcher flits into the compound, investigating a squatty elephant tree for insects. It hops stiff-tailed from branch to branch. A flap of the wings assists each hop, and yet it seems to leap more than fly. I realize, finally, that distinguishing between hopping and flying is more important to me than to the gnatcatcher, and I resolve simply to enjoy the flap-assisted hop for what it is. Whatever it is.

I break open a cold cerveza to celebrate the gnatcatcher's hop. This was probably a mistake, given the heat. A few minutes after downing the beer I fall asleep. It's the first time I've ever fallen asleep while writing at a picnic table.


## Day 8

The class went birding to La Gringa, and I have the field station to myself. Unfortunately, they took the breeze with them, and by 9:00 a.m. even the lizards are hot.

Minus the breeze and the chatter, the acoustic landscape comes alive. What at first sounds like the scratchy peeps of a bushtit turns out to be verdin, as revealed when their yellow heads turn up in my binoculars. I hear the chirp of an osprey I cannot see. Pelicans splash, gulls complain, and a distant whale spouts forcefully. I remember hearing a whale just before first light again this morning, and wonder if this is the same individual. While pondering the likelihood of this, I hear the throaty *kerrr* of a royal tern rolling its *r*'s pretentiously.

An antelope squirrel scampers across the compound noiselessly, evading absent hawks, and I can almost hear its noiselessness. But the squirrel's quiet is interrupted by a Eurasian collared-dove, sounding as foreign and inelegant as soup being slurped. Far distant, behind me, a white-winged dove proclaims its native affiliation with the Baja soundscape.

I listen for oystercatchers, but they have not shown up for roll call this morning, so I mark them tardy lest I be accused of favoritism. Just in time, a Costa's hummingbird thrums through the breezeway, "Present, present."

While I make mental notes of the birds from whom I have not yet heard—Say's phoebe, the vermilion flycatcher—I hear something I can't identify, something that sounds like a passerine's unsuccessful imitation of a hawk. I am compelled to investigate. When I turn the corner, binoculars in hand, it flies away, wren-like, permitting only a view of tail feathers. I will have to be content, for now, with the mystery.

As the morning grows warmer there is less and less to listen to, the perching birds having vanished to whatever secret places they occupy when August holds the desert hostage. While the solitude I experience is still precious, it loses some of its glint when birds no longer share in it.

We've been told that the water truck's next delivery will arrive a few days late, and that showers will not be possible until it shows up. When a merciful onshore breeze pops up around 10:00, I soak a handkerchief, strip down to my flip flops, and treat myself to a sponge bath, an activity that is permitted even though no one brought a sponge to this field station. A sponge would be amazing; I am astonished at how quickly my handkerchief dries out.

An endemic gray thrasher lands in a nearby bush. My mystery bird? I quickly loop the handkerchief around my neck, cowboy style, and grab the binoculars in pursuit. I commit the field marks to memory—smooth, decurved bill; dark breast spots shaped like guitar picks; golden eye, I think; white throat and undertail coverts; legs the same color as the bill—and after the mimid flies off I check my Sibley field guide to confirm what I've seen. Sibley doesn't list it, unfortunately, so while the field marks are fresh in my brain I trek across the sand courtyard to see whether the National Geographic field guide is more comprehensive in terms of Baja endemics. It is not, but this turns out to be the least of my problems. Before I can cross the courtyard back to where I'd left my clothing, I hear the approaching chatter of two student workers who I'd assumed had gone out with the class, per their usual custom. Fleeing as swiftly as an almost-naked man my age can move over sand in flip-flops, I barely make it back to the showers before they arrive in the courtyard.

(The Peterson field guide to Mexican birds, incidentally, lists the gray thrasher, *Toxostoma cinereum*. I discover this after dressing.)

I'd originally been tempted to embark on this writing retreat as a solitary venture along the lines of Thoreau's *Walden* or Edward Abbey's *Desert Solitaire.* I've written extensively, elsewhere, about the trope of the solitary nature sojourner, and a strong romantic impulse pulls me in that direction.

I'd opted for the field station because a dear old friend would be here, a recently retired professor who has taught me more about Baja natural history than anyone, and who has agreed to teach in my program this coming year, Dr. Awesome. Besides that, this trip ended up being so cheap that my professional development fund was able to pay for it. The noisier the station gets, however, the more I wonder whether it would have been better to strike out on my own, snatching at the Baja summer transcendentally.

There was a moment this morning when the water was wind-rippled but still flat, and when the sun was at a perfect angle where the Sea of Cortez sparkled like a brilliant field of megadiamonds. And there was no one with whom to share this, at least until now.

My hypothesis is simple: one who is alone pays greater heed to the natural world by virtue of being less distracted by human activity. When the class returns, a few of the magpies will sunbathe on the beach, as is their wont, and it will become correspondingly difficult for naturalists, myself included, to focus on antelope squirrels. Likewise, the more students who are milling about, the more constrained the wildlife will be about venturing forth.

Even if none of this was a concern, there's always noise. Once the class returns I will be unlikely to hear whales spouting or a distant osprey chirping. At that point I will become more reliant on vision to explore nature, and I will be less aware of the general ecology because vision discriminates in a way that hearing cannot. We don't see what's behind us, as a general rule, until first we hear it and turn around.

Given my present experience, I suppose that solitude more readily facilitates the transcendental experience simply because the solitary naturalist is experiencing nature more deeply.

We should not confuse the transcendental with the transformational. I have no doubt that the class in which these students are participating will transform a few of them in significant ways. Some of these kids will make career decisions based on their experiences at the field station this trip. Transformations could run the gamut from the disengaged becoming engaged to mere students becoming scholars: change takes place. To transcend, however, involves change at a more fundamental level, the level of how one perceives reality itself. Transcendental change is about finding new ways to see, to sense, and to make sense.

## Ode to My Headlamp

As I lay awake last night
Watching Perseus shower
I became aware that my trusty headlamp
Has more than earned a salute.
This is its ninth trip to Baja
And its twelfth trip abroad
But even when I ply home waters

It rides always in my daypack.
I read by it, write by it, jury-rig too,
And all it asks in return
Is to be kept relatively dry
With batteries charged and ready.
How many toilets has it helped me to find?
How many notes has it helped me to scribble?
When called upon for a midnight paddle
It anticipates my gaze.
I've pocketed it a thousand times
Dropped it, lost it, found it again
Ever ready, always faithful
Its mantra a rabbit with a drum.
A gift of a friend it was
A gifted friend it is
Campfires, guitars, reciting a poem
Projecting a beam again.


## Day 9

I went out with the class again this morning, the plan being to observe seabird-feeding behaviors in open water. The birds were uncooperative, unfortunately, and we were not able to observe the sort of multiple-species mass feeding events we'd hoped to find. I shouldn't blame it solely on the birds; clearly, the fish were not high enough in the water column in sufficient numbers to incite frenzy. Either way, we found ourselves sitting there with four pangas full of students, all of whom expected the faculty to come up with something educational.

Fortunately, a pod of twenty sea lions, *Zalophus californianus*, were rafted up on the northern end of a small, rock-and-guano island, each beast lying in the water on its side with a flipper raised high, as if they were all volunteering to be called on by the teacher, which is exactly what the teachers decided to do.

(As I explained to the students in my boat, the actual reason for the raised flippers was thermoregulation. Sea lions can dilate the blood vessels in their flippers near the surface of the skin so that they can take advantage of solar energy to warm up their blood. It's actually more complicated than that, but . . .)

We anchored the boats a little ways off so as not to spook the sea lions, and each boat got a hushed briefing on pinniped etiquette. How nice to be working with three other academics who could spontaneously provide such briefings based on deep experience rather than lecture notes!

These particular sea lions did not seem to be habituated to humans, at least not to human swimmers. Their raft broke up immediately when we got into the water, but they did not disperse. Instead, they swam together as a single unit for the next hour, never separating farther apart than the range of visibility, their behavior a mammalian version of schooling rather than shoaling. The entire group would frequently dive deep, well beyond our range.

Sea lions have big eyes, but these animals seemed to be all eyeball, watching us intently as they swam. They seemed to want us to know that they were watching us as we watched them, and that they did not trust our feigned benevolence. I noticed, as well, that their whiskers seemed more erect, faces drawn taut, than most of the previous sea lions with whom I've swum.

I noticed one other thing that I'd never before noticed when I've shared the water with sea lions: they were communicating with each other underwater via barks and yips the entire time they were submerged. It seemed to me that these vocalizations may have helped the group maintain its formation; intelligence was being communicated regardless of my ability to decipher it. The communications were succinct, polytonal, and almost cartoonish. One might say "cute," especially given the source. Later, at lunch, the other faculty would comment on this as well. We had hundreds of sea lion dives between us, and none had ever heard this sort of communication.

The moment the humans returned to their boats, the sea lions resumed their basking, packing themselves tightly together with flippers raised in worship of the sun.

We resumed our search for an avian feeding frenzy, and found thousands and thousands of birds, mostly boobies, bobbing together on the surface in groups of two hundred to four hundred. They seemed entirely satiated, even for boobies.

Suddenly, not too far in the distance, a shoal of whale sharks was spotted.

Unlike our previous encounter, the whale sharks did not seem to be en route to elsewhere. I counted seven, the largest of which was just shorter than our panga. This "lazy" behavior prompted the students in my boat, who had been actively sunbathing ever since we left the sea lions, to beg to be allowed back in the water. Not personally having authority to do anything more than identify seabirds, I responded that if the host professor allowed his students to swim, I would as well.

Picture this: a cloudless day, the breeze light and the seas flat, and a panga idles alongside a massive whale shark, head to bow, tail to stern. Inside the open panga, eight collegians, deeply tanned and clad only in their swimsuits, gaze through binoculars at another panga several hundred meters away, COM-PLETELY IGNORING THE WHALE SHARK swimming so close they could spit on it.

There are times . . .

There was finally a splash near the host professor's panga, a human splash, thus averting mutiny on my boat. We did not revert to anarchy, however, and I permitted only three swimmers overboard at a time, assuring them that everyone would get a turn. In the end, everyone other than the kindly academician running the boat had a turn at whale sharking.

We zoomed back to the field station just in time for lunch, hot, sandy, salty, and completely imbued with the sublime.

During lunch I listen intently over a too-hot bowl of *chile con queso*, eavesdropping on multiple student conversations about the morning experience. This is easy to do because no one is speaking softly—appreciation is conveyed in the form of volume. As a general rule the younger diners lack the necessary vocabulary to articulate the sublime, and must resort to comparative description such as "the coolest thing I've ever done." Awe is seldom evoked when the experience is processed. The group at my table soon moves on to making plans for a night dive after the late lecture. They want to know how long I plan to talk about my research on natural histories of Baja, since I'm guesting tonight's lecture.

Sigh.

My faith in teenagers momentarily falters, but is restored an hour later. Because the wind has shifted, Dr. Awesome and I are writing over in the breezeway by the labs when we are approached by a young scholar, fresh from a swim, who tells us she and her friend have found a squid on the beach, and asks permission to dissect it. My colleague asks whether it's a giant squid, and the teen replies, "Nah, just a Humboldt squid."

This cracks me up about as far as I can be cracked. *Just* a Humboldt squid, indeed. It takes two of them to carry the squid up to the lab, and they report that they can feel a heartbeat. They also seem to appreciate what a beautiful creature it is, even in its death throes.[1]

Two more squid are found, and my overly generous colleague offers them my writing table. He scampers away to retrieve a dissecting microscope while I pack up. I move to an adjacent table, but the noise level ultimately chases me away.

---

1. Lest these students seem callous in terms of their eagerness to dissect the squid rather than attempt to rescue it, let me point out that squid usually die soon after laying eggs, a natural conclusion to their life cycle. This is apparently why numerous squid were being found washed up on our beach.

I move to the far breezeway, where the breeze at this moment is inferior and the birding is almost hopeless. A half-dozen students are reading scientific papers here in order to prepare class presentations, and I end up functioning as the resident scientific dictionary, helping define everything from "crepuscular" to "fecund."

So now we've moved, in short order, through three unplanned activities: diving with sea lions, diving with whale sharks, and dissecting Humboldt squid. Education is taking place completely off the syllabus. Anticipated learning outcomes have not been drafted, there is no plan in place to assess student learning, and yet intellectual curiosity is being satisfied at an alarming rate. The host faculty are planning additional instruction on marine mammals to help satisfy that curiosity, which means that something else on the syllabus will need to be dropped.

I feel like standing up on the table and shouting, "THIS IS HOW EDUCATION SHOULD TAKE PLACE!" Fortunately, a student asks me to explain "paradigmatic" as it applies to wildlife management theory, and I shift back into the comfortable role of being a provider of answers. At the same time, it occurs to me that we miss tremendous opportunities if we emphasize technical vocabulary at the expense of helping students articulate affective experience, especially as it relates to the sublime. What changes in you when you go from diving with sea lions to swimming with whale sharks to dissecting Humboldt squid? What is it you learn on days like today? Are you learning anything about yourself, and about your innate abilities to learn?

I'm certainly learning something about how to teach. Rule number one, it seems to me, is to know when to abandon the syllabus.

## Day 10

A juvenile Harris's hawk flew into the breezeway just now, creating a bit more commotion than a young hawk ought to. I was walking through the breezeway at the time; at one point my head was within two meters of the hawk's talons.

This was the second Harris's hawk I've seen this summer, the previous one having been encountered on the gloved fist of a falconer walking through Paddington Station in London.[2] No kidding. It was the first one I've ever seen east of Texas.

---

2. It turns out the falconer was on his way to Wimbledon, via train, to chase away the pigeons from center court prior to the tennis matches.

Harris's hawk: chocolate brown with hints of chestnut at the shoulders. Chestnut thighs as well. The juvenile is heavily streaked below. A flare of white in the hands and at the base of the tail, and then black wingtips. Flat head, long tail, a glare that can melt steel and talons sharp enough to intimidate college professors.

The hawk clearly felt distress at being in the breezeway, giving me an accusatory glare for having trapped it, an infraction of which I was completely innocent. It seemed more angry than frightened, but I may be projecting a human emotional landscape on the animal here. Mostly, I perceived wildness. The drama was amplified because no wild Harris's hawk, even a wayward juvenile, should ever become trapped in a breezeway constructed by humanity. On that point, both the hawk and I agree.

Shortly after the hawk vanished I went for a snorkel, less to explore intertidal natural history and more to escape the heat. The plan was to take a long swim followed by a quick shampoo before returning to my writing, the water truck having finally showed up.

I contented myself, once immersed, to join a school of gulf grunion in the shallows. Silver and sleek with an iridescent blue lateral line, the grunion is about the size of a steak knife.

I've never seen a solitary grunion. See one and you'll see a few thousand. When the moon is right and they come into the shallows, they pretty much own the place, schooling so tight it makes the other fish dizzy.

I was doing my best to blend in with the fish, careful to keep my hands at my side and not splash my fins. I swam along at the grunion's pace, and they seemed to accept me as a friend of the family, especially after the first half hour.

Although I was as relaxed as I've been all summer, I couldn't get the hawk out of my mind. I was a greater threat to the grunion than to that hawk, and yet they tolerated me, swam lazily within arm's length, and were quick to forgive if ever I startled them. The hawk, on the other hand, was frantic to get away from me even though I had not entered its world so much as it had entered mine.

Are grunion any less wild than hawks? How is it that the ten seconds that I spent in close proximity with the hawk was so frenetic while the hour I spent with the grunion was so relaxing?

I wonder whether I confuse the hawk's hostility with wildness, just as I might mistakenly associate the grunions' tranquility with tameness. Part of the problem here is that I'm comparing fish with birds, but I suspect that similar disconnects can be found even when we stay within a single taxonomic order. Which bird is more wild, the hawk or the pelican? Is the pelican less wild, in our judgment, just because it appears to be tranquil more of the time?

The more I think about the wild, the more trouble I have with the concept.

The desert seems wilder to me right now, here in August, and this is undoubtedly because it's more hostile than I've ever before experienced it. When I've visited this locale, Bahia de Los Angeles, in December, or March, it is not immediately apparent how quickly the desert could kill me. The heat today is not merely oppressive—it's dangerous. The aridity is so ferocious I keep water with me constantly, even when I write here in the shade of the palapa.

As I grow older, I seem to want no less of the wild, but I seem to appreciate tranquility more. And the wildness of the pelican entrances me.

## Day 11

Cooler today—only 37 degrees Celsius in the shade. Morning clouds transmogrified into afternoon mugginess, and Isla Angel de la Guarda has vanished in an ethereal haze.

I'm limping today. En route to my swim with the grunions yesterday I'd sprinted across forty meters of hot sand, mistaking myself for a young man. Second-degree burns resulted, and the blister on my right foot is the size of a *cinco-peso* coin. Fortunately, it hurts only when I walk.

They'd planned a hike today, but shortly after I opted out they decided on a pelagic adventure into Canal de los Ballinas, thus changing my mind for me since there was a chance to see sperm whales.

Aside from seeing a couple thousand common dolphins, the first two hours were uneventful. One boat encountered a red-billed tropicbird that I didn't get to see, and I've seen only one once before so I'm feeling deprived. Another boat saw a finback whale, but once again my boat was skunked.

We finally came across a juvenile blue whale, only thirty meters in length, which means it was probably born a year ago. We got close enough to see the blue mottling of its skin without having to use binoculars. Still, I'd have traded it for the tropicbird.

The whale would spend seven to nine minutes submerged after sounding, and each successive interval seemed to stretch the patience of the students, especially when the call for silence would go out after five minutes so that we could hear the blow when the whale surfaced.

We ran to a nearby cove for lunch and a refreshing swim. The cook had prepared quesadillas, but included a bag of leftover pancakes from breakfast. We also had the standard snacks: Goldfish crackers, pretzels, and horribly sweet

Mexican cookies. And a jar of peanut butter. One of the students spread the peanut butter on his pancake, sprinkled it with a dozen or so goldfish, folded it in half, and called it a fish taco. The concept so appealed to my sense of whimsy that I immediately made a Goldfish taco for myself, as did Dr. Awesome. The rest of the students, meanwhile, behaved themselves.

It was delicious!

On the way back to the field station we encountered a cow Bryde's whale with calf, my crew estimating its length at a range from eight to eighteen feet. My own guess was five meters, which the students took to be authoritative, probably due to it being a metric guess.

When in doubt, it helps to sound correct.

We didn't stay with the mother and calf long, our reservoirs of reverential gazing having been exhausted. I learned later that things could have been worse. Dr. Awesome was a bit frosted after coming off the water. The magpies had flocked to my colleague's boat today, and the conversations lacked intellectual depth, especially when waiting for whales to surface.

Later, I reflect on whether the biggest obstacle to engaging young people in natural history is the amount of patience it takes to observe nature on its own terms. Whales are really cool to watch when they spout, but waiting nine minutes between breaths can be taxing for someone raised on today's bandwidths. The two weeks we've spent together, away from TVs, telephones, and the Internet, have taxed the magpies. Where the faculty, all of whom are birders, have been energized by the discovery of a red knot, *Calidris canutus,* on the beach a few days ago, and have been lugging spotting scopes up and down the beach every dawn in the hope that there may be others, the magpies find such activity draining rather than stimulating. After all, it's just a fat little sandpiper, right!

I feel for the magpies—it's not their fault that they are the product of their times. They've done everything right, even down to taking an excessive number of AP courses in high school. They've gone so far as to take a summer course down here in the Baja heat, far away from the nearest swimming pool. But they just can't take that final step and get up at first light in pursuit of a red knot.

The difference, from a teacher's eye view, between engaged and disengaged students is far more dramatic than between the plumages of brown boobies and their blue-footed cousins. The engaged spend hours of precious free time dissecting Humboldt squid, delighting in the discovery that they can use squid ink to write on each other's bodies. The magpies, meanwhile, work on their tans.

## *Day 12*

In celebration of a recent promotion, my department gave me a case of five-by-eight-inch Moleskine notebooks. I interpreted the gift as warm appreciation for all the scribbling I do in the field, ignoring the pointed inducement to keep at it. As of today, I will have filled an entire 192-page notebook during the trip, the first of the gifted notebooks, and will have to finish up the writing in my sketchbook, which is nothing more than an unlined five-by-eight Moleskine.

There's something fulfilling about filling a field journal. Educators don't always get to see visible results of their labors. The freshmen I teach this coming fall will not look much smarter in December than how they appeared in September. Most will have gained a bit of weight, and many will look scruffier, especially the males, but none of these changes in appearance will be the result of my labors. A few students have complained that my writing assignments have caused them to pull out their hair, but I don't really see the evidence. Other than a trail of initials following my name, the best thing I have to show for my intellectual adventures is a shelf of inked-up journals back in my office.

The journal feels sticky this morning. Like clockwork, an onshore breeze filled in at 9:00, and it has taken on a tropical affect, more like something you'd experience in the West Indies than on the edge of the Sea of Cortez. When I close my eyes I can imagine coconut palms swaying on this beach, but when I open them the keystone species is still the cardon cactus, rigid, parched, and somewhat phallic.

I'm glad to have spent two weeks writing in the Baja summer, but I will be equally glad to leave this beach two days hence, bound for a sailboat in foggy San Francisco Bay, boarding the bus home with a full journal squirreled away in my daypack. The heat has not been as bad as I'd feared it might be. You drink between six and eight liters of water per day, you keep a wet kerchief around your neck, you spend as much time in the shade as possible, and you learn to embrace the breeze. There's not much else you can do, other than to slow down a bit.

I need to learn more about slowing down. Dr. Awesome rarely exceeds fifty-five miles an hour, and yet generally arrives on time. Stores around here still close for the afternoon siesta, and yet their customers purchase no less than they would if the stores were open 24/7. Yesterday, I visited a retired professor who lives in town. He serves red wine chilled in the refrigerator, but he takes pride in getting through the day without air conditioning. When Dr. Awesome and I dropped in on him, he was wearing only boxers. He excused himself with great dignity, emerged moments later wearing shorts, and welcomed us formally and toplessly to his own personal field station. This is how things are done in the Baja heat.

Last night, when colleagues broke out a guitar, a fiddle, and a mandolin after I'd already set up my cot, my first thought was that it was too hot to play music. But I was wrong. Yes, it was hot while I tuned up, but the moment I strummed my way into their melody, the heat melted away. We played well beyond the moment when the field station switched off the breezeway lights, and when I finally made my way to the cot on the beach, sleep was possible.

I fall asleep each night atop the silk cocoon, and wake up each morning inside it, seldom remembering the moment when the transition was made. It helps to be exhausted, or nearly so, when bedtime rolls around, but the heat seems to exhaust us just enough to make sleeping in it possible. I'm told of heat waves, this time of year, where sleep was not possible until people took their sheets into the showers to wet them down before snoozing.

My other trip this summer was to Scotland, to a seaside town on the west coast where it rains three hundred days per year. We were there for two weeks in June, and never once wore shorts. As I sit here on the beach in Baja, it's hard to imagine that there are places in this hemisphere where, right at this very moment, people are wearing wool.

One of my goals at the outset of this writing retreat was not to spend the entire time writing about the heat. It would be dishonest, however, to write in and about this desert in August and not mention the heat from time to time. It animates everything, in its way, from how we sleep to what we eat to how we go about our business. Three times now I've taken short strolls out into the desert in the middle of the afternoon, and I've yet to observe activity among other members of my phylum. How strange it is to be the only chordate out and about.

If I have learned anything during this retreat it's how different this desert is from the upper Sonoran Desert in which I've lived and worked for many years, especially the high desert. There is nothing in New Mexico, Arizona, or Colorado to match the barrenness of the Midriff Islands this time of year. Likewise, there are pronounced differences between this place and the cape region, far to the south, where I take my classes. I doubt I could overstate how much more a landscape can do with twenty-five centimeters of annual rainfall than with nine. I am especially aware of the absence of some of my favorite Baja trees from the cape region—the rock fig, for instance, or the palo blanco.

Yesterday, while sitting on the emeritus professor's veranda, enjoying my first glass of wine this month, I noticed a diver walking up the beach toward town carrying a mesh bag the size of a bowling ball from which scores of octopus tentacles were protruding. I would guess that he'd harvested at least ten kilos of cephalopods, and it broke my heart to see them being toted off to market in such fashion.

When I commented on the diver's presence, my emeritus colleague exclaimed, "Those guys are not from around here—they've been coming down from Ensenada all summer, but there's nothing I can do about it!" He sipped his drink and then added, "The local divers have more respect, and always left this stretch of beach alone."

The last time I was here in Bahia de los Angeles was nine years ago, the first time was five years before that. In the rocky reefs around the islands, bony fishes seem to be faring better, especially those that spearfishers prefer. However, invertebrates such as urchins and sea cucumbers are in serious decline. The octopodes were under the same serious pressure nine years ago, and I can't see how much more of this can be sustained before that fishery collapses as well.

I am encouraged by the abundance of cetaceans I've been seeing during this retreat, especially of such species as common dolphins and pilot whales that feed at higher trophic levels. While I have no point of comparison from previous years since I was not here during the summer, we can infer that a healthy population of such fish as mullet, herring, and grunion must be present to support the thousands and thousands of Odontoceti we've seen in the past two weeks. These toothed cetaceans would simply not be here were they not able to find an adequate food supply.

A mixed report is the best I can give. I had hoped to see evidence of a resurgence in sea turtles, but it's possible that the scarcity we observed was the result of seasonal fluctuation. There can be no doubt, however, that they remain in serious decline.

We eat, as always, in the breezeway, at tables that have been cluttered with field guides all afternoon. During dinner a thirty-strong pod of bottlenose dolphins swims by, no more than a hundred meters from the beach. They are moving fast, but that doesn't stop a few of the younger students from bolting the table and sprinting down the beach, shedding garments as they run. They dive, they swim, but they can't catch the pod. The rest of us line the water's edge, shouting encouragement even though everyone assumes the quest to be hopeless.

Just as the pod begins to pull away, two of the largest dolphins turn back. A cheer breaks out on the beach, and our swimmers raise their heads to investigate. The two dolphins swim to within five meters of the swimmers, pause, and then turn back to the pod, their investigation complete.

Dolphin pods often have their own "police squads" comprised of larger males who will defend the pod if necessary. It's possible that the two animals that turned back did so just to ensure that the swimmers were no threat to the pod. It's also possible that these dolphins were motivated by curiosity, or perhaps even playfulness.

When the group returns to dinner, I lag behind, watching the two large males return to the pod, wishing I'd had the chance to get to know them better.

## *Day 13*

I slept in until daybreak this morning, and awoke to the most spectacular sunrise of the trip. One student described it as "insanely gorgeous." Wavy clouds near the horizon passed the reds and golds from side to side while the various pinks arced to the clouds overhead. This was the sort of sunrise my wife always narrates for me, as if I'll appreciate it more once I'm told the actual colors.

The moment I stir, the student occupying the nearest cot comments that this is our last sunrise. The bus will pick us up tomorrow at 4:00 a.m., and the sunrise we witness through its windows won't be nearly as poignant.

Today promises to be emotional. Final-day sentimentality sweetens our pancakes the way maple syrup never could.

The boats won't be going out today, and I am glad; I'm ready to be done playing naturalist. I have one last thing I want to write today, and the sooner I get started . . .

A huddle forms on the beach. I'm guessing it's another Humboldt squid, and I don't want to interrupt my writing for another dying cephalopod. Or maybe I do, because others, including faculty, have joined the huddle. I investigate, leaving my binoculars and hat on the writing table, my way of stating that I'm a writer this morning, not a naturalist. The squid ends up still being alive, and it flashes red-white-red when I join the huddle. I'm wearing a red shirt this morning, and a student points out that the squid matched my shirt for a moment. Solidarity? The host professor delivers an impromptu lecture on the squid's life cycle while the students document its death with their cameras.

There's so much life here in this sea that death is never far away. We find desiccated remains on the beaches of every island we visit: hammerhead sharks, the canine skulls of sea lions, pelican beaks, a few turtle shells, mystery vertebrae. The biologists pick through this detritus eagerly; to them each corpse is a lesson in anatomy. To me it tends to be a poem that ended too soon. Always too soon.

We attribute immortality to our gods even though we now know mortality to be the force driving natural selection. The survival of the fittest only has meaning if the less fit die earlier than the more fit. In nature there are no disability accommodations, nor are there provisions for assisted living. To this, the beaches of Baja give ready testimony.

This morning I can look all the way across to the farthest island without seeing a single ripple on the water. I don't see a single spout or dorsal fin, nor even the wake of a panga. Boobies are not zipping, mullet are not jumping, and undergraduates are cramming for the field identification exam. Every once in a while, one will seek me out, asking something along the lines of how to distinguish Caspian terns from royals. They complain that the caps are too similar, missing the fact that the wingtips are not.

I used to struggle with red-tailed hawks until someone directed my attention to the patagial patches. That which had been difficult was suddenly easy, even for someone unable to make out the color of the tail. There's a life lesson here for all of us: *look for what you can see, listen for what you can hear.* You don't have to memorize the bird, the fish, or the tree—just ask for its calling card.

I conducted an experiment with my own students a few years back. We all observed an unidentified gull for a full minute through binoculars. Then I instructed them to turn their backs to the gull and face me. At that point I asked them to tell me what color the gull's legs were. Most of the class immediately turned back around, raising their binoculars to their eyes. They hadn't looked for leg color.

Lesson learned.

The blue whale has distinctly mottled skin, but you won't tend to see it unless you know to look for it. You'll be too busy observing enormity to note mottle.

No system is foolproof. I remember once when a student couldn't identify a Costa's hummingbird because its yellow head confused her. She asked for my help because there weren't any yellow-headed hummingbirds in her field guide. What she didn't realize was that yellow was not the color of the plumage itself; it was caused by pollen. Likewise, another student was unable to identify a snowy egret because it didn't appear to have the characteristic yellow feet. Actually, that particular bird did have yellow feet, but it had been foraging in mud that morning during low tide, and the mud obfuscated the yellow.

For my part, I've learned a great deal these past two weeks thanks to the naturalists with whom I've been working, each of whom is a long-term Baja hand with several decades of experience teaching in these waters. My personal list is correspondingly long:

*What I've Learned*

- In a pinch, fish tacos can be made from leftover pancakes.
- Gulf grunions make great companions.
- Sea lions sometimes communicate vocally underwater.
- A red knot can be quite the exotic bird, depending on where you find one.
- Red-necked phalaropes seem to avoid me.
- Swimming with whale sharks isn't as easy as they make it seem on the Nature Channel.
- Pilot whales travel in "chorus lines"—that's actually the proper collective noun—that tend to be highly organized.
- I can write productively at a picnic table in a breezeway where someone else's students feel free to interrupt me.
- Never run barefoot on hot sand in Baja in August, even if it's only a brief sprint to the water.
- Never pull a boat on a trailer into a garage with the Bimini top up.
- The more experts who try to estimate the size of a school/flock/pod/herd/shoal, the more divergent the range of estimates.
- Red-billed tropicbirds seem to avoid me.
- However desirable it may seem, solitude is not necessary for a writing retreat.
- The ability to sketch does not come flooding back like the ability to ride a bike.
- Having a good student to faculty ratio is more important than having a good field station.
- It's easy to confuse a loggerhead shrike with a northern mockingbird if all you're seeing is the southern view of a northbound bird.
- Mandolins sound better under the stars.
- Vermilion flycatchers seem to avoid me.
- Referring to the bump on a bull sea lion's forehead as a "sagittal crest" is a quick way to impress a biologist, especially if the reference is made during casual conversation.
- If you hang out with ornithologists, they will see the birds you miss, like red-necked phalaropes, red-billed tropicbirds, and vermilion flycatchers. This is especially true if you have a red-deficient form of color blindness. One must learn not to fixate on such setbacks, and instead focus on all the extra birds one sees as a result of hanging out with ornithologists, such as the red knot, the black-bellied plover,

and the black-vented shearwater. In other words, take the birds you get.

- It can be a lot of fun helping students get good grades in someone else's class.
- Sometimes one must take it on faith that zebra lizards can run bipedally.
- Never go to Baja without hiking boots.

# 5

# Same Beach, Different Expedition

> We have a book to write about the Gulf of California. We could do
> one of several things about its design. But we have decided to let
> it form itself: its boundaries a boat and a sea, its duration a six weeks'
> charter time; its subject everything we could see and think and
> even imagine; its limits—our own without reservation.
>
> JOHN STEINBECK AND EDWARD F. RICKETTS, *Sea of Cortez:*
> *A Leisurely Journal of Travel and Research*, 1941

I suppose an apology is in order, if not to the readers of this narrative then at least to the students whose expeditionary exploits were being narrated as they attempted to circumnavigate the Isla Espíritu Santo archipelago. As I pick up the narrative threads after the interlude, we find ourselves on the same island, indeed the same beach, where the pre-interlude tale left off. It is a year later, however, and the fascinating students we were reading about are replaced by a group every bit as fascinating. This sort of thing happens to teachers all the time.

So let me set the scene: I'm sleeping in the same one-man tent as before, snuggled inside the same greenish-gold-whatever ultralight down bag. I'm still color-blind, of course, and I'm still paddling *Opsrey*. This expedition's male to female ratio has "improved" to five to eleven, depending on one's perspective. The students are all juniors and seniors. The new TA was a member of last year's expedition, so you already know her. She's great. As a matter of fact, she's probably a better TA than she was a student. The same guides lead us, of course.

We're pinned to the beach, at least for the morning. It blew all night, each capricious gust hurling a handful of sand against each tent. El Norte. I can't imagine that any of us slept for more than a few minutes at any given time. If I woke up once last night, I woke up fifty times.

It's hard not to take the north wind personally when you're sleeping in tents that flap. And the reality is that when El Norte visits a beach, all tents flap.

Responding to nature's call, two of the students climbed out of their tent at first light, and their tent almost blew away, sand anchors still attached. The taller of the two caught the flapping monster the moment it became airborne, and hung on doggedly until her tentmate was able to tame the beast by running around to the door and climbing back inside. It's the first time in four expeditions that our homemade sand anchors, constructed of squares of plywood the size of a CD jewel case, haven't held. We spend the next half hour hauling rocks to the other tents so that they won't wander off once their occupants do. Call me sexist, but it's when we haul rocks that I wish there were more males participating in these expeditions.

The guides hope that the wind will die down as the day heats up, but I'm not feeling it. Since when does El Norte bring heat anyway?

I've always worried that one of our groups will not complete its circumnavigation, and the latest long-range weather chart, its nasty-looking wind arrows pointing south, forecasts that this might indeed be the year. El Norte is supposed to be a winter phenomenon, cutting off in mid-March, but I've known this brute to visit during spring break before, although only for a couple days here and there. But this is an El Niño year, when even kayak guides get confused by the weather's mercurial temperament.

The wind is coming straight off the water, and is blowing so hard right now that the sand stings my ankles unless I stand below the high-tide line where everything is still wet. The students are going to be up any moment, at which point I'll have to conjure up the sort of cheerfulness that students find inspiring. I remind myself of something I learned back at the scout ranch: *if the staff keep smiling, there's still hope, but once the staff get grumpy, the campers all get homesick.*

One of the heartier fellows finally emerges, ready for the morning. He walks down to where I stand. He's reading my face, trying to determine whether the situation is as troubling as it seems. I smile, and then ask whether he's hungry. The question seems to surprise him; he probably anticipated a conversation about meteorological rather than culinary matters. He consults his stomach, and discovers that he actually could eat a bite or two.

"Let's get to it, then," I suggest.

We begin slicing mangoes, and he asks about the wind.

I look around, pretending just to have noticed the wind for the first time. I ponder the question for a moment, and then answer, "Inconvenient."

Two other students are now wandering over to the mango table. The first student reports to the newcomers, "Juanito thinks this wind is inconvenient."

Nervous laughter squeaks out from under a windbreaker's hood, barely audible over the howl of a fresh gust, and the behooded student steals my knife to take over the job. The other heads to *Opsrey*, the misspelled breakfast boat, to search for some *pan dulce,* sweat bread, so that we can snack while slicing fruit. Garambullo comes around to pour coffee, the same thick, awful Mexican coffee he poured the previous morning, regardless of which expedition we're talking about. Things are looking up.

Dr. Awesome emerges. Frowning. The other professor has had an awful night, and has a stiff neck. I realize, instantly, that I should have briefed the faculty on the cheerfulness thing. I tell my stiff-necked partner that the good news is that we won't have to paddle today. My colleague doesn't take the bait, and fails to ask what the bad news is. A shame, for I had a great answer: *"The students think it's windy."*

After breakfast I huddle with the guides, who are still optimistic. I tell them I will be happy enough if we can get off this beach tomorrow, and they agree without abandoning their optimism. We plan a hike up to the ridge—there's no trail but we can see the top from the beach—then down the lee side to a reef where no one ever dives. The guides prognosticate—correctly, even though they've never dove there—that we will find more coral than usual. We will hike with our dive gear in our daypacks. We will have fun. If the wind is blowing after we return to camp for lunch, we will plan another hike. It will also be fun, because this is Baja.

We all agree that this is a sensible plan.

The talus is loose and the climb is not as safe as it appeared to be when assessed from the beach. Pillow-sized rocks predominate, each sharp-cornered rock stacked on the one below it in such a way as to look stable without necessarily being trustworthy. The only real way to tell whether you can safely step on any given rock is to do so, always treading skeptically. Lacking a trail, we must zigzag back and forth, and I worry that one of the more nimble climbers up ahead will dislodge a rock large enough to create havoc among the plodders lower on the slope. We make it to the saddle without incident, however, and now the guides want to detour up the ridge to a high point overlooking the sea. One of the students has a bit of acrophobia, and this ridge is somewhat exposed, so I stay back with her. We decide to head down to the dive site and become beachcombers.

We find the desiccated remains of a triggerfish, its eyes missing but its teeth still prevalent. We also collect a brown pelican's skull with the bill intact, the tip of its beak still sharp; a recently deceased puffer fish, fully puffed; some huge oyster shells that must have been idling on this beach since at least Steinbeck's day; two unbroken urchin shells; a sand dollar; and a long backbone of indeterminate origin. (An eel? A snake? We can't decide.) We tromp over mounds of broken coral, almost all of it bleached white, coral so dry that it crunches like chalk when you walk on it. We set up a little natural history museum on the coral mound so that the other expeditioners can view our treasures. They arrive just as we complete the main exhibits, gushing about how windy it was at the very top.

The reason that no one ever dives the reef we're about to dive becomes apparent when we approach: there's no beach. Just rock piled on rock, all of it loose, some of it slippery, the talus of the slope above extending underwater. Ankle deep, I perch my tender, professorial feet on one of the rocks while donning my wetsuit, and the moment I put my right leg through the appropriate hole, a gust of wind topples me into the leeward student, who in term topples onto her leeward neighbor. Dominos. After decades of teaching, it's the first time I wipe out two students at once. We collapse into the shallow water, laughing at my quip about having succumbed to a pocket of heightened gravity.

There are times you must laugh at El Norte, lest he ruin your day.

Dr. Awesome has encouraged us to focus on vertebrates, instructing us to identify as many species as we can in thirty minutes' time. In short order we've singled out the colorful Cortez rainbow wrasse, a well-camouflaged stone scorpion fish, the majestic king angelfish, and two preoccupied Cortez angelfish, gaudy sergeant majors, austere scissortail damselfish, a blunthead triggerfish, several types of puffers, female Mexican hogfish (no males), a silvery squadron of Pacific crevalle jack, a few long, elegant trumpet fish, and a nondescript Cortez grunt. The duckies are learning the fish names fast and furious, and I'm not sure what has possessed them. It's funny, because they're completely ignoring the invertebrates, but I guess this is the nature of the exercise. When I point out *Heliaster kubiniki*, the poor echinoderm generates no excitement whatsoever. It's not his day to be a star.

The dive is over all too soon, and the wind sets us to shivering when we peel off our shorties. The hike back over the ridge warms us, and by the time we make it to the beach where our tents, mercifully, have not blown away, I note a slight abatement in the wind.

Manuelito feels it too, and immediately asks, "Do you feel that, Juanito?"

I scan the horizon with my binoculars. The waves are still white-capped, and are at least two meters high. I respond that the lighter, warmer breeze is too little, too late.

"Not for today, Juanito. *Mañana. Perfecto.*"

It takes a moment for me to realize the implications. El Norte has not defeated us yet. Tomorrow we will be able to launch the boats and get off this beach.

I am awed by how attuned our guides are to the wind and tides. When a cloud drifts overhead, I see only a cloud, while Manuelito sees the forty-eight-hour forecast. If his back is to the beach when you ask him what time the tide will be low, he doesn't have to turn around to give you an estimate. Once, when we hiked to the top of the island, I pulled out my binoculars and announced that there was a southerly blowing in the far channel. Manuelito replied, "Yes, it's been southerly for two hours now." When I asked how he could know that, since we'd just gotten to the point where we could see the channel, he simply pointed to the few clouds in the distance, adding, "We don't have as many clouds as you have in Alta California, so we pay more attention to them."

Scarcity. Paying attention. These things go together in the desert.

One of the noteworthy things about this particular expedition is how they deal with accidental scarcities. One student forgot to bring toothpaste, another forgot sunscreen, and yet another left her hat on the airport shuttle. But we're on an island now, a desert island, and there is no *mercado* down the beach where replacements can be procured. So we inventory, and we discover that we have extra hats and sunscreen, and enough toothpaste, collectively, to brush everyone's teeth for months.

Here on the island, our scarcities help define our community. If nothing else, we learn that there's plenty to go around—if we share—despite the fact that every expeditioner's personal belongings are limited to what fits into a single twenty liter dry bag.

I call the TA over, and we make quick plans to get lunch going, and organize a hike for those who want to join in. She tells me that some of the students want more diving time to work on their species lists. This is good, not only because she has become the voice of the students, which is one of her most sacred responsibilities, but also because students are pushing for more time in the water. So much better when this sort of initiative comes from the students rather than the faculty. I magnanimously grant the request, at which point the TA suggests that guacamole would go well with lunch. This, as well, meets my approval.

She gets the guacamole crew going, and I return to my writing without noticing that the wind continues to abate. I fail to notice, additionally, a squabble going on with the guacamole preparations. This is a shame, because it would have saved me a bit of bewilderment later in the afternoon.

The faculty decide to skip the hike, and this turns out to be a good thing. Without anyone insisting that hikers pay attention to critters and cacti, something of a speed hike breaks out, and the group practically jogs the several kilometers up the peak they've connived to ascend. Back in camp, meanwhile, I can't help missing the group. The wind has all but died at this point, and it's almost too quiet to write.

The expeditioners return to camp ninety minutes after they left, happy, sweaty, and completely out of water, unanimous in the judgment that I've just missed the best hike of all time. I nag them about staying hydrated, especially if they're planning to go diving again.

Blank stares. Diving?

"Kelly said you guys wanted to work on your species lists."

Oh. That. Yeah.

It turns out that Manuelito has offered to put on a roll clinic. Eskimo rolls. I reply, "If you want to roll, roll. If you want to dive, dive. But don't wear out the guides."

I begin to suit up, and only a handful of students recall the need to work on their species lists. The five of us begin making so many cool discoveries, however, that sooner or later most of the others will be drawn into the water. Someone reports having found seahorses over by a large coral head. When I swim over there, however, I spot something more unusual than a seahorse. It's spherical. Green or brown, one of those colors. Dark. Larger than a marble, but smaller than a golf ball. I've never seen anything like it in these waters, and yet it's strangely familiar. I stay down a moment too long, and then kick up to the surface, purging my snorkel just in time.

What was it? I dive back down four, maybe five times. The object seems unattached, and rolls back and forth in the light surge. I touch it, and it's hard. Smooth. Slightly slimy to the touch of my now-waterlogged fingers. After returning to the surface to refresh my breath, I return to the base of the coral head one last time and pick the strange object up. Cradling it gently in the palm of my hand, I return to the service where I realize, finally, that this specimen, although clearly biotic, is not of aquatic origin.

It's an avocado pit.

Still cradling the pit, I swim over to the nearest huddle of students to share my grand riddle with them, exclaiming, "You'll never guess what I've found." They immediately see it for what it is, however, without even having to touch it. I'm duly informed that a member of the guacamole crew threw it into the water before lunch, even after another member of the crew told him not to. That's what the squabbling I'd ignored was about.

I return to the beach to record this episode, only to realize, after I'd completely dried off, that I'd never observed the seahorses. For a moment I consider heading back into the water, but then I write this sentence instead.

While I'm writing, two of the students, one of whom will ultimately be selected to serve as next year's TA, are wading at the far end of the beach. They've found something interesting, but I can't tell what it is at this distance, even using the binoculars. I return to my scribblings until they come back to camp with the news of a large eel they've seen swimming around the shallows.

I ask them to describe what they saw, and what they report sounds fishy. When they describe the specimen itself, everything corresponds to a fully grown green moray eel, but when they describe its behavior, this critter isn't acting at all like any self-respecting moray would act, especially given the time of day. I encourage them to think of other possibilities. A trumpet fish, perhaps? Maybe a barracuda? With the sun getting lower in the water, was it possible they didn't get a good look?

We break out the fish manual, and they insist that their moray looked exactly like the one in the photograph. The panamic green moray, its distinctive green color coming from a mucus it secretes to protect its scaleless skin. Eel snot. I remain skeptical, however, and insist that the moray simply doesn't come up to bathers in the shallows in broad daylight. Impossible.

My skepticism disappoints them, of course; they both decide to add *Gymnothorax castaneus* to their species lists anyway. This is a gutsy move, except for the fact that the species list will be graded by Dr. Awesome, not me. Still . . .

There are no other interruptions to my journal writing until happy hour, which flows nicely into dinner. But when the first few students take their emptied plates down to the washing buckets, cries of "Eel! Eel!" resound through the encampment

I jump to my feet immediately, but am nearly trampled by undergraduates, who as a general rule tend to be quicker on their feet when eels are involved. The entire class gathers in the wet sand just short of the Sea of Cortez, and there is a great deal of pointing and shouting. When I finally push through the crowd, I see before me, in perhaps twenty-five centimeters of water, a panamic green moray more than a meter long.

Uh-huh.

The eel appears to be as aware of us as we are of it. It swims with its mouth open, its side turned toward us as if it wants us to see it better. I can't conceive of why a moray would advertise its presence. This animal has dropped every shred of the eel craft that is so characteristic of its night-stalking kin, the Muraenidae family of predators who tend to hide in cracks and crevices during the daylight hours.

It leads us down the beach at a slow walk, undulating snakelike and often turning its head to look at us squarely, its mouth always open, its teeth always visible. Very visible.

I notice, eventually, that our guides have not come down to the beach to witness this remarkable phenomenon. This in itself seems to be strange behavior, especially for Garambullo, who holds a bachelor's degree in marine biology and who rarely passes up a chance to vet whatever subtidal identifications the students are making. I walk back up the beach to investigate, leaving the eel to the duckies, and I can't help but notice that while the eel seemed so utterly brazen, the guides seem unusually chagrined. Has this event somehow embarrassed them?

Indeed it has. In low tones Manuelito explains that the guides from a rival company have been feeding this eel chicken gizzards whenever they used this beach, training it to come into the shallows for the entertainment of their clients. Our guides, having a stronger sense of ecological citizenship, are mortified at the actions of their colleagues, feeling that it reflects poorly on all kayak guides.

My own mortification was soon to come. Once the commotion on the beach died down, the two students that had reported the eel earlier came and sat in the sand close beside me, one on each side, and yet pretended to ignore me. Neither one said a word about the eel, so I finally asked, "Did you see it?"

Yes.

"And was it the same one you saw this afternoon?"

Yes.

"And is there a moral to this story?"

There was a moral, of course, but they were kind enough to let me figure it out for myself.

In *Zaca Venture*, William Beebe wrote about a member of his Baja expedition wading about in the sargassum and spearing four eels, "three of which were vicious green morays." Can't help wondering, in the company of these gentle students who have just witnessed a green moray gone begging, just how vicious *Gymnothorax castaneus* actually is. (*Gymnothorax*, by the way, translates as "naked breastplate," a reference to the lack of pectoral fins, and "*castaneus*" references the animal's chestnut color when it's not particularly snotty. Nothing essentially vicious connoted here.)

I have heard that morays will bite humans in self-defense, especially in instances where the human intruder reaches into a crevice where the moray is hiding. My information, however, is hearsay, and having logged more than five thousand scuba dives, I have never had the least bit of trouble with an eel of any sort. The unvarnished truth is that most of the humans who lose fingers to morays were attempting to feed the morays at the time, a simple matter of divers feeding an animal a bit more flesh than intended.

There was a time when hand-feeding a moray was a rite of passage for rookie divers. So many divers lost fingers subsequently that in some places—Australia, for example—laws had to be passed forbidding the feeding of morays. Such a shame we humans need laws forbidding us from feeding sharp-toothed predators who hunt primarily by smell. That humans, who rarely lunge during meals, seem genuinely surprised when eels lunge at whatever they eat speaks poorly of human intelligence; table manners are different for creatures who hunt from cracks and crevices underwater.

Clearly, the moray is misunderstood. One reason for this may be that it constantly opens and closes its mouth whenever it is observed, revealing some impressive dentition. This is often misinterpreted as a threat gesture, but in actuality this action is part of its breathing physiology—it's the best way to get water flowing over the gills when you're wedged motionless in a crevice for hours on end.

There's a moray eel skull back in my office, adorning a cluttered bookshelf. The largest tooth, by far, attaches not to the jaw, but rather descends from the center of the roof of the mouth. All the teeth are raked backward, the better to grasp prey, with the teeth in the back of the mouth raked more sharply backward than the incisors. I discourage students from handling the skull, for they will inevitably prick themselves, not believing the teeth of a dead animal can be as sharp as these are. So far, no one has lost a finger to my eel skull, but it has drawn blood several times.

🕊

It has not been the sort of day an emeritus scuba instructor wants to brag about. Prepping for my morning dive I was toppled over by the wind while donning my wetsuit, taking down a couple students in the process. During the afternoon dive I spent an excessive amount of time trying to identify a feral avocado pit. And after the diving was done I told two of my students that the marine denizen they'd clearly seen could not possibly be the denizen they claimed to have seen.

There are days when dusk can't come soon enough. I am glad when the expedition's Flame Queen digs the canterns out of her kayak and loads them with tea lights. These canterns—candle lanterns made from beer cans—are our own inventions. You cut the top off a regular beer can, no other sort of can will do, and then perforate them so that the light casts decorative patterns and the wind doesn't blow the candles out. On windier nights, depressions are dug into the sand to serve as an extra windbreak.

There is no need for a pit tonight, the wind has died completely. Canterns are ignited, and we huddle with the students to debrief the day. The stars are brilliant, but I cannot shake the feeling that El Norte is not finished with this expedition. Manuelito wants to get an early start and see whether we can catch up to our original itinerary, in essence accomplishing two days' worth of paddling in a single tomorrow. I have the TA team the weaker paddlers up with stronger paddlers in the doubles, but I'm hesitant about whether we can make it as far as our guide suggests. We decide to put in for lunch at the beach where we'd originally hoped to spend this evening, and then to see whether the students had the energy to put in a few more miles. They agree to this plan when we propose it to them, but I worry that they have no idea what they've just gotten themselves into.

Dr. Awesome is the first to bed, followed closely by the students. Everyone seems determined to recapture the sleep El Norte stole from us the previous evening. I sit in the dark with the guides, quietly watching nothing in particular. Manuelito finally quips, "Baja midnight." I check my watch, and it is nine o'clock, straight up. Baja midnight. Time for me to crawl into my sleeping bag as well.

El Norte, mercifully, allows us to sleep through the night undisturbed.

# 6

## Sea Sparkle

Nature is loud, and if you let it, it will speak to you.

A student journal

A wave breaks nearby, close enough to be felt through my ground pad. Shaken from my slumbers, although I intuit that dawn is not nigh, I am instantly aware that the tide is high. The water sounds close. Too close.

I'm out of my tent in a clumsy instant, headlamp in hand, glasses still back in the tent, barefoot in just skivvies and a T-shirt. The student ghetto has been pitched closer to the water than my tent, but the somber glow of my headlamp reveals that their tents are all standing. Dry. And the boats are still safely above the tide line. A quick inventory tells me that I'm the only one awake at the moment. I check my watch, but without my glasses there's no way of telling how late it is. Or how early.

Breathe. The only wind here is my own.

I check the tide line. There's still plenty of dry sand between the splash zone and the tents . . . but I know I did not dream up that wave. Or did I?

I switch off the headlamp. Baja etiquette demands that I pee in wet sand, not on the dry. I approach the splash zone cautiously, just in case another huge wave lurks out there in the dark. The wet sand, not as cold as I expected, reminds me that I'm still on a desert island.

I have to concentrate to relax enough to take care of the business at hand, and in the process I become aware of the tension in my body. Worried about this expedition, probably.

I counsel myself to unwind. The Scots have a saying that my PhD supervisor kept trying to teach me: *Whit's fur ye will no gang by ye.* What's meant to happen will happen. I suppose this even applies to El Norte, should the bastard once again visit.

By the time my bladder empties, my eyes have adjusted enough to the dark that I perceive bioluminescence in the surf. Each wave, after it breaks, glows for a moment at its base, probably the result of *Noctiluca miliaris*, a microscopic dinoflagellate taking a tumble. Sea sparkle. I make a note to point this out to the students on our next beach, whichever one we might end up camping on tomorrow night. No one should go through life without experiencing sea sparkle.

When I return to my tent I decide not to put on my glasses to check my watch. It's better, sometimes, not to track the hours too closely.

The next time I awaken, it's light, but just barely, the pinkish-gray light one sees prior to sunrise in this part of the world. Garambullo is already up, but none of the students have stirred. He waits until I sit up in my sleeping bag before he approaches, and after we exchange the usual pleasantries, I ask through the mosquito mesh whether he heard a big wave break during the night.

"*Sí.* At high tide."

"What do you suppose it was?"

"A big wave."

I am schooled enough in kayak-guide humor to realize that he's messing with me, but I pretend to ponder his response thoughtfully, professorially, regardless. After a few slow nods of my head, I answer, "You're probably right."

He asks whether I want him to wake up the camp, and I answer, "Only if you want me to make the coffee." That matter being settled, I try to remember which tent my TA occupies, with the goal of waking her first as a matter of professional courtesy. She awakens immediately, her hair askew, her eyebrows knitted, her demeanor serious. She has already sketched out the new kayak assignments, but before she can run them by me I assure her that I trust her judgment in this matter. This deepens her frown, so I suggest that she keep an eye on the new pairings, making further adjustments during our lunch stop as necessary, assuming we continue on.

As I commence with the other wake-ups, I slip somewhat automatically back into camp-counselor mode, commenting fervently not only on the beauty of the day but the fact that everyone has already missed the best part of it. When I get to the guy tents I hear myself asking the slackers inside why their tents haven't already been struck. From the other side of a rain fly a gravelly voice responds, attempting to sound manly, "Hey, hold it down out there. We're trying to write."

Right.

It is indeed a beautiful morning. The first wisps of breeze are southerly, the most gracious breeze possible to someone heading north. I don't want to miss a moment of this beneficence, should it hold, but I counsel myself not to become impatient with how long it inevitably takes, whenever college students are involved, to break camp and get the boats into the water. I've been in this business long enough to realize that badgering these kids won't get us to our next camp any sooner.

The mild southerly breeze is still blowing when we finally launch the boats, and it feels good finally to be back on the water after having spent an entire day pinned to the beach. The southerly is wonderful, but I worry that it will probably die off around noon, only to be replaced by something contrary. I know what Manuelito is thinking, that he'd love to skip lunch and ride this southerly as long as we can. I suspect that Manuelito knows what I'm thinking as well, that this is only our second day in the boats with this crew, and that it's too early in the expedition to paddle as far as we're hoping to paddle without a substantial midday break.

I value my connection to Manuelito more than I can express. We've spent a hundred days together on this island, as I write this, and we've had ample time to work through each other's foibles. There have been times when an idea occurs to us simultaneously, and all we need to do to negotiate a change in plans is to make eye contact. His eyebrows will arch a bit, asking me, "What do you think?" And then I'll nod almost imperceptibly, my way of saying, "Let's do it."

Mother Nature begins to mess with our plans within a few hours, just as soon as we round the point into the large *ensenada* where we're planning to stop for lunch. There, less than a kilometer ahead of us, is a sizable pod of dolphins, feeding. Manuelito realizes, instantaneously, that there's no way to sneak this many collegians past that many dolphins without losing at least half an hour, and at the same time I realize that it would be entirely perverse to attempt to rush these kids past a dolphin encounter. Experiencing nature is a bit more of a priority at the moment than getting the expedition back on schedule, but only a bit.

Both guides have spotted the dolphins now, and both faculty, but we don't point them out because sooner or later one of the students will make this discovery as well. Sure enough, within a couple minutes one of our sharper-eyed charges chimes up about what's ahead, and I signal the group that we should be silent.

I'm in the front now, setting out on a vector that I think will bring us close to the pod without cutting them off. The expedition trails silently, paddling fast, and once we're within a hundred meters or so I'm able to identify the animals as the long-beaked variety of Pacific common dolphins, *Delphinus capensis*. Not quite as large as bottlenose dolphins, their sleek gray dorsal areas are complemented by white bellies and a yellowish thoracic panel. The adults in the water clearly outweigh the adults in the kayaks, and the largest of these dolphins weigh twice as much as I do. I stop paddling as soon as I make the identification, knowing this species well enough to know that they'll probably initiate contact with us if they're not too busy feeding. I hold my paddle horizontally overhead, still gripping it in both hands, the signal to stop. The students drift up beside me without so much as a whisper.

Sure enough, the pod alters its course slightly in order to come closer to us. They do not suspend their feeding activity, however, which is a good thing, for if they wanted to play we'd lose twice as much time.

Close-up engagement with other marine mammals—whales or sea lions—tends to be more exciting than dolphin encounters on these expeditions, but the time spent with dolphins always seems more sublime.

I estimate that there are forty-some animals in this pod, which makes it small by local standards. It quickly becomes apparent how the dolphins have organized themselves, especially in terms of communal relationships. They move about in twos or threes, no dolphin lacks a companion. Larger dolphins tend to swim with larger dolphins, medium with medium, mothers are clearly accompanied by their calves. One becomes aware that the pod has its own way of doing things, and that its customs are animated by intelligence. The young are not only participating, they are learning in the process. And the largest animals situate themselves between us and the mother/calf pairs. Yet the entire pod seems to know that we present no danger to them, despite the fact that we're a far larger herd of kayakers than they usually experience in these waters. They seem to appreciate that we're not paddling through their lunch.

We sit there in silence, barely moving. A nearby student reaches for her camera, and I whisper that she should make certain the flash is turned off. She puts the camera away, which is a good thing, because the machine would not be able to capture the awesomeness. Our silence is nothing short of devout, although at least one student is struggling not to shout out, "OH MY GOD, I CAN ACTUALLY SMELL THEM" after catching a whiff of a fishy exhalation.

The pod moves on, and we remain motionless, listening to them breathe, until Manuelito asks, "Lunch, Juanito?"

Lunch.

Just as the dolphins chose not to play at this particular moment, we must do likewise. Feeding behavior once again takes precedence, and the guides guide us to our luncheon landing.

There is a brackish well not far from here, no more than five meters deep, dug by hand many years ago by the Mexican Army. After a quick huddle, we decide that Manuelito and Dr. Awesome will lead the students up to the well for a quick shampoo, while Garambullo and I stay behind to put lunch together in the interest of speeding things up. What this means, ultimately, is that I open and drain a dozen cans of tuna fish while Garambullo attends to the more skilled task of chopping up a vegetable salad.

I'm usually not assigned kitchen duties on these expeditions, so this is my first go-around with Mexican tuna cans. I'm pleased to learn that this tuna is dolphin safe, but it surprises me that the cans, which are otherwise in Spanish, use the English phrase "dolphin safe" rather than translating it. Garambullo does not think this strange at all, since the customers most concerned about whether their tuna was caught using dolphin-safe methods will be able to read English.

By the time the expedition returns, I've already wolfed down a tostada salad, and I deal with my looming impatience to get back on the water by pulling out my journal and attempting to be reflective. The pod of dolphins we encountered still has a grip on me, a grip I describe weakly as "psychic," but I'm too distracted to better articulate the bond I was feeling with these animals. Cetaceaphilia?

It's always difficult to write with the sun directly overhead and dolphin-safe tuna in the belly.

Rather than being able to focus on the encounter I had the last hour, my mind wanders to previous encounters with dolphins, all of which have proven to be sacramental. I recall the time with bottlenose dolphins on the Santa Barbara coast, where we could feel their echolocation clicks with our buttocks through the hulls of surf kayaks. The time with spinner dolphins in Hawaii, where a mother allowed her calf to explore the humans with whom it was sharing a cove. The time scuba diving in Monterey, where the visibility was so bad I could hear the dolphins observing me even though I couldn't see them. The time sailing in the Gulf Islands of British Columbia when they played so energetically in our bow wave, splashing us, it seemed, on purpose.

One of the students pulls out a journal to join my struggles with the muse, and I hear the TA telling her that we really haven't got time for that. Yikes. It seems wrong, here on the island, to be so rushed, but the TA is right—if we're going to afford the lay day we want tomorrow, we need to complete another day's paddle today.

I stow my field notes back in my dry bag, and then congratulate the group on doing yesterday's paddle this morning. Now all we have to do is today's paddle, right?

They seem to think this will be a cakewalk. Regardless of their optimism, I recommend that everyone have their headlamps ready just in case it gets dark before we make our next landing. This sobers them up a bit, and we manage to get the boats back into the water quickly, almost too quickly. At the last moment I remember to break out two of the large water bladders and have everyone top up their drinking supply.

We look like seasoned kayakers by the time we point our bows back to the north. This is good, I reflect, because if we've got the look down, the skills can't be far behind. I remind myself that a few of these duckies have already learned to roll their boats—we're not doing at all badly for this point in the trip.

We've lost our southerly breeze, unfortunately, but the headwind is fairly gentle at the moment. I mentally reassure myself that if it doesn't get worse, this light headwind will only cost us another half hour. I paddle up to join Manuelito at the front, wondering whether he's worried. He is not, not really, and he opines that the wind won't build enough to keep us from making our landing by sundown.

I slip back to join the slower paddlers. We'll make it when we make it, I assure myself. *Whit's fur ye will no gang by ye.*

The group near the back is singing again. They urge me to join in, but I excuse myself, explaining that I don't know the words. They find this incredible, because the songs are from *The Little Mermaid.* Everyone knows them, right?

I assure them that I grew up before mermaids could sing.

A student makes the unfortunate observation that her parents know all the words to all the songs, and I decide that it's going to be a longer afternoon than I feared.

We've passed now from Isla Espíritu Santo to Isla Partida, the second-biggest island of the archipelago. The coves of Partida are deeper, the points of volcanic rock seem to stretch out farther to the west. We'll spend the next three nights on this island, according to plan.

The breeze builds slowly through the afternoon, as has the heat, but headwinds don't seem to slow us down too much except at the points, where the chop is probably a bigger obstacle than the headwind itself. After we round each successive point Manuelito leads us immediately back to the east, hoping to duck us into the lee of the next point. This adds to the distance we must paddle, but at least allows us to cover that distance more quickly. And more comfortably. The last thing we want right now is for a student to become seasick. There's no way we will make our hoped-for destination if that happens.

We're passing up some good natural history now, like an alcove that always contains a colony of blue-footed boobies, which can be quite entertaining when one or two of the males is doing a mating dance, showing off his webbed, bright-blue feet as if they're as sexy as sunglasses. When we visited this alcove last year, one of the juveniles was practicing the dance, mimicking the more earnest moves of a nearby adult. I am tempted to narrate what we're missing, but I realize that it's probably better to keep the focus on what we're not missing. All the same, it's hard to pass up boobies during the mating season.

We fall into a routine of rafting up—boat to boat, hand to gunnel—in the lee before rounding a point in order to collect ourselves. These are good times, and the students in the snack boat are becoming adept at passing out their next round of surprises. This point is trail mix, the next is Bimbo cookies, the following will be dried fruit. The rafting sessions are therapeutic: we stretch, we reapply sunscreen, those who need to pee slip over the sides of their boat and take a brief swim. Then, when everyone is back in their kayaks, feet to the pedals, we have new energy to round this point and paddle for the next one.

After we snuggle back into the next lee, one of the students points out that the sun is getting low. I pretend not to have noticed this, but she knows I'm faking. When we come back westerly approaching the next point, the sun will be in our eyes, and its reflections on the choppy water will make it difficult to see ahead. If there are dolphins in front of us at that point, we will miss them completely. I pull my broad-brimmed hat so low on my forehead that I can barely see beyond the bow of the boat, focusing once again on matching my breathing with the strokes of my paddle. I attempt not to consider how far we still have to go, concentrating instead on how best to get there, trying to maintain the disciplined beauty of my paddle stroke. I call out that everyone should keep their grips relaxed.

The dolphins we saw earlier still have a grip on me. As we round the point I search for another pod in this last grand bay, Ensenada Grande. Although it seems like a great place for dolphins to feed, there are none to be seen.

One final point to round. When we raft up this time, this last floating congress during an unusually long day, there's less attention to snacks and hydration. Students are digging out their cameras, intent on capturing the sunset, which is already hinting of the ruby tones to come. They think it's cool to be paddling this late in the day, and I'm glad they're less apprehensive about what lies ahead than I am. Perhaps they've forgotten how quickly darkness follows sundown at this latitude. For my part, I'm fairly certain that we're going to get our butts kicked rounding this point because now we turn permanently to the east, having come near the top of the archipelago. Balance will become an issue. I tell them not to stiffen up, but to keep their hips loose and move with their boats. All rudders in the water. Lean forward, keep together, dig deep. We're almost there.

Manuelito and I both drop our rudders for the first time this trip.

I make it a point not to let my fatigue show. The students reciprocate by pretending to have plenty of energy to make it to the landing. We cheer each other on, as the raft breaks up, and I realize that now that we're running on adrenaline, it's going to be all the more difficult to keep the stronger and weaker paddlers together. I signal to Manuelito that I'll be dropping back with Garambullo, and he nods appreciatively. Dr. Awesome wants to know what to do, and I quietly ask the other professor to take up the rear of the front group if possible, should the group split in half. I realize, in a moment of existential gratitude, that Dr. Awesome is digging as deeply as the rest of us, perhaps even deeper.

Manuelito makes the turn wide, keeping us away from the worst of the reflector waves ricocheting off the cliffs. For most of the students this is their first time in confused seas where the chop is coming from multiple directions, but they seem to be handling it well. One of the duckies in one of the slower doubles asks me how she's doing, and I insist that she's kicking butt.

"Really?"

Really. We're all kicking butt, and if we can make it one more kilometer in this slop without any of the boats capsizing, we'll have something to brag about.

As I'd feared, we break into two groups, and we do so just as the sun disappears under the horizon. Some of the more powerful students have actually pulled ahead of Manuelito; they're like horses heading for the barn once they see the tiny beach we're aiming for. This discourages those of us at the back, because even though the slower paddlers are kicking into their last-mile sprints, we're falling farther and farther behind. To me it feels as if we're sprinting in boots full of water.

El Embudo. The funnel. The beach we're heading for looks smaller than usual, a speck of sand funneled by steep cliffs on each side. The sand reflects the deep red of the sunset. From here we can clearly see that the beach lies at the mouth of a narrow canyon that climbs to the top of this island. I know the canyon to be steeper than it appears from this vantage.

Sunset flares its final, glorious flames. I notice that Isla San Francisco, far to our north, has disappeared in the growing twilight. It seems suddenly dark, but then I remember that I'm still wearing sunglasses, and that the lenses are so caked with salt at this point that I probably wouldn't be seeing much even in broad daylight. I remove them, letting them hang by their lanyard, and realize that there is still plenty of light to make the blurry landing safely.

The last hundred meters lasts an eternity, and my butt feels quite literally as if it has been kicked. Mercifully, some of the fast kayakers have remained knee-deep in the water, cheering us on, and one of the fellows braces my boat while I pull my legs out of the cockpit. I straddle a leg to each side of the boat, and he offers me his hand, pulling me to my feet. I feel as if I haven't stood in months.

We previously instructed the students that, as a standard procedure, the first order of business once we've gotten the boats out of the water is to erect the shade canopies. They've already pulled them out, a matter of habit although it's only our third day on the island, and I point out that shade might not be our most immediate need now that the sun is down. They freeze, turn toward me as a unit, and give me the so-now-what-do-you-want-us-to-do look.

I suggest that the faster they pitch their personal tents, the sooner we can celebrate happy hour.

You've never seen a dozen tents erected so quickly.

Before I can get to the business of setting up my own domicile, I am distracted by an earnest conversation in Spanish between our two guides. They are speaking in a clip too rapid for me to follow, but when they catch me eavesdropping they switch to English. Manuelito points to a collection of ash up on the rocks, the remnants of an illegal campfire, and says, "Poachers, Juanito."

"*¿Pulpo?*" I ask in Spanish. (Octopus?)

"No," he replies in English. "Sea cucumbers."

"How do you know?"

"You go dive here tomorrow. You will see."

My tent is the last to go up, but I manage to place it in the exact same spot I've chosen the past two years, as far as I can get from the student ghetto on this particular beach. The propane lantern has been lit and the dinner crew has already gone to work by the time I start digging holes for my sand anchors.

It's officially dark when the TA comes over to hand me a Cuba libre, wanting to know how we did today. She knows perfectly well that it was a fabulous effort, but she wants official confirmation from a representative of the university. We speak with our headlamps off, and I tell her that I'm proud of everyone, especially her, and that we should probably reward the group's effort by letting them sleep in tomorrow morning. She agrees, even though she realizes that faculty and students define "sleeping in" differently.

She returns to the now-glowing kitchen area without me, no doubt spreading the news regarding tomorrow's sleep-in.

Alone again in the dark, I sip the Cuba libre, hoping that the caffeine will work its wonders and give me sufficient energy to scratch out a few field notes after dinner. I still want to write about those dolphins, although I have no idea what I want to write about them. The memory already seems distant.

Dinner is being served, and I am being called. I quickly slip out of my paddling shorts and a shirt that has too many salty miles on it, and I actually feel a chill as I switch into clothing appropriate for such a late dinner. I realize, in the process, that I've been avoiding the group, who have grown noisy as they aggregate around food, almost boisterous in celebration of what they've accomplished today. What we need tonight is a campfire, somewhat desperately, but we won't build one because we're not poachers.

I slip in at the back of the dinner line, my customary place, and I'm led to believe that my presence was missed at happy hour. I explain that it took me longer than usual to dig in my sand anchors, which is only partially true. The part of the truth that I'm not telling is that I'd need to be half my age to match the group's energy right now, and it felt better just to take my time, alone, setting up my one-man tent in the most solitary location I could find, which on this minuscule beach in this tiny cove with its steep, sheer, sound-intensifying walls is never quite solitary enough.

I have a funny relationship with this particular beach. I've long fantasized about occupying it alone for a couple weeks, asking it to serve as one of my periodic writing retreats. There would be fewer distractions here than just about anywhere else I could conceivably go; the birding here isn't all that good, nor is the diving. No trees; no reefs. Straight-up cliffs on each side. There's only really one hike out of here, a steep up-canyon climb directly away from the water, and it's one I could easily pass up, having hiked it enough times already.

The plan would be to bring a small writing table and a chair that I could set up under a shade canopy. A cooler for beer would be nice, and a glass of wine for dinner every night. Otherwise, I could make do with a one-burner camp stove, a carton of canned food, and a large bag of carrots to stave off scurvy. Throw in a couple bags of tortillas, raisins, and a jar of peanut butter. And a coffee pot. The more austere the dinner menu, the more I'll appreciate my return to civilization once I do so.

I'll hire a *pangero* to drop me off and then to leave me as alone as I can be left. Pick me up at such and such a time on such and such a date, weather permitting. And please don't forget I'm out here.

I actually submitted a grant application to the Ellen Meloy Fund for Desert Writers a few years ago, proposing that they subsidize my fantasy. I have no idea why I didn't receive the award other than that this seems to be the story of my life: *the more I crave solitude, the more I end up spending sojourns in the desert with classes filled to their enrollment capacity.*

This current group is pretty special, however. They're already making plans for reunions once they get back to school. There's talk of getting commemorative tattoos as well, an activity in which I'm enthusiastically invited to join. I suppose that if I'm destined to spend time on this beach with humans, it may as well be with these humans. *Whit's fur ye will no gang by ye.*

After dishes I insist that all lights, headlamps as well as the lantern, be turned off. We gather at the water's edge to watch the sea sparkle.

# 7

## Red Sky at Morning

Today is the best day of my life.

A student journal

One of the problems with El Embudo is that the sun rises opposite the cove, which means that someone wanting to sleep in until sunrise has to guess when the event occurs. I watch from the shadows as the blue-gray dawn begins to tinge with oranges and reds. I arise as soon as the water reflects daybreak's palette.

The students are determined to sleep away half the morning, no doubt, but my bets are on the Baja sun, which will crest the cliff walls funneling behind us soon enough. It's a cool morning, but the cool will dematerialize the moment *El Sol* strikes this beach.

I sit here, enthroned in sand on the steep edge of the high-tide line, a little more than an hour after having proclaimed sunrise to be a fait accompli, watching a solitary Brandt's cormorant work a school of herring just beyond the intertidal zone. Every time the all-black bird dives, an explosion of silver erupts as herring attempt to escape the hook at the end of the long, straight beak.

Baja: birds underwater, fish airborne.

It's lay day, and it's glorious. Although we technically had a lay day two days ago, that one was El Norte's idea. This one is ours.

I am stiff, but I am writing.

I kayak year-round in order to be able to keep up with these kids for ten days every March. My weekend paddles have evolved to take the place of church. Unless it's windy I religiously use a larger paddle than the one I bring on these expeditions, hoping that the increased resistance builds more muscle tone. During the winter quarter, when it's especially important not to skip a weekend, I might even go out in the rain. One of the fundamental tenets of my sect is that a hooded, fluorescent-yellow spray anorak with latex cuffs will protect me from all evil.

This morning, unfortunately, my torso feels as if the paddling muscles were used yesterday for the very first time. The trapezii feel especially tight, and they shouldn't be. Were I someone who believed in psychology, I'd be blaming this stiffness on the stress I'm feeling about whether this will become our first group not to complete a circumnavigation. Something about this sunrise wasn't quite right. Red sky at morning . . .

By the time the sleeping-in students begin to crawl out of their tents, I have placated my muse sufficiently to have made up for the sin of ignoring her yesterday.

Two sets of tentmates, all female, head immediately into the water for a dip before breakfast. After dropping their towels down beside me they invite me to join them, but I indicate that I'm writing. I remind the one in front to do the stingray shuffle. She shuffles to the point where the water comes just below her navel, and then dips her shoulders in, keeping her hair dry. She then asks what I'm writing about.

I read the text back to her, *"She shuffles to the point where the water comes just below her navel, and then dips her shoulders in, keeping her hair dry."* She thinks I'm teasing, certain that a college professor would have more important things to write about.

There's a bit of splashing, and it causes a general stirring in those tents that are already sun-stricken. The expedition doesn't want to miss anything, least of all today. And it must already be getting warm inside those tents.

Walker Percy, in his essay "The Loss of the Creature," writes about how a "symbolic complex" can keep us from making our own discoveries when we encounter a new place. Instead of benefiting from our own observations, the modern-day sightseer tends only to see through the eyes of those who have previously encountered the landscape. We never really observe the Grand Canyon, according to Percy. We just see the cultural landscape that's been packaged for us.

I fear that the same thing has begun to happen to our lay day on this beach. If the members of last year's expedition have told the members of this expedition anything about what they'll experience here on the island, it's about today's adventure. Today is the day we snorkel with the sea lions, *el lobos del mar*,[1] and according to the forecast it will be totally cool.

The largest of the bulls we'll swim with today will weigh around 380 kilos. That's slightly less than all five of my male students combined. Fortunately, we'll be spending a lot more time with the pups than the bulls. This is standard procedure.

North of the border, the sea lion population has been growing by about 5 percent per year since the 1970s. Down here, it's been declining. The animals here are no less protected than they are in the United States, but the problem in these waters is that their food sources will no longer support the population densities we saw in the 1970s. The master narrative for these animals has been overfishing, and the tragic twist is that the local fishermen blame the declining fish stocks on the sea lions.

Fishermen do this back in my country as well.

The scholars currently in the water have goose bumps. When the first one takes a step back toward dry land, the rest follow immediately. A male in a tank top comes along while they are toweling off, and asks what I'm writing about.

"I'm writing about the cormorant over there preying on the herring."

I notice, suddenly, that the cormorant is no longer with us. Probably took off the moment the four *Homo sapiens* first waded into the water, at precisely the point I was no longer writing about it.

"Well, you ought to be writing about the sea lions."

There it is, the symbolic complex. Mr. Tank Top could probably sit down right now and narrate the dive he'll be taking in a few hours.

"My rule is: observe first, then describe."

Perhaps this is my symbolic complex: I somewhat blindly trust that these islands will teach us something worthwhile if we will first learn how to see.

The original four bathers are writing now, perhaps because the only other alternative was to begin preparing breakfast. I resist the urge to ask what they're writing about. Another group makes its way to the water's edge. For a moment it appears that they may join the writers, but they opt for a swim instead.

The entire camp is wearing tank tops today, as if someone circulated a memorandum at sunrise. I observe that neither the faculty nor the guides seem to have received the memo.

I look over to see how many are still in their tents, and observe a student beginning to strike his. I yell over that he's allowed to keep his tent up on a lay day. He crawls back inside, and his movements seem stiff from a distance. It makes me feel better to realize I'm not the only one.

---

1. Literally, "wolves of the sea." While this metaphor is no less incorrect than calling these animals "sea lions," in actuality their faces appear more canine than feline in structure.

The TA comes along, finally, and asks whether she should get breakfast going or have a crew erect the shade tarps first. I answer, quietly, professorially, that I want her to make this sort of decision without having to consult me first. She decides, correctly, to begin with the shade. Had she decided otherwise, that would have been fine as well. Either way, we'll be eating breakfast in the shade, and I harbor the unspoken wish that this will happen soon.

I stow my writing toys, now that writing has become fashionable on this beach, and grab my diving toys.

"We're not snorkeling before breakfast, are we?"

"Just a quick survey of the sea cucumber population."

I take my time slithering into my wetsuit, wanting the morning sun to warm me as much as possible before I dip in. By the time I submerge, there are no students left in the water. The herring seem to have abandoned the cove as well.

I hug the rocky wall to the north of the cove, which is where the water has been in the sun the longest. The water feels cool, despite my wetsuit. Even though it's officially spring, the Sea of Cortez retains a touch of its winter chill.

The first large head of cauliflower coral I come across, *Pocillopora elegans*, is partially bleached, the microscopic algae called "zooxanthellae" having been expelled as the result of stress. We see this more during El Niño years, but a fair number of the corals survive. I make note of the position of this coral, hoping to visit it a year hence and check its health. Other corals in the area still have their color, but they appear dirty, as if there's too much algae in the neighborhood. Or too few of whatever fish are in charge of scrubbing these corals.

There are few gorgonians around, the bluish, fuzzy-looking sea fans that were numerous when I first dove in this cove more than a decade ago. I pause to inspect one, and find myself wondering whether I've acquainted myself with this same gorgonian in the past. It seems to be an old friend—more properly a colony of old friends—but I realize that I tend to err on the side of sentimentality when making such assessments.

No chance of doing that with a sea cucumber. Especially not here. It is as the guides had predicted when discovering the fire pit the poachers left behind: there isn't a sea cucumber to be found.

I recall the words of a former classmate, Andromeda Romano-Lax, in her book *Searching for Steinbeck's Sea of Cortez: A Makeshift Expedition along Baja's Desert Coast*. "A holothurian, as members of this class of animals are called, will not sidle on up for a back-scratching, or look you in the eye. It has no eyes. Basically a cucumber is a faceless rubbery or leathery gut—a mud-eating tube" (144).

But there are no holothurians here today.

I wish I was a skilled enough ecologist to understand how the absence of sea cucumbers is affecting this cove's ecosystem. Outside of the Asian seafood market, I honestly don't know what predators eat sea cucumbers. After this dive, when I consult our guidebook, *Sea of Cortez Marine Animals*, written by an old friend, Dan Gotshall, I still won't know. It will not be until I get back to the university and Google on "sea cucumber predators" that I'll discover that they are eaten by crustaceans, sea turtles, and many fish, as well as humans.

Steinbeck and Rickets wrote about the sea cucumber in the very first paragraph of *The Log from the Sea of Cortez*. They asked, somewhat philosophically, "Why do men, sitting at the microscope, examine the calcareous plates of a sea-cucumber, and, finding a new arrangement and number, feel an exaltation and give the new species a name, and write about it possessively?" (1).

On March 20, 1941, when Steinbeck and Rickets visited Isla Espíritu Santo, they stopped at a beach a few kilometers south of here and wrote:

> The dominant species on this beach was a sulphury cucumber (*Holothuria lubrica*), a dark, almost black-green holothurian which looks as though it were dusted with sulphur. As the tide dropped on the shallow beach we saw literally millions of those cucumbers. They lay in clusters and piles between the rocks and under the rocks, and as the tide went down and the tropical sun beat on the beach, many of them became quite dry without apparent injury. Most of these holothurians were from five to eight inches long, but there were great numbers of babies, some not more than an inch in length. We took a great many of them. (77)

"Literally millions." Was "literally" used here to denote "without exaggeration"? Could there literally have been millions of sea cucumbers in any given cove of this archipelago within the last century?

I am nearly late for breakfast when I return, which would have been unforgivable given the fact that we're about to devour two jumbo frying pans of *chilaquiles*. This traditional Mexican breakfast never fails to transform me, not even when I'm weighed down by environmental doom. Our recipe on the island begins with quartered corn tortillas, *sausa de molé*, egg, and some pulled chicken. Add some *crema Mexicana* and *queso fresco*, and you'll never again want to face French toast in the morning so long as you live.

The panga, *Pato Loco*, shows up early, which is not a good sign. This portends afternoon winds strong enough to convince our *pangero*, Manuelote,[2] to make an early run.

---

2. "Manuelote" translates "Big Manuel," thus distinguishing him from our guide Manuelito, or "Little Manuel."

A giant of a man, not only is Manuelote the best *pangero* in the entire Sea of Cortez, he is *buena gente*, good people. I call out to him in my most enthusiastic Spanish, *"¡Capitán, es bueno verte!"*

*"¡Igualmente! Es* good to see you too, Juanito!"

Manuelote, working alone, spins the boat around and drops an anchor off the bow before backing the panga toward the beach. He cuts the engines just as the anchor line goes tight, ending up in knee-deep water at the transom. If he's done this once, he's done it a thousand times, and he probably hasn't misjudged his landing in decades. When I offer my hand to take the beach anchor, he shakes it first.

The panga contains a half dozen blue, nineteen-liter bottles of *aqua purificada,* the large type of bottles designed for office water coolers. Although we carried enough for the week from the outset, one never passes up a chance to resupply water here in Baja, and it's good to have the extra safety margin should unexpected situations arise, such as if El Norte decides to pin us to a beach indefinitely. When we fill up the empty bladders during these resupplies, I'm always a bit shocked at how much water a score of kayakers can drink over the course of a few days.

While the students deal with the water under the direction of the capable TA, the guides consult with the *pangero*. They speak in low, fast Spanish that I'm unable to access, but I clearly hear El Norte being discussed. Manuelote has brought us the weather forecast, and it is not at all promising. My heart sinks, having naively hoped that we'd beaten El Norte the previous day and that the winds would therefore be favorable from here on out.

Once the bad news has been appropriately digested, Manuelito turns to me and asks how much of the conversation I understood. I reply that I didn't get the part about exactly when it's supposed to blow.

*"Mañana."*

Manuelito has a plan of course, having dealt with such contingencies dozens of times before. He proposes that tomorrow, if we're able, we'll backtrack along the lee side of Isla Partita, going into Caleta Partida to camp for the night. That way, although we won't be able to circumnavigate the entire archipelago, we'll still be able to make it around the windward side of Espíritu Santo if conditions are better forty-eight hours from now.

I attempt to conceal my disappointment, but these guides are too good at reading my face. Garambullo, always the optimist, counsels, "Let's have a happy dive first, and wait to tell the students until happy hour."

I turn to the beach and yell, "Gear up, duckies! Life jackets! Towels! Sunscreen! Water bottles! Windbreakers! Dive gear!"

"Journals?"

"No journals," I reply. "If you make it back alive, you can write about it on the beach."

Just having fun, of course. If you don't mess with the students once in a while, what's the point of teaching?

We sit shoulder to shoulder on the enormous panga, probably squeezing a few more bodies aboard than we ought to. It will be a short ride, literally just around the corner, and I'm surprised when we clear the point, catching a glimpse of Los Islotes, that some of our group didn't notice the islets in the twilight last night when we finished our paddle. They are as surprised by their observational lapse as I am: "Really, we could see Los Islotes last night? Are you sure?"

Trying to sound neither pedantic nor sarcastic, I point out that one tends to see what one is looking for, and last night the group was looking for a beach on which to land, not the gleaming white islets that were practically glowing in the gloaming.

Were it not for the amount of guano decorating the rugged crags of Los Islotes, the islets would appear to have been designed by Disney Studios. Rising straight up from the water, the promontories are higher than the islands are wide. Devoid of vegetation, the flat top is thickly forested by birds: frigates, boobies, gulls, and terns. It's not a place you'd want to be if you didn't have wings.

A strong swell is running, and it takes me by surprise even though I know that lousy weather is forthcoming. How could the swells from this storm get here before the wind does? Manuelote forgoes his usual spin around the island, opting instead to pick up a mooring on the lee side where we will be protected from the swell. It goes without saying that he doesn't want seasick passengers. The question now is whether we'll be able to enter the sea cave that punches through the island on a north-south axis. While Garambullo begins his predive briefing I quickly don my mask and fins to go check the conditions.

The water feels colder, and I blame this on my earlier dive back in the cove. Even though the water felt chilly this morning, my shorty wetsuit seemed up to the task, but now it disappoints me thoroughly. Figuring that I'll warm up once I start swimming, I kick over toward the sea cave, escorted by a mature sea lion cow who seems mildly bored with my presence, perhaps because she outweighs me.

I hyperventilate twice at the cave's entrance and then dive down three or four meters to see how strong the surge is along the bottom. It's not bad—at least the students will have the chance to swim through the cave should they want to. Back on the surface I signal to Manuelito, who has been watching me intently, that the cave is OK for diving. I do not signal that the water feels unusually cold; he's always been more sensitive to water temperature than I have.

While I wait for the students to enter the water I recall other times I've swum Los Islotes. Once, when accompanied by a group of grad students, before we could pick up a mooring an enormous school of mobula rays swam by, circling clockwise around the windward point. The guides and I grabbed our masks and, without bothering to don our fins, dove immediately overboard and swam toward the rays, being fortunate enough to watch a few so-called devilfish launch themselves from under water before the entire shoal vanished. On a different occasion, this time with undergrads, we dove Los Islotes right at sunset. None of the adult animals were in the water at that point, only the pups, and they were more playful and affectionate than I've ever seen them during the day.

Awash in memories, I swim slowly back to the boat, still chilly, arriving just as Garambullo finishes his briefing. The students are gearing up now, but it will still be several minutes before a critical mass is in the water. Students tend to futz at this point, regardless of which expedition they belong to. I assume a resting position facedown in the water, hoping to relax my bladder enough to heat up my wetsuit the easy way. Unfortunately, I am unable to achieve significant warmth.

Finally ready, we snorkel over for our first encounters. The sea lions seem every bit as tentative as the students at first, as if they're picking up on human nervousness. A bull swims by, the sagittal crest on its forehead prominent. Rolling ninety degrees as he passes, he shows off the enormity of his girth, but he's not at all aggressive. At best, his attitude is dismissive.

I gather the students around and explain that the sea lions will come and play once they're ready. I suggest we swim over to the cave, ignoring *Zalophus californianus* for the moment. Sea lions, especially the young, can't stand to be ignored.

What I don't tell them is that I'm still unusually chilled, and I covet the warmth that swimming should provide.

While we're swimming over toward the cave, one of the students swims up from behind and asks whether I realize that my wetsuit is unzipped in the back. Completely unzipped. In my haste to check out the conditions I'd ignored an important detail in my predive ritual. The student zips me up and the transformation is nearly instant.

We swim through an enormous school of yellow-striped sergeant majors, so thick below us that they make it difficult to see the more interesting Cortez angelfish beneath them, the black juveniles with their alternating gold and electric-blue stripes looking demonic in comparison to the more stately, angelic adults. An elderly female sea lion, her muzzle nearly white, swims through the sergeant majors and they ignore her completely, as if her teeth pose no danger to their well-being.

At the mouth of the cave, I yell out that although it's going to be choppy at the surface the surge isn't bad down below. Almost showing off, I execute a classic jackknife dive and swim toward the windward side at a depth of two meters, making it most of the way on a single breath. The stronger swimmers among the group mimic my technique, while the others bob along behind cheerfully. A student surfaces next to me and wants to know whether the gorgonians are soft corals. I explain, as succinctly as possible while treading water, that they're in the same class but a different order. Mercifully, the student doesn't ask the name of either order. Some conversations are better held back on the beach, and this is one of the questions that Dr. Awesome is far better equipped to field.

It's a bit rough on the windward side of the island, but it's absolutely gorgeous. The water is as clear as I've ever seen it, and thanks to the surface chop the rays of sunshine dance their way up and down the rocks below. These are tough conditions for beginners, however, and I reluctantly decide that we should spend no more than a couple minutes on this side of the island.

The sea lions have other ideas.

They come in three wavelets: first, two pups; then, four more pups; then, the final two. They are all the same size, no more than a meter long, and I'm guessing them to be two years old. Perhaps I should be calling them "subadults" rather than pups, although they are clearly prepubescent. They are possibly at the point of maximum playfulness as far as their life cycles are concerned.

The pups quite actively—and, it would seem, intentionally—lead the students away from the cavern to an area between two boulders where the surge is less pronounced. The students follow compliantly, all of them realizing as if by instinct that we are dealing with pups. I'd told them, weeks ago back in the classroom, how pups play when the games include humans, and the entire class seems to recall this snippet of lecture, even those who have forgotten the meaning of "sagittal crest."

A few of the pups play the zoom game, swimming at full speed toward a diver's face mask, not diverting until the last second after the diver has already winced. The more aggressive pups will sometimes bark at the point closest to collision, a ring of bubbles emerging from their mouths as they zoom by, but none of these do so, which is a good sign. They don't want to intimidate.

One pup, clearly the most affectionate of the octet that had joined us, hovers upside down in the water, floating motionless is if to invite the students to try suspended underwater headstands themselves. A few do. Another pup seems fascinated with the mane of long, curly hair that emanates like an underwater explosion from one of our students. The pup nips at her hair a few times until Dr. Awesome intervenes, pushing the pup away. Another pup, finally, takes active interest in my fluorescent-yellow split fins, a technology it has apparently never examined closely. It grabs my left fin in its teeth and pulls, but does so gently enough to not damage the fin. I appreciate this; ever since retiring as a scuba instructor I've had to purchase my own fins.

It's difficult to tell one pup from another based on individual looks. All have the same canine muzzle and the same huge eyes, and the only thing that keeps them from looking wolfish are their tiny external ear flaps, properly called "pinnae." Individual pups, however, behave differently from each other, and it would not be a stretch to claim that they have distinct personalities. I think of one as "Hair Nipper," another as the upside-down pup, and yet another as "Sprinter" for how it accelerates with only a few kicks of its flippers. One is distinctly shier than the rest, preferring to sneak up behind rather than approach divers frontally, and there are two who stick together constantly, special friends among the cohort. It would be wonderful to know how these animals characterize the humans with whom they are playing.

Sea lion pups are so lithe that they seem not to have backbones. They can twist while they bend, corkscrew while they flip. The students attempt to mimic their gyrations, but look clumsy and inelegant by comparison. Upside-down pup is able to arch its back so that its snout actually touches its hind flippers, as if involving itself in a pinniped version of yoga. Shy pup can execute a 180-degree turn within its own body length. Sprinter banks and turns more like a swallow or a swift than a marine mammal. The entire group, taken as a troop, seems to understand the depth of our delight at watching their performance.

Garambullo joins us after a few minutes, and asks whether I want Manuelote to bring the boat around to retrieve us. I agree that this would be a good plan, explaining that I've completely lost control of the situation. He smiles through his mask and exclaims, "I can see that!"

We end up playing with the pups for a good half hour after the panga arrives. Dr. Awesome and I keep an eye out for shivering, sending students back to the boat once they seem uncomfortably cold. A handful of students were so enraptured by the sea lions that they'd become oblivious to their own comfort, and at one point I thought I might have to drag the final two expeditioners away. The pups, of course, follow us all the way back to the boarding ladder, not abandoning us until we finally abandon them.

I seldom get the students' best writing when they describe their adventures at Los Islotes. Writing suffers as much from too much energy as from too little, and overstatement is always deadly, even when it's justifiable. Too much marvel, and the writing becomes strangely commonplace. Students will often complain, in their journals, that they can't write well enough to capture how wonderful the experience was. Bits of brilliance poke through, however, like when one writer observed that it was the first time he'd ever looked a wild animal in the eye close enough to see it blink.

There is something that needs to be said for the experience of being a guest in the habitat of wild creatures who could easily do you harm, especially when those creatures are within arm's length. The students, when chronicling these encounters, will often write about their awareness of being out of their element, understanding in fresh ways how water functions so much better as the sea lion's element. Students universally acknowledge how the sea lions are so graceful in a medium in which we are so awkward. I imagine that sea lions feel much the same way when they watch humans cavort with Frisbees on a beach.

In the afternoon we head upcanyon to a large dry lake bordered with cliffs. We have to do a bit of scrambling to get down to the lake bed, and as soon as their feet hit the flat ground they break into a run   it's the first chance anyone's had to run in a great many days. They run, instinctively, to the east, to a point where they can peer down over the cliffs to the side of the island we're supposed to paddle tomorrow. It ties a knot in my heart that we haven't yet told them that it will be too rough tomorrow to voyage around the northern end of the island as planned. Indeed, the waves below are already white capped. Tomorrow, this stretch will be a cauldron.

Happy hour comes all too soon. The moment at hand is one I've feared for years, telling a group that they will be the first expedition in the school's history to be unable to circumnavigate the archipelago.

We huddle together under the shade tarp closest to the spaghetti pot where the margaritas have been concocted, and Manuelito tells the group about the weather forecast. Having heard the bad news, one of the students raises his cup and says, "I don't care what we do tomorrow, I'm having a great time."

The entire expedition raises cups in agreement. We clink each other's plastic tankards in a muffled group toast, and then make plans for an early departure. The tough part will be the first two kilometers, backtracking to the point where we'll be able to turn south and let the wind do the work. The biggest challenge will be for the single kayaks; we'll put the better paddlers in these, and ask those in the more stable doubles to hold back so that they can rescue any singles that capsize. Manuelito warns that once we turn south, retreating back to this beach will not be an option. El Norte will see to that.

"The hardest thing tomorrow," Manuelito predicts, "will be to stay together. You will not be able to hear me in the wind, you must always watch for my signals until we all get around the second point into Ensenada Grande."

"Stay together," I echo. "This will be our mantra."

We are a well-oiled machine the following morning, breaking camp as if we've done this hundreds of times. The northerly breeze is up, but it's not yet ferocious. I climb the cliff some fifteen meters on the north side of our encampment, high enough to where I can see the first point we'll have to round. It appears navigable from this vantage. Manuelito joins me, and I pass him my binoculars. He agrees, almost whispering, "This group can make it."

Yes. It's less about the wind, at this moment, and more about the group. This group will make it.

We stretch, we pee, we launch. Rudders are lowered, chin straps are tightened, sunglasses are tethered. My boat feels more teetery than usual, but I realize that this is just El Norte psyching me out. I pull the foot pedals tighter, sacrificing a bit of comfort for control. This is my way of telling El Norte to go screw himself.

We paddle.

There's not much more to tell. One of the students in one of the singles got seasick, but she paddled gamely on until we could duck into the lee of a point where it was safe to switch her to a double. No one capsized. The more the wind blew, the tighter the group got. By the time we landed at Caleta Partida, the sand spit on the southern tip of Isla Partida, the expedition had become epic.

All was not yet lost. We had another chance to get to the windward side of the archipelago the following day by cutting through the narrow gap between Isla Partida and Isla Espíritu Santo. If we couldn't circumnavigate the entire archipelago, perhaps we could at least circumnavigate its largest island.

After another early start, we gave it stouthearted effort, encouraged by our success the day before, but on the windward side the swells were so high that sometimes you couldn't see the kayak over in the next trough. Little more than a kilometer into our voyage a roguish wave picked up one of the doubles and slammed it sideways into *Opsrey*. I was able to perform a high-brace maneuver that kept me from capsizing, but just barely. This was a brace that beginning kayakers would not be able to perform reliably in such conditions. I spun around to signal Manuelito, back in the sweep boat, that we should turn back, but he was already signaling the group to turn around.

There would be no circumnavigations for this expedition.

Later on I asked Manuelito why he waited so long to signal a retreat, and he replied that he was wondering the same thing about why I had not made the signal earlier. Clearly, we were both reluctant to disappoint this plucky group.

Here's the crazy thing: this was not only the first of our groups to fail its nominal task—they were also the tightest community of any class I've ever taught. The night we returned to campus they didn't want to break up quite yet, so they decided to go out en masse for Mexican food. They were a little disappointed that I didn't want to join them, but understood how I might want to visit my wife for the first time in weeks.

The following evening, just as Carol and I were finishing up dinner in our on-campus apartment, we heard the voices of the expeditioners serenading us from down below. "*¡Juanito, Juanito, vamanos!*"

The group had been home almost twenty-four hours and had still not split up! I joined them, of course, but only for a couple cervezas. It was a school night, the eve of the spring quarter, and some of them needed to do laundry in the most desperate way.

The following weekend, several of them got their tattoos, perfect outlines of the archipelago they'd failed to circumnavigate.

The story is still being told that it was the greatest expedition of all time.

# Second Interlude

## June in the Sierra San Pedro Mártir

Curiosity plays an important role in the life of scavengers.
Condors must continually investigate the activity of other species
if they are to be consistently successful at foraging.

MICHAEL WALLACE et al., 2007

There is no ivy on the walls of the Beckman Center for Conservation Research, and the building still retains its pristine sparkle despite the decade that has passed since the first scientists moved in. Constructed of textured brick ramparts topped by plate-glass parapets, it was a bit more stout than I'd expected it to be, even considering that it constitutes one of the three campuses of the San Diego Zoo.

There are signs on the front gate requesting that no animals be allowed through. I'm hoping, after my long drive south, that humans are excepted from this policy. In short order, a primate belonging to the class Mammalia, the phylum Chordata, and the kingdom Animalia, announces himself over the intercom, and the gate slides open as if by wizardry.

Dr. Michael Wallace, coordinator of the California Condor Recovery Program, waits for me on the landing of the central stairs as I push through the heavy front doors. The first thing I notice about him is the Leatherman multi-tool hanging from his belt.

After nearly a year corresponding with Dr. Wallace, I was slightly intimidated meeting him. When I had asked him, last Christmas, to recommend some reading to help me prepare to visit the California Condor Field Research

Station in the northern mountains of Baja, he sent me his curriculum vitae. This was not vanity, I would learn; reading through the man's scientific papers was simply the best way for me to get up to speed on the issues surrounding condor restoration.

A soft-spoken man whose full head of hair belies the fact that he's three years my senior, Mike has devoted an entire career to vultures. It becomes immediately apparent that this man is more at home rappelling into a nest cavity on the side of a cliff than entertaining a visiting scholar in his office. We chat cordially while we begin to navigate the necessary paperwork, but I can tell that he's distracted, concerned. He receives periodic satellite texts from the field station staff, and greets a few of these messages with a frown.

I had expected that on my arrival we'd shake hands, sign the waiver form, load my gear into a zoo vehicle, and head south for the border. Such was not to be the case. Among other things, Mike had just learned that a formal "letter of engagement" had to be written to the Mexican national park director requesting permission to enter restricted areas for my research—there seemed to be concern as to why a nonscientist such as myself would require the type of access I had requested.

There is a great deal of caution whenever endangered species are concerned, and with the Baja condors these concerns are magnified because two sovereign governments sharing a sometimes-troubled border are collaborating to protect them. I would end up spending the night north of that border on Mike Wallace's couch, sharing the living room with two snoring dogs, grateful not only for the hospitality but also that he would personally be driving me to the field station the following day, assuming everything worked out with the authorities. This was no small favor—the drive takes six hours each direction, a bit more if we stop at one of Ensenada's ubiquitous fish taco stands. I will soon discover that, regardless of the fact that we've both come to specialize in *tacos de camarones*, Mike's taco-stand research is more extensive than my own.

But I'm getting ahead of my story.

Not everything was working out on the other end. A condor was missing, and not just any condor. Over the course of the next hour I was briefed that condor no. 217, who had been nesting, was no longer showing up on telemetry. Back at the field station the biologists, who were scheduled to depart two days from now to present papers about their current research, were making a concerted effort to find the missing bird, and the results were not promising.

Before we left his office, Mike handed me a studbook in which the lineage of every California condor in existence was listed. I discover that 217 was sired by Topa Topa, condor no. 1, a bird captured back in 1967 that had become the keystone of the breeding program. As I flip through the studbook I recall reading somewhere that it had taken Mike five years to convince Topa Topa to breed. On the maternal side, 217 had equally impressive bloodlines, her grandsire being AC2 (studbook no. 6) and her granddam being AC3 (studbook no. 10). These were three of the last birds alive back in the dark days when only twenty-two condors still had a pulse.

I have difficulty keeping up with Mike as our vehicles climb the curvy road leading to his orchard in the hills above Escondido, my older, compact, environmentally correct pickup not having the gumption of his shiny-new zoo pickup, with its huge off-road tires. During the drive I resolve not to pester him with condor questions all evening, not realizing that he plans to use me, along with his brother and a few hired hands, to move a pool table from a neighbor's farm to a patio near his barn. After that, I will earn whatever questions I might want to ask while shucking the corn for dinner.

We spend most of the evening talking about falconry. I had noticed a few pencil sketches of hawks—a northern goshawk and a Harris's hawk—in the living room, and Mike explained that these were some of the birds that he'd trained. While we cooked dinner I learned that Mike was a master falconer, one who began training hawks at an age when most of us were still playing with slingshots.

Dawn comes all too soon. My host harvests a grocery bag full of avocados from his orchard, careful to select representatives of all the varieties he grows. I add tortilla chips to my mental list; we're planning to shop for groceries on the far side of the border. I will be cooking for myself most evenings, which adds considerably to the adventure I'm about to have.

When we finally head south, I discover that if you really want to get Dr. Michael Wallace talking, you don't ask about condors in the abstract. Rather, ask him about a specific bird. Both hands on the wheel as we navigated the pass down from Tecate, Mike spoke about no. 217 as if she'd hatched yesterday rather than on April 3, 2000. The first thing he told me is that she'd been the most subordinate bird of her cohort. "She was meek and mild, and then, by accident, became the first breeding female in Baja."

It turns out that no. 217 was one of the first three condors transferred to Baja. This happened when she was two years old. She was to be part of an experiment Mike had conjured up. In all the other release sites, condors raised by hand puppets,[1] which were used so that the chicks wouldn't imprint on humans, were released alongside condors that had been raised either by their parents or

---

1. In the captive breeding program, the first egg laid is taken away from the parents in the hope that a replacement egg will be laid a month later, a process called "double clutching." Chicks hatched from these original eggs are fed from behind a curtain using realistic condor hand puppets, a system conceived and designed by Mike Wallace.

by surrogate parents. Most experts speculated that parent-raised birds would adapt better to the wild than puppet-raised birds, but Mike had his doubts. So when it finally came time to initiate the Baja project, Mike proposed that the first eleven birds released south of the border all be puppet-raised birds to field-test the theory. And when Dr. Michael Wallace suggests something in the world of condors, it usually gets done.

Mike had personally selected the site for the field station up in an old-growth forest of Jeffrey pines, lodgepoles, sugar pines, and white firs situated high along the ridge of the Sierra San Pedro Mártir. The aviaries are seventy-five kilometers east of the Pacific Ocean, a place where offshore winds and radical topography combine to provide enough lift for inexperienced, newly released condors to fly.

I was originally hoping to participate in a release, but now that wasn't going to happen. In Baja, it's the birds who dictate the schedule, not the fellow with the keys to the aviary.

The initial release of three females, nos. 217, 218, and 220, was not entirely successful, and had to be aborted after two weeks because the condors were being hassled by golden eagles. This had previously happened in Arizona during the earliest releases there; three condors were killed in the Grand Canyon before the eagles remembered that condors are a benign presence. The Baja condors were recaptured without incident, it being a simple matter to put out a carcass in a pen with the door open, and then shut the door while the condors glut. The vultures spent the winter in a large pen, to be rereleased the following summer.

The second release was more successful, but had its tense moments. A fire broke out that year on the Fourth of July, and although new birds that were still awaiting release had to be evacuated, the three already-released birds would use the huge plumes of smoke as thermals, circling within them to gain altitude. At that point, a tentative claim that they were wild condors could be made.

To date, no. 217 has had to be recaptured twice for health reasons. In 2007 she suffered symptoms of lead toxicity, and after recapture she needed to undergo chelation therapy, which consists of intramuscular injections of calcium edetate, administered pectorally, twice a day for five days. The therapy was successful, and she was released back into the wild. A year later she was again symptomatic, but a blood test determined that her exposure level was a relatively low twenty-five milligrams per deciliter, so she was again released.

Of the three pioneer birds, no. 218 was initially dominant, and therefore most likely to mate. Unfortunately, she was attacked by a golden eagle, who grasped her leg in its talons, puncturing it repeatedly. Eagles and other raptors often lock talons with each other midair, spiraling around each other as they fall toward the ground. Vultures, however, do not have talons; their feet are never used for killing but are adapted, rather, for ground locomotion, at which they are surprisingly adept. Several times I've watch condors run in the vicinity of a carcass, seemingly on their tiptoes, and they are remarkably swift. Unable to do this with any grace after her injury, no. 218 lost social status, and 220 became the dominant female.

That didn't last long either. The Sierra San Pedro Mártir has a healthy puma population, "puma" being the preferred term locally for animals commonly called "mountain lions" or "cougars" in other regions. As Mike explains it, a puma had taken up residence for some days under a manzanita bush near a burro carcass that had been left out for the condors. Although no one saw it happen, at one point during the puma's encampment condor 220 was found to be missing all her tail feathers except one. Although she could still fly with only a single tail feather, she lost social status during the eight months it took to grow back new feathers. Mike explains that condors are keenly aware of how each other look and behave; a bird that looks goofy and flies poorly isn't going to retain dominance for long. The dominant male, no. 261, lost romantic interest in her, and that was a good thing for 217.

Condor 217 nested twice, both times in eagle nests, which was a mistake. Condors tend to select nests in small, protected caverns that are almost impossible for egg thieves to access. But they don't build nests other than to scratch out a clean patch of sand. Eagles build nests of stick, and although they will reuse a nest, they tend not to do so in consecutive years because if they do, parasites will build up. This is precisely what happened with 217. Mike visited the nest a couple times to determine the health of the chick, and it was not quite as large as it should have been on the first visit. When Mike returned to the nest two weeks later, he was bitten more than two hundred times by poultry bedbugs, and the chick had vanished.

No one knows what happened the second time 217 nested. The second nest was more remote than the first. From the GPS and telemetry data Mike could infer that a chick was hatched, but it was never seen.

The problem, this third time, is that they can't even find the nest.

In 1981, when controversies raged as to whether a captive breeding program was an appropriate way to preserve condors, "archdruid" environmentalist David Brower published an essay, "The Condor and a Sense of Place," in which he wrote, "Condors are soaring manifestations of the place that built them and coded their genes." I recall these words as Mike's pickup climbs into the Sierra San Pedro Mártir. The higher we get, the more perfect this sierra seems to be for gigantic birds that require dramatic vertical topography. Even the trees seem to have conspired to welcome condors; not only are there plenty of ancient snags still standing, but many of the most senior trees are topped with naked branches that should provide ideal roosts for birds with three-meter wingspans.

Brower also described the wildness condors require, writing that an appropriate home for this species "requires space to nest in, to teach fledglings, to roost in unmolested, to bathe and drink in, to find other condors in and not too many biologists, and to fly over wild and free." In other words, it will have to be remote. When we reach the locked gate to the restricted area, I note to Mike that from the time we turned off the coastal highway until we reached our destination two hours later, we did not pass another vehicle in either direction. He replied that this was often the case, even on weekends.

We arrive at the field station shortly after the team returned from a long day of searching for 217. The mood is heavy, as befits a lack of radio telemetry from a historic bird. When Mike and I walk into the field station, a single word, "*Nada*," is spoken by a scientist in a terry-cloth bathrobe, her hair wet and her bare feet leaving a moist trail of prints across the concrete floor.

Nothing.

There is a quick conversation about whether a search plane should be called in to try and locate the nest. Although this would be an expensive option, it will cost only a fraction of what's already been invested in 217 over the past fourteen years.

I stand in the background, barely inside the station, taking it all in. A few days ago I was still in the classroom, frantically bringing the spring quarter to its conclusion. Opting to assign a ten-page paper rather than give a final exam, I graded everything in two days, heading south to San Diego on the third. There has been no time to decompress, other than for two long days of driving. Still, the ambience of the field station makes the aggravation of getting here seem worthwhile. We are in the thick of a mixed conifer forest, and the entire station is awash in the aroma of pine-scented vanilla. And shampoo.

The scientist in the bathrobe interrupts herself, noticing me and apologizing immediately for not having welcomed me properly. She extends a warm hand, and when I respond, "*Mucho gusto*," that I am pleased to make her acquaintance, I mean it sincerely—this woman has lived on site for twelve years, summer and winter, and she is as much a part of the station's ambience as the conifers that surround it. I would like to inquire how she accomplished her recent shower, since the station still doesn't have running water, but the time doesn't seem right for such questions.

She apologizes again, this time that all the scientific staff will have to leave tomorrow, and asks whether I can extend my stay so that we can get properly acquainted once everyone returns.

We exchange pleasantries for too short a time; the searchers skipped lunch today, and were not adequately hydrated either. Fortunately, Mike picked up dinner ready-made from town, two rotisserie chickens that have begun to fill the field station with a torturous aroma.

Dinner is a pleasant affair, conducted back and forth between two languages. I am asked whether I'm related to the Farnsworth who invented the world's first fully electronic television system, and when I report that he was my grandfather's cousin, they want to hear my entire family history. When I get to the part about my kid sister being a lead painter and art director for animated features at Disney Studios, a murmur of deep appreciation fills the room.

There is irony here—these people live in a field station that is completely off the grid, far from the nearest broadcast TV signal. The closest town is over a hundred kilometers away, accessible only by four-wheel-drive vehicles, and one would have to drive a couple hours beyond that to get to a city big enough to have a movie theater. I become aware, as I'm telling my family history, even though I'm using a language that not everyone here speaks, that this is the best entertainment the group has had for a while: someone whose story is not already known.

I have a special surprise for dessert, zucchini bread that my wife baked from scratch the day before I left. It's not as fresh as I'd hoped it would be, my arrival having been delayed a full day, but it's consumed with gusto and I'm made to promise to send the recipe along.

Mike falls asleep sitting upright on the couch before the dishes are washed. The weary searchers are equally bushed, and by 8:30 I'm the only one left at the table, the only one who has not yet gone to bed. I take advantage of my solitude to scribble a few pages of notes about condor 217, not realizing until I've completed this task that I have not yet seen any of the Baja condors.

The next morning, before heading back to San Diego, Mike takes me down to a newly constructed aviary, explaining that I'm the first outsider ever to view it being used. Indeed, few nonbiologists will ever lay eyes on this pen, and when birds are here in preparation to be released, the field station staff will only come here at night, a precaution against what Mike calls "mal-imprinting" a bird. The pen has been constructed high enough to include two full-grown trees inside, and it's obviously been built by zoo professionals: it's as sturdy as it is roomy, with its edges footed in concrete so that coyotes can't dig their way in. A blind has been built into the far side of the aviary from which postdocs can conduct behavioral research during the day, but the birds will never see the researchers, and the experiments will all be conducted with ropes and pulleys.

There are two condors in the pen now, juveniles, soon to be shipped to the Phoenix zoo to serve as "ambassadors" for the project. These birds had been scheduled for release into the wild, but were mishandled by Mexican veterinary students who posed for condor selfies, holding the birds on their laps, and then publishing the resulting snapshots on their Facebook pages. As a result, the birds are now considered tame. They have been separated from their cohort so that they will not act as a negative influence on birds that are less habituated to humans. Mike adds, curtly, that the experimental program to train local veterinary students was suspended indefinitely.

As I gaze at two birds that will never fly free, perched shoulder to shoulder high in a pine tree, David Brower's words, written decades ago, echo in my memory. *"A condor in a zoo, however elaborate the enclosure, is to be pitied."* While pitying these two juvenile condors, however, my mind flashes back to the hawk sketches in Mike's living room, and I connect the fact that a master falconer's knowledge of how to tame raptors translates directly into Mike's theories about how to keep condors wild. With birds this intelligent, they must either be wild or tame; anything in between increases mortality.

Mike takes me to an escarpment—which I will call "Estación Juanito" to protect condor privacy—where I'm welcome to set up my own observation station. We choose a tree I should sit under to make me less conspicuous, a massive boulder behind me to provide further concealment. He briefs me that if a condor lands nearby I'm to pick up a branch and make threatening gestures in hopes of reinforcing its "aversion training." If that doesn't work, I should go so far as to chuck a pine cone in the direction of any condor getting too close. "Don't treat them like they're endangered," he counsels. "We don't want them thinking that humans are friendly."

The field station's caretaker, Rogelio, who will be the only one remaining behind with me for the next eight days until Mike can return to pick me up, has been instructed to drop me off here whenever I feel the need to observe condors. I'm almost certain to see nos. 218 and 220 from the original cohort around my station. It goes without saying that I should train my binoculars on the patagial[2] tags in the event that 217 shows up, in which case I'm to contact Mike immediately. I'll also be keeping a close watch for 261, 217's mate. Seeing him repeatedly could be a bad sign.

---

2. Because condors defecate on their legs in order to thermoregulate, leg bands cannot be used. Rather, a wing tag is clipped to the patagium, the soft tissue on the leading edge of each wing that makes the wing aerodynamic.

By the time we return to the field station, the scientific staff are all gone. Mike follows them north shortly.

It's probably safe to say that every field station is a work in progress, constantly evolving to meet needs that are evolving even faster.

This station is all about the condors, and has been constructed with an urgency that reflects the plight of critical endangerment. Built two kilometers from the aviaries, it replaced the tents and trailers from which the staff originally conducted their mission, an encampment that must have been challenging once the snowfall began to accumulate each winter. As a result of this history, the field station is a bit of a fortress, a place of refuge for people whose work demands they spend long hours outdoors.

I have come in as someone outside of that history, and at first I am annoyed that this structure isolates me so from the fabulous landscape in which it sits. Several times I will have to remind myself that the station wasn't built for gringo college faculty who visit in June. For example, there's a lovely porch outside, one where I'd love to sit on tranquil evenings, but the deck is lined with a dozen five-gallon gasoline cans, two large freezers for carcass storage, a high-capacity pump used to fill the five-thousand-liter cistern at the end of the porch, and a small table saw. Regardless of my own desire to commune with nature, this is not a place to watch sunsets. It's all about business here, the business of saving nature, and the structural rhetoric suggests that natural historians who want to stop and sniff the wildflowers had best find someplace else to do it.

Despite whatever aesthetic critiques I might offer, I love field stations. These are places where natural history still has standing. Field stations tend to be remote, and they tend to be staffed by people who enjoy solving problems.

It seems that every field station I've ever visited has more scientific equipment than places to store it. Remote stations are universally cursed with a surplus of ice chests and empty propane cylinders. Lying about any field station one will discover uncataloged collections of feathers, skulls, and either antlers or seashells. Windowsills will inevitably house glistening minerals that I can't identify, and bits of folk art left behind by postdocs who walked off with books from the station's library. This station is too new to have a library, but the antler collection is well under way.

Rogelio, a slender, painstakingly polite man in his late thirties, greets me with a ready smile despite missing his two front teeth. His English is less developed than my Spanish, which doesn't bode well for conversation. His voice always soft, he gives me a tour of a lower building, just completed, half of which is a garage for snowmobiles and all-terrain vehicles, the other half of which is a state-of-the-art veterinary clinic, complete with a portable X-ray machine. Most of the medical gear is still in boxes, and the solar array for the lower building has not yet been erected.

Uphill from the upper building, the "casa," is a pen in which there are currently three sheep. I guess, correctly, that these will soon become condor food, but I keep this information to myself. Why spoil it for the sheep?

There's something a bit creepy about feeding condors, at least at first. Someone—a safety expert, I suppose—sent up labels with Mike yesterday that are to be affixed to the freezers used for condor food, one of which currently holds a dozen unbutchered sheep. The labels say, "Animal food only," and they say it only in English despite the fact that every permanent resident of this field station is Mexican. Were I one of the scientists, rather than a well-mannered guest, I'd already have stuck one of these labels onto the kitchen fridge, just to remind us all of the taxonomic kingdom to which we belong.

## From the June 11 Field Notes

I had no idea that conducting radio telemetry[3] could be so exhausting. Today's survey involved some of the gnarliest off-road driving imaginable, a wee bit of scrambling, and enough rock hopping to worry the knees. I probably should have brought the new boots, they'd have been broken in already, and this granite will make short shrift of the tread remaining on the boots I'm wearing. I'm as weary as my old boots right now, but I'm not quite as weary as Tigre, the boxer/pit bull mix that accompanied us in order to chase condors away from a microwave transmitter the vultures have recently discovered. When we get back to the field station, Tigre hobbled directly to his sleeping mat near the hearth, and could be heard snoring before Rogelio and I opened our sorely needed cervezas.

A new bird for me today, a red-naped sapsucker, *Sphyrapicus nuchalis*. For a moment I mistook it for a Nuttall's woodpecker until it took flight, revealing the white wing bars characteristic of its genus. The new bird is not the day's major headline, however, for the vistas were more noteworthy, including one

---

3. Radio telemetry involves sweeping the horizon, usually from a high point, with a device that looks something like an old-fashioned television antenna. The receiver is held at arm's length while the operator revolves 360 degrees searching for a signal. After the signal is recorded and annotated, the operator switches to the next bird's frequency, and again revolves 360 degrees listening for the next bird. A trained telemetrist can tell a great deal from the sound of each signal, such as how far away the bird is, and whether it's flying.

from near the dome of the 2.1-meter telescope of the Mexican National Observatory where, from the summit, one can see the Sea of Cortez far off in one direction, and the distant Pacific Ocean in the other. From any of our telemetry sites we could look down at least three hundred meters, usually more. Straight down, sometimes. At one point Rogelio wondered whether I was scared of heights because I was breathing hard, but I assured him it was just the altitude. He backed off his pace from then on, which I appreciated greatly.

Nothing but static on no. 217's frequency. We are officially hoping that she's nested deep inside a crevice, but . . . Tomorrow they're sending a climber up the canyon with a telemetry receiver, a fellow who is reputed to be the best climber in this sierra.

I spot condor 682 hunkered down on the knife edge of a granite ridge no more than 250 meters from where we are scanning, looking every bit the juvenile with a still-black head. Condor 682—gotta love that high number—is one of the two chicks hatched and fledged in the wilds of this sierra. Makes me wish I hadn't left my scope back at the field station.

When we climb down from the summit, Rogelio says, "*Ahora conoce la sierra.*" Now I know this mountain range. A lovely sentiment, but it usually takes me a bit longer to become intimate with an ecosystem. My various introductions, however, are moving along quickly. En route to the next telemetry site we get a good look at a bobcat standing tall, pointy ears perked, holding its ground until the dog barks from the back of the pickup. As it turns tail and flashes away I am delighted to hear Rogelio refer to it as "*gato montés.*" Mountain cat. Much more fitting than how we refer to this noble feline north of the border.

Carne asada tonight, grilled in the fireplace over manzanita coals, while a bucket on the hearth heats water for "showers." Despite the fact there isn't a cell phone signal within a hundred kilometers, I keep my iPhone on the table so we can look up vocabulary on the Spanish-English app. Rogelio starts dinner by cleaning all the ash out of the fireplace, piles up a half-dozen pine cones, adds an armload of dried manzanita, explaining that he won't use pine because of the resin, and then lights the pine cones. The fire flames quickly, blazes a hot white flame, and then reduces to coals almost as quickly as it caught. When the flame has almost vanished, Rogelio grades the coals level using a two-meter-long *removador de brasas* that he welded himself from rebar capped perpendicularly by a short length of one-inch angle iron. He places a hand-built grate over the coals, and once it's hot cleans it with the flat part of a halved onion skewered by a long fork. Then he places the meat gently on the grill, four thin steaks the size of dinner plates. There's enough carne asada here for several meals, which is precisely the plan: the leftovers will end up as burritos to be consumed over the course of the next three days. I will soon learn that here at the field station, burritos are as much a breakfast food as anything else.

We make a guy meal of it, just steak and frijoles. At the last minute I mix up some guacamole from one of Mike's avocados to make sure we have something green on the table, just in case my wife reads these notes.

### From the June 12 Field Notes

I awoke this morning to the "quick three beers" song of olive-sided flycatchers. I had to laugh, there in my cot, my sleeping bag askew, because the supplies I brought to the field station include a ration of two beers per day. I should have known that the local wildlife, this being Baja, would be critical of my not-so-wild life at the moment.

I resolve to ignore the flycatcher's injunction. At this altitude, three quick beers might put me under the table, and even one quick beer might be deleterious in terms of my literary output.

There's been a last-minute change in today's telemetry schedule. Someone back in San Diego remembered that the condors need to be fed, and relayed the orders to Rogelio. What this means, for me, is that I will be dropped off at Estación Juanito to spend some time alone, hopefully with condors. I'm beside myself with anticipation. As much as I've enjoyed lending an extra pair of eyes to the telemetry searches, this has been at the expense of my own project. And I'm finding that too much moving about makes it more difficult to connect with the environment. My plan is to park myself under a tree, set up a spotting scope and a camp chair, and stay the hell put. I'm committed to doing this at least thrice over the course of the next week, at least five hours at a time, whether condors come by or not. Maybe every other day?

I've been asked to record the tag numbers of the birds I spot, so I'll at least be contributing to the effort in a small way, but my greater intent is to take the pulse of the landscape, or in this case the skyscape. I want to know how a sierra feels when condors are reestablished.

It's been fascinating to watch Rogelio go about the process of keeping the field station functioning. After watering the sheep, dogs, and cat this morning, he rigged a pump to transfer water from the huge five-thousand-liter cistern outside to the two two-hundred-liter drums inside. From there we will hand-ladle water to be used for dishwashing and bathing. Our supply of potable water for cooking and drinking is separate.

I've begun monitoring my consumption of drinking water, realizing how easy it will be to become dehydrated at this altitude. The field station's weather-monitoring system, which sits right over the dining table, reports a relative humidity of 10 percent this morning.

Not certain of how strict the field station's water-conservation program is, I ask Rogelio how often people tend to bathe here. He indicates that I should wait until I'm "*sucio*," a word I have to look up. It means, of course, "dirty."

The field station is defended by two large dogs, Tigre and Frieda, and an enormous cat, Yoda. Whenever I grab my binoculars and step outside, the dogs insist on coming along for my protection. The dogs are very much aware of coyotes and pumas, constantly ready to answer a distant chorus of yips with indignant barking. As a result of my protectors, I've come to despair of spotting any mammal larger than a chipmunk during my time up here on the ridge.

The mountain bluebirds, *Sialia currucoides*, almost make up for the lack of four-legged observables. They are two shades more brilliant than the western bluebirds, *S. mexicana*, whose feathers would seem plenty blue were it not for the ostentatious cousins overlapping their range. Every time I walk outside there are one or two bluebirds drinking from the dog's water bowls. I watch two mountain bluebirds leave behind an azure trail as they streak away toward the sheep pen, where I notice that Rogelio throws a small pad of hay to the doomed animals. They consume it eagerly.

Not long afterward, his morning chores almost completed, Rogelio squeezes a dozen limes into a liter container, adds a coffee mug full of sugar, adds a level teaspoon of salt, and fills the jug with water, shaking vigorously. After that, he dons his hat and announces, matter-of-factly, that he is going to kill the *borrego*, the sheep. I know from one of Mike's papers that the protocol is to use a captive-bolt gun, the system used by most modern slaughterhouses, because this is considered the most humane way to dispatch an animal that will later be consumed. Rogelio asks whether I'd like to watch, and I pass, indicating that my field notes need attention. He looks at me curiously, and I tell him in my best Spanish that I'm writing about bluebirds.

While Rogelio tries to make sense of my answer, I briefly consider asking why he'd fed the sheep so soon before killing them. But it occurs to me, before

I can figure out how to pose the question in Spanish, that the sheep's breakfast this morning was an act of compassion. Compassion doesn't always have to make sense.

Rogelio returns to the station house a few short minutes after he'd departed, but without his usual cheerfulness. I expect that he will get over it soon; you can't work with condors if you can't deal with death.

Observations from the first day at Estación Juanito:

The auditory landscape of my observation post rivals the vista itself. The greater part of the San Felipe Desert lies below, undeveloped, creating a background silence that's almost audible. The winds here do not cancel out the silence; they complement it.

Wind comes in puffs, and is almost never steady this early in the day, sounding a constant pattern of crescendo and diminuendo that seldom holds pitch longer than a moment. One hears a puff embrace each stand of trees individually, and then dissipate into far thickets. Birdsong accounts for the soundscape's treble notes, the unseen birds contributing the most distinct trills. If one listens extra hard, one will hear the wingbuzz of insects mixed in with the far-away chatter of swallows.

When the condors whooooosh by, they bring the wind with them, increasing its fervor. A group of three circle around my perch, each one sounding as if it's being chased by angry bees whenever it banks into the wind. This close, this fast, it's hard to read their wing tags—I can get 69 and 82, but the other is a blur. I concentrate anyway, simultaneously trying to determine whether I can distinguish the sound of one condor from another.

Imagine a flock of Harley Davidsons gunning their engines down Main Street, and you will approximate the effect of when condors circle Estación Juanito. These birds haven't evolved an iota of stealth, which seems appropriate when you consider that pure scavengers never have to sneak up on their prey. But I never expected *any* bird to be quite this noisy. Indeed, the wing noise of a dozen geese gliding to a landing doesn't quite match the cacophony of a single condor.

Lowering my binoculars because there are too many birds to fit the view, I notice that all the birds—there are seven now—have full crops. They are freshly gorged, and this seems to be their victory lap.

They see me, and circle close as if to show that they can tell I'm hiding. I pick up a branch, as per my briefing, and try to look evil. They seem to understand that I'm one of the bad guys, and they break my heart by whooshing away, as they've apparently been trained to do. It's hard to make friends with birds who have been through aversion therapy.

A lone turkey vulture wings by, seeming almost as diminutive as it is silent. Unlike the condors, it doesn't seem at all curious about me. If I'm not dead, why should it care? In this regard, it is not at all like the condors, who seem curious about everything.

Another condor, this one alone. My heart skips a beat when I read the numeral "1" on its patagial tag, but the whole number turns out to be "18," condor 218, one of the three from the original cohort. I send out a quick prayer, petitioning the bird to find its sister and to bring her back to us, assuming of course that she's not nesting.

A kettle has formed behind me now. Three birds become five, become seven. Circling tight. They are playing with the very air that keeps them aloft.

Two break away from the kettle simultaneously, as if they were reading each other's minds. I track them instinctively with my binoculars, and sure enough, a "follow flight" ensues, a follow-the-leader ritual that is part of the pair-bonding process for vultures. The lead bird banks so hard it's amazing no feathers come off in the process. I can tell that the following bird is having a difficult time duplicating her moves, and my heart goes out to him. She flaps once, twice and vanishes behind the crag directly east of me, her pursuer flapping as well. I try to will them back into my visual range, to witness what happens next, but they have vanished for the day.

I am suddenly alone, just sharing the space with a lizard on the nearest rock and a chipmunk on the downed tree behind it. The sky feels empty without condors.

Toward the end of my time at Estación Juanito this afternoon I was watching a squadron of a half-dozen turkey vultures flying low almost three hundred meters away. I scanned each bird individually with my binoculars to determine whether any condors might be with them, but all the birds had the turkey vulture's classic dihedral shape and teetering flight pattern. Suddenly, as they crossed over a cluster of Jeffrey pines, one of the birds folded back its wings into a hawk-like stoop, diving straight down—clearly not a turkey vulture!

I wasn't close enough to observe any distinguishing characteristics such as the yellow feet or the white band on its tail, but based on the behavior alone I'm certain this was a zone-tailed hawk, *Buteo albonotatus*. With their gray flight feathers they often mimic the flight of turkey vultures in order to surprise their prey, either lizards or small birds that have learned to ignore harmless turkey vultures.

This one fooled me as well, for a while. I would still be looking for the first zone-tailed hawk of this trip were it not for that stoop.

### Reflections after a Day at Estación Juanito

I needed to get today out of my system. I was a gawker today, an amateur naturalist at best, one "given to exclamations of wonder," as Linnaeus put it. Even without the condors, my station would have been sublime; with them flying about it was glorious. I went into the station prepared to observe the birds, so I thought, but completely unprepared to have the birds observe me. Condors don't miss much, and they don't view the world peripherally, the way a pigeon does. Rather, they swivel their heads as they're flying by, observing whatever interests them with both eyes, binocularly. My big discovery today was that the condors were as interested in me as I was in them.

Watching a condor in the wild isn't the same experience as observing a red-tailed hawk. The hawk remains constantly aloof. Red-tails have decided that humanity are not part of their agenda, and have therefore written us off. I've watched thousands of red-tails fly by on Hawk Hill while counting hawks for the Golden Gate Raptor Observatory, and can't remember a single instance of making direct eye-to-eye contact. Indeed, wildlife photographers will sometimes bring along a stuffed owl and situate it right above the camera to get those shots where the hawk seems to be glaring into the lens.

A condor is different, starting with the fact that there's nothing stealthy about how a condor goes about its business. It has nothing to hide, including the fact that it might be curious about anything novel. There was a new human in the home territory today, doing something different from the few other humans they routinely saw. I wasn't conducting telemetry, I wasn't moving about, indeed I wasn't doing much of anything. Just sitting there, watching them watching me.

Now I know why Mike Wallace insists on what he calls "aversion training" for the condors. There's a linkage between a condor's learning ability and its curiosity. These birds watch, they learn, and then they adapt, the whole adaption process being driven by curiosity. It's one thing to read about condor curiosity in a scientific paper, and another thing completely to sit under a Jeffrey pine and be circled by a bird that so obviously wants to know what you're up to.

It was breathtaking—I don't care what Linnaeus would say.

## From the June 13 Field Notes

Over the VHF radio, word has been passed along from the park's ranger station that a ranger is available to show me the park's natural history museum. Someone, somewhere within Mexican officialdom, has decided that the visiting college professor needs to see this newly constructed facility. A courtesy has been extended, and I have a hunch that it would be discourteous of me not to accept it graciously. I will be given my own private tour of the museum, the privacy of which somehow makes sense in a national park with more condors than tourists at any given moment. I've been instructed that I should bring a headlamp; they haven't yet raised money to purchase the solar panels, and sometimes the portable generator won't start. Rogelio, whose brother happens to be one of the local rangers, snarks that sometimes they run out of gas.

I resolve not to be snarkish myself. In the past year I've been given special access to rare manuscripts in the Natural History Museum in London and in the American Museum of Natural History in New York City. But so far, the only museum ever to honor me with a private tour is the Museo de Cultura e Historia Natural en el Parque Nacional Sierra de San Pedro Mártir.

The standard uniform for Mexican park rangers, at least in this national park, is an untucked ranger shirt worn over blue jeans, augmented by a baseball cap. No badges, no flat-brimmed campaign hats, no sidearms, no olive-green military overtones. My ranger spoke passable English, which was revitalizing after so many days struggling to communicate with my limited array of irregular Spanish verbs.

Although the natural history exhibits were informative, most notably the one on local mushrooms, I found myself drawn more to the cultural artifacts, especially a room full of hand-blacksmithed tools such as a hammer fabricated entirely from iron. This hammer had been used for decades on one of the local rancheros, at a time not long ago when a multiday burro trip to a *mercado* large enough to carry tools would have presented far more difficulties than building the hammer oneself. The crude tool was indeed precious enough to have earned its way into a museum.

My biggest hope for this visit was to get my hands on a comprehensive checklist of birds found in the park, but my ranger guide informed me that no such list existed, and encouraged me to develop one myself. It hadn't occurred to me, up to that point, that such a list would not be readily available for the asking. This was an object lesson, and I will never again grumble at having to pay a couple bucks for a checklist in one of the California state park visitor centers.

I was relieved to return to the solitude of the field station, where I could stop playing the role of college professor. I was free to invest what remained of the day catching up on my writing—and some birding—while Rogelio went out to conduct telemetry. Before he left, I admonished him to watch out for *las serpientes de cascabel* just to demonstrate that I'd learned something at the museum.

### From the June 14 Field Notes

Before dropping me off at Estación Juanito, Rogelio asks whether I would like to hike to the summit of a nearby hill to help with telemetry. Eager to stretch my legs, I agree, and it pleases me that I'm finally adjusting well enough to the altitude to keep up with him without wheezing.

Halfway up the hill we come across a concentration of large bones. "*¿Vaca?*" I ask. "*Vaca, sí,*" he replies, "*y caballo tambien.*" (Cows, yes, and horses also.)

I'm shocked. "You carried these animals up here?"

Humble Rogelio pantomimes that he quartered them first to make it easier to carry them. A bit higher we come across the remains of an observation blind, what must have been a large, tentlike structure before it was crushed by a falling tree. Rogelio explains that Mike had set this up to watch the birds eat, and I am left to imagine what sort of science this blind produced, guessing that, if nothing else, it would have provided a way to monitor which birds were dominant. Rogelio interrupts my speculation to tell me that the tree was his *amigo*, the fallen pine having relieved him from needing to drag more dead horses up this hill.

After the telemetry, when Rogelio drops me off above Estación Juanito, he reminds me to keep an eye out for condor 217, and he requests that this time, when I record the tag numbers of whatever birds I identify, I should also write down the time of the observation. And the color of the tag. He adds a final instruction in English, insisting that I "watch the rattlesnakes."

*Por supuesto.*

He punches the transmit button on the walkie-talkie on his belt, listening for the resultant hiss from my unit in order to confirm that I have turned it on.

He drives off, apparently still concerned for my safety, and I lug my gear down to the same contorted Jeffrey pine in the protection of whose shade I'd spent the previous day. I hear numerous alarm calls while I'm setting up my tripod, and when I glance up I see an American kestrel, *Falco sparverius*, circling overhead, resplendent in the sunlight. With my binoculars I can almost see through its fanned tail when it banks. It's a beautiful bird, but I hope it goes away soon so that I can spend the day listening to birdsong rather than alarm calls.

My first condor, no. 498, doesn't arrive until 10:00. It seems to be hunting, and will probably end up over at the feeding station soon. I will have a long wait before I see another. I hear Rogelio on the radio, calling both the observatory and the ranger station to ask whether anyone has seen condors this morning. No one answers; all I hear above the squelch is the apple in my daypack calling my name. I decide to wait until 11:00, but the apple is so persistent that I give in to temptation at 10:55. No sooner do I take the first bite when condor 469 swoops by, moving slow for a condor.

Have you ever tried to look through binoculars while holding an apple with your teeth?

Another condor comes by, and I switch to the spotting scope because it's too far away for me to get the tag number with my trusty 7x42s, which I'm now convinced were a mistake to bring on this trip in lieu of optics more powerful. I watch the bird fly away, and am distracted by a zone-tailed hawk, my second of the day. It begins to glide, folding its wings back for speed as it takes advantage of wind curving up over the cliff. I follow the glide in my scope as the hawk accelerates, chiding myself all the while for allowing a hawk to distract me from a condor. But I'm too much of a hawk watcher not to appreciate this show, and the condor is only giving me tail feathers.

Scanning the skies again, I spot a red-shouldered hawk, *Buteo lineatus*, a rarity for these mountains. After so many days watching dark-feathered birds, the red-shoulder seems luminous, as if sparkling in this crisp sunlight.

Another zone-tailed hawk, directly overhead. I get a great look through the binoculars, so good that I can identify the genus of the whiptail lizard clutched in the zone-tail's talons. I watch the hawk soar along the ridge for at least a kilometer, and then watch it climb a thermal, circling eight times before it glides south, presumably to feed the lizard to hungry chicks.

A red-tailed hawk hails behind me, but my view in that direction is blocked by trees. I'm tempted to walk around to try locating it, but that would make me too conspicuous to the condors, none of whom are present at the moment. Indeed, it feels like a condor drought, at least in comparison to my previous stint at Estación Juanito, but I realize that it's unseemly to complain about only seeing *Gymnogyps californianus* at the rate of two per hour.

I settle into my camp chair and wait impatiently, thinking that an eagle would be nice right about now. Instead, a Costas hummingbird hovers a meter from my face, its gorget flashing such a bright purple that even a color-blind guy ought to be able to see it.

Rogelio calls, as much to see whether I'm having any luck with the birds as to make certain I'm still alive. I give him the few tag numbers I've observed, along with the reassurance *"todos bien,"* that all is well. I sign off in a hurry as no. 508 glides by close enough to be heard.

By the end of my session I will have had one good kettle of condors. Five birds at first, and then three. Although circling, the three seemed to be flying in formation, in communion with each other as if by telepathy. At one point, all three dropped their legs simultaneously. At another, all three flexed their wings deeply downward into an inverted *U*, losing altitude together in the process. I don't really know how they synchronized so well, and I'd love to know whether they were relying on auditory clues from the clamor of each others' feathers.

After they wheeled together clockwise and glided off to the north, I realized that in my fascination with their synchronicity, I'd neglected to notice their tag numbers.

### Reflections after a Second Day at Estación Juanito

I've read about these mountains so many times, and I've had previous acquaintance with the great majority of the flora and fauna here, but my environmental imagination was not up to the task of visualizing what this sierra was going to be like. Until I got here a few days ago I was somehow missing the taste of the air, the strange aridity of the sea breeze, the brilliant quality of latitude 31° sunlight, the fickleness of the morning wind, the snow-rounded character of the granite, and how thickly the forest would be carpeted with cones.

When I return to campus I'll reread a few narratives about early treks through this range, just to determine whether the problem is with the writers who introduced me to the Sierra San Pedro Mártir or with me as a reader. Meanwhile, I am confronted with the question of how a writer evokes an ecosystem, especially a mountain range.

I'm feeling the same way about the condors. In the six months between when this trip was approved and when it finally happened I've read a mountain of material about *Gymnogyps californianus*, everything from scientific papers about restoration methods to histories about how they became a conservation icon. Still, I had no idea what it would be like to have one land in a tree above me, or how exhilarating it would be to watch a kettle of condors party with each other.

The other day I came across a primary feather lying on the ground. Any temptation I may have had to hide it in my daypack was tempered by the fact that it would never have fit within my pack. I picked the feather up in my right hand—how could I not?—and extended my left arm horizontally, placing the feather's quill against my ribs. The feather extended past my watch, halfway over the palm of my hand. One feather!

## From the June 15 Field Notes

Today is *Domingo*, Sunday, not only the Lord's Day but Father's Day as well. After breakfast, Rogelio announces that he doesn't have to work today, being the father of two teenagers. Then he proceeds to sweep and mop the floor.

What he apparently means by not having to work is that he doesn't have to deal with carcasses. And no night visits to the aviary. More to the point, this means we don't have to use the pickup truck, which means we'll zip around in the *motos,* the four-wheel-drive, all-terrain vehicles more akin to motorcycles than jeeps. The one to which I'm assigned, a Yamaha Grizzly, looks especially raptorial. You have to wonder why anyone would name an all-terrain vehicle after *Ursus arctos horribilis.* More to the point, why would the San Diego Zoo purchase such a predacious machine?

My first fifteen minutes are pure terror, and I'm quite literally left in the dust by Rogelio, who seems to find this mode of travel invigorating. I'm not really certain where we're going, only that we'll be going to places a four-wheel-drive pickup truck can't navigate. I'm left to assume that this is a good thing.

I slowly learn to trust my machine, and once I stop fighting it and start riding it I can throttle up to a respectable speed without screaming, at least on the flat stretches. I can't help thinking how ironic this is: for many Americans, Baja is nothing more than a place to play with their off-road vehicles. For my part, however, I prefer the tranquility of a sea kayak.

We make a couple stops in usual places to conduct telemetry, with Rogelio on the electronics and me doing visual identifications whenever possible. After the second stop, Rogelio tells me that now we're going to take a *camino estrecho*, a narrow trail. When he holds up four fingers I'm to shift into four-wheel drive. When the trail slants, I should shift my weight uphill. He demonstrates, and I cringe.

The narrow trail doesn't seem to have been traveled recently. Some places are so thick with pine cones that my grizzly seems to be sledding on them, rarely making solid contact with firm ground. Twice we must make drastic stops because trees have fallen across our trail. In one case we can go around, in the other we must use caveman technology to create a gap through the downed snag, busting it apart with rocks and muscle. Finally, we come to a tree too stout to go through, and too long to go around. Rogelio switches off his engine and says, "*No mas camino.*" The road, if you could call it that, had ended.

We grab our daypacks, and I notice that Rogelio isn't bringing the telemetry equipment. When I point this out, he replies, in perfect English, "Not this time."

We descend into a U-shaped swale studded with large granite boulders—monoliths, really—looking proudly batholithic. The forest has an ancient feel. At one point Rogelio stops and whispers, "*Crótalo,*" a word close enough to the genus name, "*Crotalus,*" that I get the message and start listening for rattlers. We begin climbing at this juncture, until finally we arrive at a summit of sorts, a place where the view opens up to the southwest, expansively, and there is no sign of human artifact, not even a road, within this view. My immediate impression is that not many humans have gazed out at this vista, at least not recently.

Only one word is spoken, "*bonita,*" Spanish for "beautiful." I realize, at that moment, why we're here. This has nothing to do with condors or with making a living. This is about *Domingo*, the sacred day for a father who only gets to see his kids once a month. This far from priests, from churches, and from family, Rogelio has led us to the most sacred space he knows, and has called it by its proper name, "*Bonita.*"

I am emboldened on the ride home, and keep close enough behind Rogelio to become covered in dust. As I become more and more expert riding my grizzly, I keep thinking about my wife, and my students. What would they say if they could see me right now, having turned sixty within the past fortnight? Would they worry that I'd gone over to the dark side, or just worry that I wasn't wearing a helmet?

When we return to the field station I leave my dusty daypack outside, not wanting to contaminate Rogelio's clean floor. I take off my sunglasses, and Rogelio bursts into laughter. He grasps my arm above the elbow and drags me over to a mirror. I look like I'm wearing a raccoon mask, my face clean where the sunglasses protected it, the rest as brown as Baja itself.

What a glorious Sunday!

### From the June 16 Field Notes

Having passed my driver's test, apparently, and now that I know my way around the sierra, I am invited to drop myself off at Estación Juanito today riding the grizzly—a solo outing except that I must take the radio, just in case. This works well for everyone; Rogelio wants to get as much work done as he can today so that tomorrow, during the World Cup soccer match, he can visit the ranger station and help the rangers cheer for Mexico as it goes up against Brazil on their satellite TV. I am left with the impression that the telemetry sweeps will take place more swiftly if I am not present.

I resolve to drive slowly, softly, safely enough that there's no chance of supplying the condors a superfluous carcass.

While I will still continue to monitor patagial tags, especially given the chance that no. 217 could still show up, my objective today is simply to enjoy the condors. How many people get to do that? Tomorrow, I will put away my pen and notebook and fire up the laptop computer because I want at least to begin the composition of this interlude here in the rarified air of the sierra, hoping for thoughts as fresh as the Pacific breeze when it scrubs through these pines.

For now, however, I will watch.

I arrive at Estación Juanito precisely on schedule, having taken only a single wrong turn in the process of getting here. I park the grizzly under a large pine at least a hundred meters away from my station, and lug the gear I'll need for the day in a single trip. Shortly after I've set up my tripod and camp chair, two condors, 529 and 682, alight on the largest snag behind me. I have not had condors land in any nearby trees all week, but the condors are not looking in my direction, and there's no way to tell for certain that they know I'm here.

The two birds ignore me while I record the tag numbers and the time, but when I pull out the camera to a snap a few photographs they stare directly into the lens. I judge the birds to be just out of pine cone range, but I pick up the best available missile and sidearm it in the birds' general direction. The pine cone whistles toward them, straight and true, but fizzles less than half the distance to the targets, falling to earth short of the base of the snag on which my audience is perched. They watch, unfazed and unruffled, kind enough not to laugh at my effort to frighten them. They are not, after all, ravens.

Figuring that the birds are smart enough not to come within pine cone range, I snap a few more photographs and then turn my back to the intruders, hoping that they become bored with me.

Within fifteen minutes, two more birds arrive, 549 and 468. I consider abandoning the station at this point, but I'm reluctant to do so. With the earlier interruptions, it took me a half hour to get everything set up . . . and, after all, this is my last day at Estación Juanito . . . and . . .

My thinking is interrupted by another condor. I train my binoculars on its patagial tag, still hoping for 217. But this is 551, and it drops its legs a good fifty meters out, the way a 747 extends its landing gear on final approach, aiming at a tree nearer to me, one clearly within pine cone range. After listening to the landing I decide that if any of these birds are destined to become zoo birds, it will not be on my account. The hell with pine cones; I will abandon my station.

I don't waste time packing the gear—binoculars, camera, spotting scope, radio—into protective cases. I jumble everything into my daypack, hoist the tripod up onto my right shoulder, and grasp the chair under my left arm. I turn 360 degrees to make certain I haven't forgotten anything and, as I complete my turn, I spot another bird gliding in from the north. It's too small to be a condor, and too dark. Without the assistance of my optics I have trouble identifying it until one of the condors emits a loud hiss from the tree behind me. The new bird streaks past, not twenty meters away, a golden eagle that would have appeared majestic ten days ago.

It looks so tiny! I realize, instantly, that the condors have altered my perspective.

Two of the condors flap away, not at all happy to be sharing airspace with an eagle. The other three remain behind as I load my gear into the grizzly's basket, strapping the camp chair to the rear rack. I fire up the engine and lope away from Estación Juanito, a bit saddened to be doing so.

Out on the main trail I stop briefly to repack gear and figure out what to do with the rest of the day. By the time I get everything organized, there are three condors perched atop a nearby tree. They're clearly investigating me at this point after having all but ignored me during my first few days on station. I decide to strike out for a meadow a kilometer away where I can check out the wildflowers and enjoy a solitary lunch. The irony of this plan is not lost on me: Is it possible that I'm the only birder who, during this current millennium, has deliberately sought out a space away from condors?

There are no condors near the meadow, and none of the earlier birds have followed me here. I delay lunch for half an hour, just to make sure, and spend the time photographing wildflowers and compiling a list of all the condors I'd been close enough to ID so far today: 218, 362, 468, 469, 498, 508, 549, 551, 562, 675, and 682. Throw in a close encounter with a golden eagle and it wasn't a bad morning, aside from losing my observation station.

I'm particularly glad that I didn't see 261, the mate of 217. We'd picked up his signal once earlier in the week, and it would have been troubling had he stayed around. The fact that he's been missing from the telemetry the last few days could be interpreted to mean that he's with 217, helping her attend to a chick in a nest so remote that their radio telemetry signals are out of range.

I call Rogelio on the radio and let him know that all is well, *todos bien*, but that I'm slowly returning to the field station. I rein the grizzly in on the way home. It's a noisy beast, and I'll be glad to be done with it soon. I pass some pines infested by a vociferous scold of pinyon jays, at least fifty dull-blue birds in all, and I turn off the engine so that I can listen to them spread derision through the forest. Tree by tree they slowly migrate east, always at full volume, and when they're gone I'm left feeling a bit blue myself. Today I became aware that the wildest condors here in North America might still be a little bit tame, lacking an essential aversion toward humanity. Still, I'd rather have them this way, complete with patagial tags, than not have them in the wild at all.

On my way back I pass through a section of forest that had been logged illegally by poachers, two local ranchers who were not caught until after they'd desecrated a dozen hectares of ancient forest. The logs were never transported out, and remain stacked to this day as evidence. It doesn't seem to be a place where condors would be happy.

As soon as I let out the dogs back at the field station I scan the skies for condors, seeing none. I feel a bit elegiac about this—I've clearly gotten to the point where I want my skies filled with big birds.

### Reflections after My Final Day at Estación Juanito

If I've observed anything during my time on station that I didn't learn about in all my preparatory reading about condors, it's how these birds maintain particular friendships. Although much has been reported about the social aspect of condors, I don't remember reading about cliques, buddies, or cronies. Here in the sierra I see birds roosting shoulder to shoulder in treetops, I see the joy they experience flying with one another, and I see how the threesome that flew together yesterday is still enjoying each other's company today.

Over the course of time, I'm just beginning to notice the same birds hanging out with each other, and I'm wondering what sort of patterns emerge in their friendships beyond the nominal patterns of dominance. There seems to be something deeper going on here, and I regret that I've only been here long enough to notice it, not to really study it.

Are the Baja condors aware that 217 has been absent from the central flock for so long? Will they mourn her at some point, or perhaps have they already done so? With a life expectancy of sixty years, do they view the passage from life to death differently than other wildlife?

So much to learn.

*Field Station Bird List*

California condor, *Gymnogyps californianus*
Turkey vulture, *Cathartes aura*
Golden eagle, *Aquila chrysaetos*

Zone-tailed hawk, *Buteo albonotatus*
Red-tailed hawk, *Buteo jamaicensis*
Red-shouldered hawk, *Buteo lineatus*
Cooper's hawk, *Accipiter cooperii*
American kestrel, *Falco sparverius*
Prairie falcon, *Falco mexicanus*
Peregrine falcon, *Falco peregrinus*
Common raven, *Corvus corax*
Mountain bluebird, *Sialia currucoides*
Western bluebird, *Sialia mexicana*
Spotted towhee, *Pipilo maculatus*
Pinyon jay, *Gymnorhinus cyanocephalus*
Violet-green swallow, *Tachycineta thalassina*
Tree swallow, *Tachycineta bicolor*
Costa's hummingbird, *Calypte costae*
Blue-gray gnatcatcher, *Polioptila caerulea*
Olive-sided flycatcher, *Contopus cooperi*
Dusky flycatcher, *Empidonax oberholseri*
Mountain chickadee, *Poecile gambeli*
Dark-eyed junco, *Junco hyemalis*
Pygmy nuthatch, *Sitta pygmaea*
Northern flicker, *Colaptes auratus*
Red-naped sapsucker, *Sphyrapicus nuchalis*
California quail, *Callipepla californica*
Mountain quail, *Oreortyx pictus*

### From the June 17 Field Notes

I had planned a full day of writing today, and indeed was plugging away shortly after daybreak, but at 9:00 a.m., when Rogelio asked whether I'd like to help with telemetry one last time, I jumped at the chance.

It turns out that I wasn't much help at all. At Punta San Pedro we heard nesting peregrines vocalizing from the cliffs below. I lagged behind, searching with my binoculars while Rogelio, after commenting that he liked the wind, went on ahead to check telemetry. It seemed a strange statement at first, but as we separated I noted that it was indeed an excellent breeze, steady and warm, perfect conditions for the formation of thermals, ideal not only for condor flight, but also for me to bid farewell to Sierra San Pedro Mártir.

Rogelio set up shop atop a boulder some ninety meters away, in a place where we could both see each other but where my listening wouldn't be interrupted by the noise of the telemetry receiver.

The peregrines would chirp, screech, and call—*kak kak kak*—every five minutes or so, and it definitely sounded as if they'd set up housekeeping down below. It would probably have been easier to spot the falcons had I been down on the canyon floor looking up, but I had no desire to be down there where it would be so much warmer, and the vistas would be so much less expansive.

I spent about an hour listening without making any visual contact, and it felt like an hour well spent. It had taken a bit more than a week, but I'd finally slowed down enough to listen with equal amounts of curiosity and reverence.

Finally, I heard a whistle, and turned to see Rogelio pointing up. There, to the south, a kettle of eight vultures had formed.

At first I thought the telemetry boss might want help getting visual confirmations of the tag numbers, but this was not the case. He just wanted to make sure I wasn't missing this spectacle, one that can only happen in a handful of places on this continent. I joined him, asking quietly whether 217's radio blip had been heard this morning. It had not.

The birds did not seem to be circling so much to gain altitude as to use the opportunity of a thermal to check each other out. Through the binoculars I could clearly see their heads swivel as they watched each other fly. It was obvious that these birds all knew each other, and could visually determine how everyone else in the kettle was doing. One glance could tell whether the neighbors had full crops, how much social status was reflected in the facial colors of adults, whether somebody's feathers were ruffled, who was molting, and whether the juveniles were ever going to grow up.

Watching this kettle, it became increasingly apparent why the collective noun for condors is "party." Just as one might reference a gaggle of geese, a murder of crows, or a scold of jays, it is entirely proper to refer to any gathering of condors as a party. And this was indeed a party, a social occasion where friends and acquaintances gathered, however briefly, not only for their mutual entertainment but also to check how everyone seemed to be holding up. At this particular party, it should go without mentioning, the participants were all getting high.

After the kettle dispersed, Rogelio asked whether I'd noticed the colors of the desert down below. Not knowing the Spanish term for "color-blind," I told him, *"No puedo ver colores,"* which didn't seem exactly right to either of us. I probably should have said, *"No puedo reconocer colores,"* because I can see them, I just can't seem to recognize them.

Rather than discuss desert hues with someone neither linguistically or physiologically up to the task, Rogelio beckoned that I should follow, and led me down a rocky non-path through a thick, low-lying copse of Encino oak, the small, sharp, stiff leaves having no difficulty pricking through my lightweight nylon shirt. We emerged from the bramble at the precipice of a cliff, at which point he warned me to be careful, which naturally set me to wondering whether I'd better start watching for rattlesnakes again. We stood at the edge, both holding on to slender oak branches, and he pointed out, on the adjacent cliff, the nesting site used last season by condors 284 and 269, two of the birds that had evicted me from Estación Juanito the previous day.

Following the line of Rogelio's outstretched finger, I was able to locate the nest cavity. Thinking on behalf of a vulnerable condor chick, I said, "It looks safe."

My *compañero* shook his head and held up three fingers, saying, "Not safe. Three rappels down."

We drove back to the field station in silence. When we got to the top of the ridge, I suggested that after another ten days of this, we'd surely be fluent in each other's languages. Rogelio chuckled at the suggestion.

Mike called on the radio when he was half an hour away. The park had closed its gates right after dark, so we headed down to the ranger station to find someone to open things up for him. It was 9:00 p.m. before we got back to the field station. When he climbed out of his pickup he was grinning like he'd just won the lottery. Keeping his secret as long as he could, he did not break the news that condor 217 was alive until we finally got inside the field station.

The climber who started down below from the desert side had picked up her signal on telemetry, both on a cliff where she was suspected of nesting and in the next canyon over, where she was probably foraging for her chick. The signals were typical of a nesting condor. Since this is Baja, it took a few days for the news to make its way to San Diego and then back down to the field station, Mike having only gotten word that afternoon, right before leaving to come retrieve me.

We are ecstatic. This could mean that three chicks will fledge this year, bringing the total number of Baja condors born in the wild up to five. And best of all, condor 217 has not perished in the process of restoring her species to the Sierra San Pedro Mártir.

Mike cautions us not to become overly optimistic, there's still plenty that can go wrong before that chick is introduced to the local party of condors. But his admonition falls on deaf ears; for now, all that matters is that a lost bird has been found.

David Brower has concluded that condors are "five percent feathers, flesh, blood and bone. All the rest is place."

He's right. Anyone spending time with *Gymnogyps californianus* in the Sierra San Pedro Mártir would come to the same conclusion. The place and the bird fit each other. The condor's problem, however, isn't about the places where it's being reintroduced—it's about the times in which it lives.

Going as far back as the early 1900s, wildlife biologists have accused the condor of being a relict species, a holdover from the Pleistocene. Interestingly, the folks who make this claim tend to leave out the fact that the species giving the condors so much trouble, *Homo sapiens*, evolved during the Pleistocene as well.

It's time for a new understanding of California condors. Most people who make a casual acquaintance with these animals, especially in zoos, never get past the impressive three-meter wingspan. That's a mistake, because condors are more about lifespan than wingspan. Any bird that we can reasonably expect to live for six decades should, from an ethical perspective, be given a chance to live for six decades.

The problem isn't with the condors; this is not an inherently senescent species! The problem is that we've provided them too many novel ways to die: ingesting lead, ingesting microtrash, ingesting poisoned varmints, risking electrocution on power poles, being shot for feathers, being shot for sport.

After I crossed back over the border, I purchased a newspaper and a half bottle of California cabernet, this having been the longest I've gone without a glass of wine in recent memory. My change consisted of three pennies and a California quarter, the tail side of which depicts John Muir gazing out at a California condor soaring over Yosemite Valley. My eyes went immediately to the condor.

In *My First Summer in the Sierra*, Muir wrote, "When we try to pick out anything by itself, we find it hitched to everything else in the universe. One fancies a heart like our own must be beating in every crystal and cell, and we feel like stopping to speak to the plants and animals as friendly fellow-mountaineers."

Despite their aversion training, condors are indeed friendly fellow-mountaineers. After my too-short visit with them in Sierra San Pedro Mártir, I cannot help but fancy that a heart very much like my own must be beating within them.

# *Essay*

## The Cove of Departure

I found it and I named it, being versed
in taxonomic Latin; thus became
godfather to an insect and its first
describer--and I want no other fame.

VLADIMIR NABOKOV, from "On Discovering
a Butterfly," 1943

Of all the beaches we camp on during our time in the archipelago, the one at Caleta Partida is the least pristine. Neither is it picturesque, although in its defense it could be pointed out that it's the only beach on our itinerary from which both sunrise and sunset can be viewed. A sand spit, formerly an isthmus, it tails from the southern end of Isla Partida, paralleling a sister spit that emerges from the northern tip of Isla Espíritu Santo. The two spits overlap, forcing the water to carve a sharp, elongated S between the islands. The water flowing between the spits is seldom deep, and at low tide the channel can be waded without getting one's crotch wet. Although it's too shallow for navigation by boats larger than a panga, it's handy for kayaks. Once, due to a storm that was still a few days away, we cut through this channel and did a figure eight, circumnavigating Isla Partida counterclockwise in order to transit the windward side before it got nasty.

Fishing shacks huddle together at the end of the spit, a remnant outpost of the *ejido* that sold this archipelago to the Nature Conservancy in 1998. Part of the deal was that the fishermen from the collective could live out their days fishing these waters according to a management plan. We maintain cordial relations with the fishermen. In an emergency, we would not hesitate to ask them to run a student to the hospital in one of their pangas, and they would not hesitate to provide this service, even in the dead of night.

There are no good trailheads here at Caleta Partida, nor is there any good diving within a reasonable swim from the beach, and much of the time it's too shallow to swim. The only activity we typically schedule when we camp here is tidepooling, and although we always make a cool discovery or two, the tidepooling here borders on mediocre, with too many fireworms and too few octopodes.[1]

Despite its pedestrian topography and a serious lack of megaflora, this beach has character. Materiality. Behind is mostly pickleweed, a low-lying, salt-extruding plant that tastes like dill pickles minus the garlic. The endemic black jackrabbits, *Lepus insularis*, who with their dark pelage look like bunnies that joined a motorcycle gang, congregate within the pickleweed. They come out at night, hopping up and down the beach in the company of ghost crabs. The jackrabbits have habituated to kayak campers, the ghost crabs have not.

At high noon there is no shade on this beach other than that which we fabricate ourselves. On a hot day, after a full morning of kayaking and half an afternoon of tidepooling, we tend to congregate under the two shade tarps. Most of us write, some sketch, some sleep, all crave sundown.

Day or night, this place breeds contemplation.

While Caleta Partida is idiomatic of "the cove at Partida Island," a literal translation could be "Cove of Departure." My most major departure at this cove has been intellectual: it was here that I became convinced that matter, even a seemingly inanimate sand spit, has agency. Having made my own material turn, I stopped viewing natural history as being merely analytical, mostly scientific. Instead, I have begun to view it, at least in part, as an art, an art grounded in observation, description, and narrative.

I readily concede the art of natural history to intersect with science, and indeed to generate science. Lepidopterist-novelist Vladimir Nabokov seemed to glory in these intersections, insisting that there can be no science without fancy, no art without facts. Recently, however, I've become aware of thresholds where natural history necessarily transcends science. Just as there is a place for the objective within natural history, there is also need for the subjective. Within the subjective realm, the reenchantment of nature often takes place.

There are numerous points of confluence between natural history and the fine arts. Like the visual arts, natural history bases its process in observation,

---

1. Well into my dotage I will insist that "octopus" is derived from the Greek *oktōpous*, not Latin, and that "octopi" is not therefore as proper a plural as "octopodes." My dictionary suggests using "octopuses," a word that looks too wrong to belong anywhere other than a footnote.

always attending to discovery. Like poetry, natural history attends to description, not merely drawing inspiration from nature but attempting its expression as well. Like music, natural history delights in pattern, attentive to the harmonies of how various elements act on each other. We sketch, we compose, we learn our craft by studying repositories of art, especially in field guides. Reverence is taught in our classes.

Unfortunately, interest in natural history, as in the arts in general, is waning.

A colleague, Thomas Fleischner, defines natural history as "a practice of intentional, focused attentiveness to the more-than-human world, guided by honesty and accuracy." I concur with the definition, but with the caveat that "focused attentiveness" need not merely be of a scientific nature. (And I am impressed that Tom felt it important to insist that our discipline is guided by honesty and accuracy. How many college professors teach their students to be honest anymore?)

We keep species lists during our time abroad, and the students are graded on their lists. This is where honesty can become more challenging than accuracy. The ethic here is that when your tentmate comes back from a midnight pee and reports having seen a ghost crab, you are not entitled to add the ghost crab to your own list until you get out of your sleeping bag, go out onto the beach, and identify one for yourself. It is only then that you will note how the crab tiptoes sideways through the sand, how its eyes articulate independently on extendable eyestalks, and how well camouflaged it is in the light of a gibbous moon. Only then will you discover how quickly it can bury itself in soft sand, vanishing ghostlike. In that moment will you understand how this organism earned its name, and once you understand this, you will feel connected to the ghost crab forever. This is why honesty is so important to us: not because we're trying to be morally pure, but because this is the only way to become, truly, a natural historian.

It's hard to drag yourself out of a warm sleeping bag in the middle of the night just to add a ghost crab to your species list, especially after a long day of sea kayaking and tidepooling. I have students who will do this, however, and not just because they want to earn a good grade. More important, they want to connect.

Once, when we were camping on Caleta Partida, a student got up in the middle of the night specifically to search for ghost crabs, one of her assigned *amigo* organisms. This is the best beach for them on our archipelago, and she had not been able to find them elsewhere other than for burrows and tracks in the sand. Her hunt was not successful, however, and she ultimately went back to bed with a blank spot in her list.

I took a short walk at first light the next morning, as is my wont. There are days when this is the only solitude I get—just me, my binoculars, and desert birds piping the sunrise. This can be the holiest time of day for local birds—likewise for birders.

Returning to camp after sunrise, I spotted from afar one of our students, a kid from Hawaii who was in the process of earning the expeditionary nickname "T-Dog." He sprinted across the sand and then dove headfirst, his arms stretched forward, sand spraying everywhere. The lunge having missed its prey, T-Dog began digging frantically, the way a dog goes after a gopher. He was almost to his elbows when he finally snatched the ghost he was after. I caught up to him shortly thereafter, and offered my upturned hat as a temporary detention facility. He explained that he'd learned to catch ghost crabs this way as a boy, and he wanted to find this one for the classmate who'd failed to see one during the night. We transferred the crab to an empty dry bag, took it to her tent, awakened her, and then followed along as she set the crab free just above the high tide line. Her delight was supreme; her honesty its own reward.

I could tell a thousand stories like this, and perhaps I should. Each time a student connects, there's a happy ending.

Let this be my thesis, then: *that the point of connection—naturalist to nature—is the point where natural history becomes indistinguishable from art.*

The first corollary is that this is why we welcome amateurs to the ranks of the naturalist. If the point is to connect, isn't it better if more are encouraged to do so?

Not all would agree. Harvard's E. O. Wilson, one of the foremost naturalists at work today, writes of having once been instructed that he couldn't call himself a naturalist until he had identified ten thousand species. Even if such suggestions are made tongue in cheek, attitudes like this are not only elitist, but counterproductive to natural history as a discipline. One can claim to be a naturalist the moment one realizes the importance, not to mention the difficulty, of identifying organisms more precisely than at just the genus level. That critter out there is not just a deer, it's a particular kind of deer that relates to its environment differently than any other species of deer. The naturalist notes that one rarely sees different species of deer inhabit any given habitat; one species always seems to outcompete the other in a particular landscape. (Scientists call this "Gause's law of competitive exclusion.") This is why natural historians attend to range: if I am here, then the deer here probably belong to a particular species. The art behind all this is to try to figure out why, and the why question itself becomes another point of connection.

One could argue that such taxonomic concerns are those of the scientist, going as far back as the "science" of Carl Linnaeus. I respond, thoughtfully rather than dismissively, that I don't do science. I most certainly don't design experiments to test hypotheses empirically. What I do is different: I stalk; I observe; I describe; I read; I learn. I pay particular attention to how colleagues describe the natural world, especially colleagues engaged in literary natural history. While I'm interested in reading biological naturalists such as E. O. Wilson to learn how they can inform my investigations, I personally make more connections per page reading literary natural histories written by the likes of Annie Dillard, Ellen Meloy, Terry Tempest Williams, Ann Zwinger, or Kathleen Jamie.

Those who require proofs will do themselves a favor by reading through the seminal works of the women listed in the previous paragraph—Dillard's *A Pilgrim at Tinker Creek*; Meloy's *Raven's Exile: A Season on the Green River*; Williams's *Refuge: An Unnatural History of Family and Place*; Zwinger's *A Desert Country near the Sea: A Natural History of the Cape Region of Baja California*; Jamie's *Findings: Essays on the Natural and Unnatural World*—and discover the art behind the process of natural history. Keep in mind, while you read, that writing is a reflexive process. These writers didn't connect with nature and then go write about it subsequently; rather, they connected with nature *by* writing about it. This is where nature becomes reenchanted: we hear nature telling its story, and then we pass the story along.

The better naturalists don't merely keep lists. In Baja, I encourage students to sketch in their field notes, but at the same time I discourage them from copying out of a field guide. To some students, this requirement at first seems unreasonable. "I didn't get a good enough look at that bird," one might protest. "It flew away before I could find my journal." I respond that they need to learn to get a better look next time, and keep the journals at hand. Sketching is a way to train yourself to observe more deeply, to see detail that your mind might otherwise not bother to note. The point is not to produce art; the point is to connect better with an organism or a landscape. Even scientists sketch.

Years ago a mentor in my MFA program advised us all to dabble in a second fine art while we studied writing as our primary art. The objective here was to experience how the second art would inform the first. I chose drawing, and enrolled in a handful of drawing classes over the next several years. The biggest thing I learned during that process was to spend less time looking down at my sketch pad and more time observing my subject, noting such things as the negative spaces, the play of light, and the subtleties of perspective. As luck would have it, these lessons not only informed my writing, but also informed how I go about observing the natural world. When one observes *Falco mexicanus* prowling overhead, one must become attuned to what's happening simultaneously with all the little birds close to the ground, for they are probably more acutely aware of the falcon than you are. Those birds, for whom falcon watching is a matter of life and death, create the falcon's negative space.

I recently went through a summer-long training, followed by a season's apprenticeship, to become a hawk watcher with the Golden Gate Raptor Observatory. Through it all, I was amazed at what the more senior members of my team, many of whom have more than a decade of experience counting raptors, would attend to during our six-hour shifts up on Hawk Hill. I would be frustrated by a blurry falcon swooping past because it moved too fast for me to identify the field marks I'd memorized. Was it an American kestrel or a merlin? The veterans knew the bird instantly to be a merlin. "Look at the chest," one would counsel. "Notice how robust it is. Kestrels are such flimsy things." These same artists can tell a sharp-shinned hawk from a Cooper's hawk just by how it handles itself in a breeze, and can differentiate between a red-shouldered hawk and a red-tailed hawk at great distance merely by how it flaps its wings, the former being much "flappier" to the trained eye than the latter, which seems relatively stiff in the carpals. This is an art, not a science, regardless of how much citizen science we accomplish while practicing the art of identifying hawks.

Natural history has always leaned toward the observational rather than the analytical. This makes it fundamentally sensuous. When something is sensuous, aesthetic is involved, and when aesthetic is involved, we move into the arts. This begins to happen the moment observation is translated into description.

By way of a second proof, I offer an explication of a short passage from Gilbert White's *The Natural History of Selborne*:

> In the centre of this grove there stood an oak, which, though shapely and tall on the whole, bulged out into a large excrescence about the middle of the stem. On this a pair of ravens have fixed their residence for such a series of years, that the oak was distinguished by the title of the Raven Tree. (letter 2)

Note how White goes beyond the merely empirical in his description. The tree itself is "shapely" on the whole, but "bulged out" into something the author terms an "excrescence," which marks it not only as an abnormality, but as something unattractive. These are aesthetic judgments based on values about how healthy oaks should appeal to the senses. He follows this up with a bit of cultural layering where his readers learn that this oak was "distinguished" by having been conferred with a proper name, Raven Tree.

The art here exists on two levels. The observations themselves are filtered through cultural aesthetics regarding how a proper oak tree ought to appear, as well as how a particular specimen of oak appeared through the lens of local culture. Then, the description of those observations becomes artistic on its own, not only because of the eloquence of the writing, but because this passage successfully introduces a short, tragic narrative about the ultimate demise of the oak and its raven occupants.[2]

It would be errant to dismiss Gilbert White as a throwback from the early Enlightenment, a parson-naturalist whose approach has long since been transcended in favor of flavorless scientific description. Tedious description that amounts to mere taxonomy shouldn't be confused with natural history per se. Taxonomy has its place—stoking the fire within which natural history is forged—but when natural history becomes artless it loses its power entirely. This is one of the reasons it's been in decline. At a fundamental level, natural historians must be storytellers.

My students experience Baja's natural history as a narrative in which they are taking part. The most accessible part of that narrative begins with European colonizers, continues through early explorers, is translated by nature writers and academics, and has been picked up by previous expeditions from the university they attend. My students study the earlier natural histories not only in order to learn about the ecologies they will soon experience but also to learn where they themselves fit in the process of discovering, describing, and evoking Baja's ecosystems. The moment they begin the process of keeping field notes, they assume creative roles in moving Baja's natural history narrative forward, much in the same way that every person who walks across a meadow is part of establishing a trail. The first to pass creates the trail, others widen it, others maintain it by keeping to it; some create new shortcuts, the results being what the builders of officially sanctioned trails begrudgingly call "social trails." Sooner or later, someone erects signposts.

Attending to natural history can be a fundamentally creative process. Within that process there is room for personal discovery, as when a twitcher adds a new bird to a life list, and for discoveries that expand the realm of human knowledge, as when a naturalist such as Nabokov describes a butterfly species that has never before been cataloged.

2. The Raven Tree is cut down during the nesting season, and the noble raven dam, refusing to flee her nest, perishes when the oak crashes to the ground "though her parental affection deserved a better fate."

An excerpt from my Baja field notes from the Caleta Partida encampment of the 2011 expedition:

> The ghost crabs were particularly active outside my tent last night, and the gibbous moon seemed particularly bright. I had to crawl out of the tent at one point and rig my windbreaker as a moonshade. Despite the moonlight, I couldn't tell what the ghost crabs were feeding on. I had always assumed that they were scavengers and/or detritivores, but there was clearly some predatory stalking/charging/grabbing behavior going on by moonlight. There was also a great deal of sand being thrown around. I assume that these later behaviors are related to burrowing, but there in my tent, lying on my stomach, my vantage was too low to see the actual burrows.

In my rambling way, the above musings articulate the question of what sand crabs prey on in this particular locality, which could be—but is not necessarily—a scientific question. It is also a nature writer's question, calling to mind Nabokov's dictum that a writer should have the precision of a poet and the imagination of a scientist.

For the scientist, perhaps the most empirical way to determine an answer would be to capture a few, dissect them, and examine their digestive tracks for evidence of recent feeding. Let's assume, for the moment, that this turned out not to be a successful strategy because whatever we found in there was too ground up to be identifiable, at least short of expensive laboratory analysis. What next? As naturalists, here on an island without microscopes or spectrometers, how would we determine what these crabs are eating? It will do us no good to search the Internet, not only because we don't have Internet access on the island but also because most sites that describe ghost crab natural history, such as E. O. Wilson's *Encyclopedia of Life*, will tell us merely that the ghost crab is an omnivore. Even the terrarium sites aren't much help, advising us merely that to keep ghost crabs healthy we should avoid too much dietary repetition.

Think for a moment of how we might go about solving this mystery. Should we employ night-vision optics? Infrared photography? Fine-mesh collecting nets? Black lights? Should we schedule our next trip to this beach to coincide with a full moon so that we might see better? Should we devise an observation platform under which the crabs might hunt so that we are looking down on them from a better vantage point? Perhaps if I just pitch my tent lower on the beach during next year's expedition . . .

Think also about the negative space, what we don't know about the behavior I've described. Is this a nightly behavior? Is the behavior specific to this locale, or do ghost crabs behave this way throughout their range? Does the behavior only take place during certain seasons, certain tidal phases, at certain temperatures or at certain points in the moon cycle? Is wind a factor? Were the crabs being opportunistic because of some sort of hatch on the beach, or do they regularly eat whatever they were preying on when I made my initial observation? Could I have confused some sort of mating ritual or territorial defensiveness for predatory behavior? Has anyone studied this before? Is there an answer contained in the literature from the 1920s that hasn't yet been cataloged on the Internet?

The question of value suddenly raises its head. Solving the mystery of the ghost crab diet on Caleta Partida under a gibbous moon in early spring is probably not going to win me a Nobel Prize, nor will it lead to the cure of a major disease. It fact, it probably won't even qualify a scholar for tenure, at least not at my university. It's doubtful that the National Science Foundation will be interested in funding this study, and it's entirely possible that once I write up my results I'll have trouble finding a natural history journal that will consider the paper important enough to publish. Because ghost crab populations are not threatened or endangered, no important conservation decisions are likely to be impacted.

We have arrived at the cusp of natural history as art. The decision to proceed with the investigation, merely to get to know the organism and its ecology better, is not dissimilar to the sorts of decisions made by practitioners of the arts. It's the banjo player pushing himself to master a new finger roll, or the mandolin player teaching herself to crosspick. As a natural historian I realize that I will never really understand this beach fully until I understand the behavior I witnessed that moonlit evening. All I need to do, ultimately, is make an accurate observation, but crafting an approach to do so will require creativity, originality, and a fair amount of study. And the better I am at my craft, the greater my chances of success.

For my own part, I delight in overlaps between the arts and the sciences, especially considering the creativity it often takes to find answers, however tentative, to natural history questions. This would work even when we're combining the imagination of poets with the precision of scientists, rather than vice versa.

Consider another journal excerpt written again on Caleta Partida, but a year later, in 2012:

We are sitting on the sand spit at Caleta Partida, crammed under two shade tarps. A reddish egret serves as our sole source of entertainment as it hunts the shallows, wings spread, chasing down its supper of crabs. Twice now we've seen it fold its wings and run out of the water in order to defecate on the beach before returning immediately to its hunt. This is not a behavior I've ever witnessed before, nor one about which I've ever read. I've asked the students sharing my shade what they think, and there's a great deal of speculation/hypothesizing going on, the prevailing opinion being that it doesn't want to contaminate its food source, possibly concerned about spreading disease or parasites. Others, myself included, think that the behavior has more to do with hunting success (not alerting prey to the predator's presence), while R. hypothesizes that the behavior might be counterproductive since the guano could serve to attract prey. The reddish egret repeats the behavior a third time while I'm writing this, right after I've pointed out to my young colleagues that we really don't know whether all reddish egrets behave this way, or whether we're observing the world's only sanitation-conscious specimen of *Egretta rufescens*. This throws a momentary wrench into the wheels of our science, but a new round of hypothesizing begins despite a serious lack of data. The general consensus seems to be that if we're lucky enough to find another reddish egret, we'll observe the same behavior.

On my return to campus, I conducted a literature search on reddish egret defecation, and came up empty. However, when I expanded the search to other ardeids (egrets and herons), to my amazement I found three papers, written in 1972, 1978, and 1980, that had noted this same behavior in great blue herons, a close-enough relative of the reddish egret. Unfortunately, there was no strong consensus between the papers, and while it was theorized that the behavior may be implicated in parasite or disease prevention, it was also suggested that it might be a measure for reducing prey avoidance.

In the last of these papers, R. D. Bayer's "Social Differences in Defecation Behavior of Great Blue Herons," the author employed a systematic, scientific approach to the question of why some herons defecated in the water while others left the water first. Bayer observed herons for one thousand hours over a six-year period on the Oregon coast, differentiating between territorial and nonterritorial birds. He noted a statistically significant pattern that the nonterritorial herons tended to defecate in the water immediately before leaving that area to hunt elsewhere, while the territorial herons tended to leave the water, defecate, and then return to the same water to continue their hunt. In essence, a bird that still wanted to hunt in its home waters tended not to empty its bowels there.

By reading Bayer I came to understand more fully how the sciences function differently from the arts. Were you to compare the field notes of a naturalist such as Bayer and one such as me, you would immediately note the difference of approach. Bayer could not have written his paper without constantly noting patterns of behaviors of territorial and nonterritorial herons alike, painstakingly recording the circumstances every time defecation occurred. His modus operandi is to document repetition, looking for patterns that become statistically significant. I, on the other hand, am less interested in repetition, more in what is novel and unique.

Here is the type of observation more likely to be made in my own field notes, this one composed at Caleta Partida during the 2013 expedition:

> We woke up to discover a juvenile mobula on the beach, flapping feebly as if to climb completely out of the water. Its disk width no more than 500 mm. [Not measured.] The smallest mobula I've ever seen. No signs apparent of disease or injury—I ask myself whether it separated from its shoal due to exhaustion. Could it be that they were moving too quickly through the night for this little one to keep up? Dr. Awesome lifted it gently and pushed it out into deeper water, but it circled back around and once again stranded itself at the water's edge, giving every indication that it had not beached itself accidentally. We leave it alone, and it is just close enough to where we are cooking breakfast that the gulls will not venture in to pluck out its eyes. After breakfast, when I head down to the water's edge to rinse my dishes, the mobula has vanished.

For me, the significance of this event is its mystery rather than any scientific certitudes I might be led to. The largest fact my observations tend to reveal is how little we know of how the natural world functions, a fact that should lead us to interact with nature in a spirit of humility. The mobula ray is an organism about which Wikipedia says, "Despite their size, little is known about this genus, much of it being from anecdotal accounts."[3] I can do little to ameliorate this situation aside from adding yet another anecdotal account to the record, one that tends to highlight the mystery surrounding this organism.

This simple, unadorned sand spit between two islands continues to be a place of discovery for me even though I have camped there now on at least a dozen separate occasions. Perhaps the most spectacular of these discoveries happened a few years back when we were launching the kayaks. We had already schlepped most of the boats down the beach, and I was part of a ten-person

---

3. "Mobula," Wikipedia, accessed February 23, 2018, https://en.wikipedia.org/wiki/Mobula.

crew portaging the doubles. We put one person each on bow and stern, and then assigned four to a cockpit, two on each side. I was handling the starboard side of the forward cockpit, working in tandem with a student who stood behind me as we lifted the boat. This boat was heavy, as I recall, and our feet sank deeply into the sand. We took a few steps forward and then the student behind me shrieked, jumping away from the boat. She had just stepped on a tiger snake eel, *Myrichthys maculosus*.

When you see a tiger snake eel underwater it resembles a medium-large snake the size of a full-grown Baja rattler, its skin the color of the sand other than for dark, round spots that always appear slightly blurry. Unlike the moray eel, which tends to hunt in rocky crevices, the tiger snake eel tends to hunt out in the open sand. But it tends to do this underwater, not up on the beach.

This eel was a good ten meters away from the water's edge.

The team having dropped the kayak, I grabbed a paddle and attempted to herd the eel toward the water. But it would have none of this. Instead, mouth opened wide in a great display of teeth, it tucked its tail into the dry sand and began to burrow backward. Within seconds, it had vanished, closing its mouth at the last moment as it backed underneath the sand. When I wrote about this later, I honestly, accurately, recorded the fact that it was the damnedest thing I ever saw.

We all stood there, slack-jawed, and I asked Manuelito whether he'd ever seen such a thing. He thought about this for a moment before responding, *"Yo creo que no,"*[4] and then adding, "Never!"

The more I think about this event, the more mysterious it becomes, beginning with the question of why a snake eel was so far out of the water in broad daylight. Preying on ghost crabs? And how had this poor student managed to step on it when I had not, even though I was walking directly in front of her only inches away? Had this eel been startled enough to pop out of a ghost crab burrow? If it was startled, why didn't it just burrow deeper, since we know from experience it had this ability?

My best answer is to admit, humbly, that I have no idea. If anyone else has ever seen a tiger snake eel, alive, hanging out during daylight hours on a beach in dry sand, please write me—my email address is easily found on the Santa Clara University website. Send photos if you've got them.

Lest you conclude that Caleta Partida is some sort of haunted sand spit, I hasten to add that not all my novel experiences here have been inscrutable. Once, at low tide, I was wading in the sand channel between the two spits, idly contemplating how long the two islands had been separated. It was almost slack low tide, the water was especially warm, and at its deepest level it just covered

---

4. Roughly translated: "I do not believe so."

the tops of my knees. I was wearing flip-flops, board shorts, a long-sleeved nylon shirt, and a broad-brimmed hat. My binoculars hung loosely around my neck.

Just downstream I noticed a large fish boil, at least a hundred fish breaking the water at once to escape whatever predator was attacking them from below. This was a perfect situation for roosterfish, so I waded toward the boil, which at the same time was moving toward me. *What a shame,* I thought to myself, *not to have a proper fly rod handy.*

The fish boiled again, and I was not the only above-water predator to notice it this time. A squadron of nearby pelicans dove into the water not thirty meters away, driving the prey fish in my direction. Chaos broke out, and dozens of fish immediately crashed into my shins, not hard enough to cause injury but certainly hard enough create anxiety.

I was suddenly in the middle of a feeding frenzy, a place where humans, even naturalists, tend not to feel comfortable. Fish were now striking my legs from all sides, and one leaped from the water, spanking my hip with its tail. Gulls and terns soon joined the pelicans, mounting an earsplitting cacophony as they demanded to be sated, guano dropping everywhere. The splashing of nearby birds had completely soaked my shirt.

It dawned on me, somewhat slowly, that my safety here was in no way guaranteed. I stopped moving and decided to keep my head down, focusing on the fish as they continued to bang into my legs. I covered my crotch protectively with my hands, but this proved to be an unnecessary precaution.

Within thirty seconds, it was all over; calm was restored, albeit a calm with a manic grin. I turned back toward camp, spotting Garambullo on a beach nearby. He placed his fist, thumb down, on the top of his head, the kayaker/diver's signal asking whether I was okay. Lacking a signal for "I'm exulted," I signaled back the affirmative.

For the first time in my life, I knew the feel of frenzy from the inside.

What the arts add to natural history is the articulation of place. One doesn't get this from science, where documenting repetition takes precedence, and rightfully so. Where science requires data to fuel its fires, the arts can be open to such tools as metaphor to describe place as deeply as Wordsworth described the Lake District, Thoreau described Walden Pond, and Gilbert White described the village of Selborne. While science can tell me a great deal about places like Caleta Partida, it will never, alone, be able to capture the placeness of the Cove of Departure, at least not the way I have attempted to do so in this makeshift essay. (And science will never tell you that *Lepus insularis* look like bunnies that joined a motorcycle gang.) But our mistake at times, and of this I am as guilty as my scientist friends, is treating the arts and the sciences too much as unlike things, forgetting that when it comes to natural history, the arts and the sciences are equally delighted in discovering a butterfly.

Let us give the last word, then, to Nabokov, who succeeded in both art and science:

> Dark pictures, thrones, the stones that pilgrims kiss,
> poems that take a thousand years to die
> but ape the immortality of this
> red label on a little butterfly.

# 8

# *Death and Poetry in the Sand Dunes*

The desert rewards those who live simply, even if
it does not reward them with much.

ANDROMEDA ROMANO-LAX, *Searching for*
*Steinbeck's Sea of Cortez*, 2002

All teachers have peeves. Even me.

One of my peeves gets triggered when the word "just" is included in the description of an organism, as in "It's just a turkey vulture."

I try not to scold. Rather, I make the professorial turn, raising my binoculars, examining the bird as carefully as if it were a dark morph *Buteo regalis*, and then respond with something like, "Ah, *Cathartes aura*—an adult."

Then I wait. The better students might ask to be reminded how to differentiate adults from juveniles. At that point I might explain that when *Cathartes aura* becomes sexually mature, somewhere around the age of four, its bill turns from a drab gray to a gleaming white. *See, the bird appears to have a headlight when flying head-on toward us. And have you noticed the red coloration of the featherless head? Take another look. You won't see the red on a juvenile.*

I like "*Cathartes aura*," a name that translates "purifying breeze." These birds have a tough job, and are particularly good at what they do. They teeter when they fly, not so much because they're unstable but because they generally fly low enough and slow enough to take advantage of their incredible sense of smell. They rule the turbulence down low where eagles and falcons haven't got bragging rights.

March is a great time to watch vultures. Down here in Baja, it's the season of love. Spring birders who pay attention to *C. aura* sometimes get to observe follow flights where a pair bonds with its territory in an aerial version of follow-the-leader. On a good day, the following bird mirrors every turn, twist, and flap of the bird ahead.

If you're particularly attentive, you can tell the female turkey vulture from the male because she's slightly larger. And she's usually the one in front. You can ascribe gender even more certainly if the one in the back ever attempts to dive onto the one in front in a copulatory manner, in which case the one in the back is most certainly male. Be forewarned, however, that you may have to watch the follow flight for several hours before such things happen. But by then you'll know for certain that they're not "just" turkey vultures.

Barring something as major as a volcanic eruption, Expedition 7 will become the fifth expedition to circumnavigate the entire archipelago.

It is our final full day on the island, the most challenging day for those expeditions fortunate enough to circumnavigate. On this day we paddle a full eighteen kilometers, not because I wanted to design a long slog into the program, but rather because there are no closer beaches on which we can camp. Topography dictates this challenge: once we head south from the cove of departure, Caleta Partida, it's Playa Bonanza or bust.

On calm days, such as today, we are able to enter a series of sea caves and caverns, spooky places where crabs coexist with bats, where waves actually echo, and where the Sea of Cortez sometimes sighs. But each cavern entails at least a fifteen-minute delay, so I'm reluctant to explore too many of them. Otherwise, it's all cliffs and wash rocks. Along this stretch paddlers can expect osprey high above, and a constant view of fish below in water so deeply blue it's hard to understand how it can be both colorful and clear at the same time.

Halfway through the paddle we set an anchor and raft the boats in the shadow of two colossal monoliths called, simply, "the Stacks." They stand together like Hyperion and Theia, monuments to the passing seasons, shoulders square but both heads cocked toward the cliffs from which they were birthed. In all but the worst conditions we can paddle the narrow gap between the two landmarks, but for now shade is more precious than adventure. Taking advantage of the respite, we pull out gringo food for the first time this trip—peanut butter and jelly sandwiches that we assembled right after breakfast—and I encourage the students to swim a bit to stretch their legs and tend to their bladders. My PB and J disappears quickly, and I force myself to savor a crisp apple slowly.

There is little more to report about this day's paddle: just south of the Stacks a noisy shoal of mobula rays feeds at the surface but resists my attempts to herd it toward the group; an almost constant cloud cover keeps us cool, and a humpback whale breeches in the distance. It might have been a perfect paddle had not the wind gods sent a southerly breeze along right at the point where we normally receive the blessed assistance of a northerly. This adds significantly to the level of buttocks fatigue we all suffer throughout the last five kilometers. Curiously, my left cheek has the best of it, holding up nicely while the starboard buttock feels as if I'd begun the day with a tetanus booster. Not for the first time today I wish I was paddling my own boat, the darling yak back in Sausalito, which is sooooooo much less painful after a fourth hour in the saddle.

Our destination finally materializes. A steep, white-sand beach forming a crescent nearly four kilometers long, backed by vegetated sand dunes topped with the yellow of acacia blooms. We will camp on the southern end of the crescent where the dunes flatten out enough to accommodate our dozen tents. Playa Bonanza ought to be called "Playa Milagro," because it's a miracle no one ever built a resort here. There was a plan, of course, but the Nature Conservancy was miraculously able to thwart it.

The last kilometer of our paddle takes the longest, but we get there. Young or old, we'd all love just to collapse on the beach for a while, but instead we form up into three teams: one to haul the boats up the steep, shelly beach that happens to be the steepest beach of the entire trip; another to put up some shade; and a third to make a refreshing salad. Cheered by our industry, Dr. Awesome and I invite the expeditioners to join us on a late-afternoon stroll in search of loggerhead shrikes, which normally rule the roost in the sand dunes behind this camp.

All but two of our party decline the invitation, wisely citing the need to attend to the penultimate writing prompt, which asks them to describe a section of the intertidal zone in such a way that they could return to this beach ten years from now and determine, on consulting their field notes, whether the ecosystem was more or less healthy[1] than before. Word on the beach is that this exercise serves as something of a final exam for the course. The four of us more

---

1. Dr. Awesome, one of them, objects to the metaphor of ecosystem health, not only because it's a metaphor but also because of the difficulty of measuring it empirically. When I ask, "But what about biodiversity?" Dr. Awesome protests that diversity is not an adequate measure of health. Part of me wants to reply, "Well it's a good start," but I remain silent on this point. One should never argue with a doctor named "Awesome."

concerned about birds than exams grab our binoculars, trade our sandals for sturdy footwear, and proceed up into the dunes.

The first bird we see, as luck has it, is a loggerhead shrike. A male barely taller than my clenched fist, it perches atop a corpulent cardon cactus with a view in all directions. Distinctly three-toned—black, white, and gray—it strikes a raptorial pose, as if warning passersby not to call it "passerine."

They call these masked beasts "butcher birds" over in the UK, a tribute to their predatory nature. In Baja, shrikes will kill lizards, large insects, small birds, and even kangaroo rats. Lacking the talons of a raptor, they've learned to impale their prey on mesquite thorns and cactus spines, often storing their kills conspicuously in a macabre cache contrived to display hunting prowess. I suppose it's no different from the stuffed moose heads mounted over the mantels of *Homo sapiens* (except for the fact that *Lanius ludovicianus* still gets to eat his trophies). Regardless, my plan throughout this hike was to be attentive to the thorns, looking for impaled lizards ornamenting the mesquites.

During the past year I have been attempting, with inconsistent success, to do my birding by ear as much as possible. This is especially difficult when hiking with college students, whose penchant for chattering is more pronounced in the wild than in the classroom. Better to hear, I separate myself from the group a bit. I am almost immediately befuddled by a soft bleating noise, something sounding distinctly ungulate, goatlike, and yet so quiet . . .

Signaling to my companions that I might have something, I proceed in the direction of the bleats, winding my way through the vegetated sand dune, its widely spaced shrubbery seldom exceeding two meters' height. Moving quietly and listening intently, I notice how the alleyways of sand between shrubs are crisscrossed by the parenthetical trails of snakes. Were snakes fleeing the source of this noise, or am I following snakes toward it?

I've been fooled often enough by desert resonance to know to suspend judgment regarding the noise I was trailing. While it seemed clearly goatish, it also seemed small, perhaps even tiny in timbre. Too soft for a goat? Could some unknown-to-me reptile make such a noise?

I am surprised by a guttural hiss off to my left, and I instinctively step away. Peering through underbrush, not daring to breathe, I spot something big and black hopping grotesquely. It takes a moment before I recognize *Cathartes aura*, a juvenile, but I instantly realize that this couldn't have been the source of the bleats; turkey vultures don't have vocal organs, and can only hiss. Within moments I notice a second and a third—finally counting six of them—hopping about clumsily in the vicinity of what could only be a carcass. Then I hear the bleat again, coming now from my right.

I see it the moment I glance away from the vultures: a kid goat. Black and white, looking exceptionally clean, exceptionally tiny, certainly no more than a couple weeks old, its head not yet as high as the heads of the vultures feeding on its mother. In between bleats, the kid would nibble pathetically on the tips of a leafless limber bush, perhaps more to notify me of its hunger than to find sustenance. It clearly wanted to be cared for.

My companions join me at this point, and we slowly deduce what has taken place. A section of old fishing net woven of transparent monofilament had been strung across a gap between plants, apparently on purpose. We are within a ten-minute walk to a fishing shack on the island's southern coast, and we conclude that the fishermen must have designed this as a way of using worn-out gear to ensnare feral goats. A clever, low-tech way to supplement a diet of fish.

The kid appears healthy, and while it seems desirous of our companionship, it becomes skittish whenever we approach closer than ten meters, bounding away on thin, stiff legs that appear to have been constructed of spring steel.

The vultures withdraw begrudgingly, staying close enough to indicate their intent to return to this lovely fresh carcass the moment the intruding bird-watchers remember to mind their own business. We urge the kid to follow us, but it is reluctant to abandon its mother's remains. The tragedy of this situation is lost on no one: an unweaned animal watching vultures consume its mother, her udder still full.

At moments like this students expect faculty to provide wise counsel, but I have nothing particularly astute to offer. The Baja I so often romanticize in the classroom has shown its other side, the ugly one where scarcity, death, and poverty dominate the narrative.

We haven't got the means to put this animal out of its forthcoming misery; it's the first time in all my years exploring Baja I wished I had a gun handy, and I say as much to Dr. Awesome, whose voice cracks in agreement. Unable to euthanize the animal, we do the next best thing, hiking toward the fishing shacks to notify the fisherman where they might find some *cabrito* if they act quickly enough to get it before the vultures do. On our way there we run into Manuelito, who has come from our encampment to invite the fishermen over tomorrow morning to take our leftover fruit and vegetables before we leave the island. There isn't much—onions, a few mangoes, a half kilo of limes, a pineapple, and two avocados—but it will be greatly appreciated in the fishing camp. Manuelito agrees to deliver the message about the goat as well.

We return to camp silently.

Later, right before dinner, Manuelito pulls me aside and tells me that the fishermen plan to take the kid back to La Paz in a few days. It will be consumed in a month or two, once it has grown enough to make the effort of butchering it worthwhile. I thank him for this information, feeling strangely grateful that the vultures didn't get it.

I will meet these fishermen the following day when they beach their panga near our camp kitchen shortly after sunrise. Both are in their late sixties, but seem far older given the effects of so many years in the sun. The more widely they smile, the older they look. They will be wearing cheap, polyurethane bib pants, yellow, outfits that will most certainly become uncomfortable in the heat of day. Their heads will be hatless.

It was men such as these who originally introduced goats to the island, unconcerned at that point about the environmental havoc such animals might wreak. Goats provide food, and food is good. Why can life not be this simple?

If Mexico has taught me anything, it has been the necessity of transcending environmental self-righteousness. Those to whom food comes easily should be slow to critique those who must kill their meals. I need to be aware that I would probably weigh the environmental consequences of introducing goats to an island ecosystem differently had I ever lived the life of an artisanal fisherman. In this case, a relatively small initial investment resulted in a lifetime source of alternative protein. The goats virtually took care of themselves, proliferating in an ecosystem where they had no predators, providing sustenance without needing to be tended by humans. String up a few old fishing nets, and they even catch themselves.

There are ongoing campaigns to eradicate feral goats and cats on Isla Espíritu Santo, and these programs are environmentally important. But it's equally important to realize that there are no villains associated with how these animals originally came to inhabit the archipelago.

The southerly breeze dies at sunset.

Our final night on the island concludes with an after-dark poetry slam held back in the sand dunes. Even without the breeze, it's chilly enough that we all wear windbreakers. As if there was a general consultation about appropriate uniform, all the females have donned black yoga tights in which their legs can disappear in the darkness. My right buttock, still tender from the long paddle we completed so many hours ago, is beginning to stiffen, and as we trudge up the dune in the dark I scold myself for not having stretched at some point. I've instructed the Flame Queen, who this year is male for the first time, to set up the poetry altar far enough back from the water that the waves won't make it difficult to hear the poets. He has chosen a hollow between two dunes in order to protect us from wind that no longer blows. The protectiveness of the hollow feels good, regardless, for we're all bone weary after the long paddle.

My syllabus stipulates that participation in the poetry slam has no bearing on student grades. It is, rather, a point of honor. Contestants are permitted to recite poetry written by others, but the great majority read their own compositions, which tend to split evenly between rap and doggerel. Bless them all. The timid get away with a quick haiku, and sometimes these are the best poems entered even though they have no chance of winning. There's always a poem or two about the experience of using "Paco," the prodigious porta-potty with panoramic views, but otherwise the competition tends to be worthy.

The guides team up with the TAs to form a panel of judges. Last year they blundered inexcusably by awarding me the prize, so tonight, for the first time in our seven-expedition history, there's a defending champion with whom to contend.

The Flame Queen has outdone himself this year, constructing a knee-high double arch weaved of twigs and lined with shells, bits of coral, and the magnificent skull of a frigatebird. And the candles, of course, that have comprised our "campfire" all week. We gather around the structure tight, shoulder to shoulder, every one of us wondering how the time has passed so quickly. Everyone takes a seat, and the hush lends the dune a churchy feel once the candles are lit.

I instinctively know that the doggerel I've composed this time won't be competitive. It lacks the sentimentality of last year's poem, and kayak guides will only vote for the sentimental or the crude, nothing in between. I like the poem anyway, it corrects a mistake I may have made on previous expeditions. And it should be perfect for candlelight with its ABXB rhyme scheme.

## Little Gray Birds

No matter how often I come here
There's always a new bird to learn
Not hawks, not boobies, not frigatebirds
Not a trophy for which one might yearn.

These days it's the little birds, little gray birds,
That I add to my lifelong list
Birds with less color than orioles
But birds whose songs are hard to resist.

My new bird this trip is a mouthful
"Black-throated gray warbler" its name

But it probably isn't as new as I think
And for that goof I must take the blame.

I most certainly must have seen one before
When my birding was still somewhat narrow
In less accurate days I probably thought
I was seeing a black-throated sparrow.

What does it matter, one might ask,
To tell look-alike birds from each other?
They're both little peckers that won't hold still
Why should anyone bother?

I don't have answers for questions like that
I can only report what I see
That a warbler's a bird with a song in its heart
A song sung sweetly for thee.

The final writing prompt, one attended to during the travel day back to campus, asks the students to reflect on what they've learned. I don't ask them to compose essays; bullet points are fine. If ever there's a time in a collegiate career to make a list, this is it.

I myself have learned a great deal from reading these lists. For example, I've learned that sand can be considered a condiment, that brittle stars are not as brittle as they're made out to be, and that words such as "awesome" and "amazing" can be insufficient descriptors. Indeed, according to expeditionary field notes, we sometimes experience sunsets that are "beyond awesome" and sunrises that are "beyond amazing."

There are years when I learn more than the students, which is a good thing because a college professor can never know enough. On one particular day during expedition 7, a day when I was keeping track, I was asked questions about the ignimbrite geological strata of the island, I was asked to identify the lower jaw of a puffer fish found on the beach, I was asked to diagnose a faulty paddling stroke, I was asked the best Cointreau-to-tequila ratio for margaritas, I was asked the best "natural" way to deal with constipation, I was asked how to access the battery compartment on an LED headlamp, I was asked the name of the constellation between Pleiades and Orion, and I was asked whether I thought Stanford had a chance of making the Final Four.

A few items from my most recent "What I Learned" list:

- A hand lens is not just for examining the stamens of wildflowers. This year, as the result of a conversation with a student who was intrigued by Baja's sand, I've been using my loupe to get better acquainted with sand diversity. I've learned that the sand on one beach can be drastically different than the sand on the next beach, even on the same island. This beach is fine-grained, the next is course and contains far more ground-up shell material. The southern beaches are whiter than the northern beaches even though the northern sand contains so much quartz that it sparkles in the sunlight. The sand spit at Caleta Partida seems to contain a higher percentage of biogenic sand, with numerous tusk-shaped calcareous fragments that I could not identify. Scaphopoda?
- I've learned that all who teach natural history must realize how consistently we will be wrong despite efforts to be accurate and honest. I assured this class that they would hear a thousand canyon wrens for every one they saw. On our first hike many of the students heard a canyon wren for the first time. Despite what they'd been told in the classroom, they looked and craned as the wren's song cascaded down. Then, the damned thing stopped singing and flew to the other side of the canyon in full view of the class.
- I learned a bit more about the ephemerality of time in an island environment. None of the students this year wore watches. It was explained to me that "in real life" they generally consulted their smartphones to determine the time of day. By monitoring the temporal disorientation of my unplugged duckies, I learned that today's college students, by and large, have no concept of how time relates to the position of the sun. One day we got up, made breakfast, ate, broke camp, kayaked eight kilometers, and then set up the next camp before noon. During lunch I suggested that we wait until 1:00 to go snorkeling, and the students were dumbfounded, thinking that it must have been late afternoon at that point. Several students, in their "What I Learned" reflection, said something to the effect that "I learned that I might actually be a morning person."
- I've learned a new meaning for "climate change." It's when you stop wondering *when* the drought will end, and start wondering *whether* it will end.
- I've learned that one of the best ways to make new discoveries is to train new eyes. After dinner one of the students asked whether moray eels ever have spots. He'd been walking along the beach, equipped with only his LED headlamp, and in the shallows had seen a number of spotted eels within a few meters of the water's edge. Dr. Awesome and I hastened to

accompany the student to identify these mystery eels, and within a couple hundred meters of beach had identified six spotted morays patrolling the littoral, apparently hunting. I was particularly dumbfounded at this discovery, having camped on this very beach at least a dozen nights previously. But I'd probably never noticed these eels because after dinner I've pretty much stopped exploring for the day. This student, bless him, had not switched off his exploratory mode, and was aptly rewarded.

- I've learned that questions that may at first seem impertinent are sometimes quite genuine. I earn a living convincing people in their twenties that it's a good thing to know what semipalmated plovers and semipalmated sandpipers have in common, while contemporary culture teaches them that all knowledge generated prior to the founding of Google is, at best, suspect. When the modern student learns that "semipalmated" means semiwebbed, a reference to the feet of some wading birds, she is bound to ask, "Why don't they just say that?" This sort of question almost always deserves an answer. And a chuckle.

- I've yet again discovered that learning opportunities tend to arise when you least expect them. While riding the vans to our campsite in the Sierra de la Laguna, one of the students requested we turn on the radio, and the entire crew was incredulous to hear that no radio stations reached this far into the mountains. We had to switch on the radio and scan the entire broadcast spectrum before they would believe. Meanwhile, as we traveled a dusty, unpaved road devoid of electrical lines, we passed ranchero after ranchero not yet connected to the electrical grid. Even if the broadcast were available, there'd be no one out here listening.

- I've also come to realize that, when done correctly, natural history can be transformational. Whenever a naturalist accurately describes a landscape, or perhaps even an organism, she has in some fundamental way redescribed herself. When Steinbeck reflected on Darwin's observation that "all nature seemed sparkling with life," he concluded that it was actually Darwin who was sparkling. All adroit natural historians understand this: when one describes a landscape, one ultimately defines one's relationship to that landscape. The subject becomes irretrievably subjective once the naturalist realizes "I'm part of this."

I go to the desert to hear my heart beating. If I listen closely enough, its rhythm is echoed in wingbeats, waves, wildness. There are times, however, where all I hear is the discourse of heat.

We bring our own noises to this place: pen scratches paper; sandals flip-flop through the sand. Students can sometimes be heard, insisting to be taught.

There is noise here, always. Yes, there are days when you can hear lizards scurry across sand, but more often we listen to the wind being pierced by thorns.

Before a rain shower, they say you can hear the mesquite beg for droplets. Afterward, they say you can actually hear the bloom of the flowers. Wings flap, tails twitch, lizards bob up and down. The acacia calls to the bees.

But we always return to campus.

The transition back to civilization inevitably jars the senses. We spend the night at a funky backpackers' hotel in La Paz, the place with the Model T pickup in the courtyard, its wheels having fallen off years ago. A mangy stuffed monkey wearing a weathered fedora sits in the driver's seat, its arms raised. The walls are festooned with antique flatirons, harpoons, glass fishing floats, rusty old rifles, whale vertebrae, stirrups, spurs, skulls, and a branding iron. Last year, kittens prowled the paved courtyard; this year they've been replaced by a rooster, its spurs unclipped. Although pitifully small, it thinks itself the largest bird in Baja. I have no idea what color it is—perhaps a greenish orange—and I'm too close to a shower to care. We called ahead from the outfitter's base to ask the patron to turn on the boiler so we'll have hot water. This will be my first shower since leaving California, and I already know it will be glorious.

It always seems to take longer to get home than it took to get out here. We return to campus a good sixteen hours after the rooster goes off. The students turn in their field journals when they alight from the bus, and hugs are distributed generously in the dark.

Dr. Awesome has arranged to sleep on the couch in my dorm apartment tonight, and we drag our luggage dormward together: dirty laundry, sandy field guides that feel significantly heavier than when we departed, filthy binoculars, my broken dive mask, and the sandals my colleague had to duct-tape together on day 3. The rifle case protecting carbon-fiber paddles. Sixteen field journals within which a great deal of ink has been poured by budding naturalists.

There is no one in the lobby; an elevator awaits. We enter it, not bothering to drop our luggage, and face the door as it closes. We wait. We wait some more, still holding heavy luggage. After almost a minute, Dr. Awesome says, "It seems slow."

I look at the control panel; we are still on the lobby level. Quietly, I announce, "We forgot to push the button."

We laugh like gulls at a grunion run, and I drop the rifle case in the process. We bump fists, still laughing, and realize that a significant part of us is still back on the island.

# Tailwind

Pilgrimages seem to be almost instinctive, or at least
derived from behaviors now so ingrained in our species that it's
difficult to distinguish between genetic and social origins.

JOHN JANOVY, *Vermilion Sea: A Naturalist's Journey
in Baja California*, 1992

An expedition has its own life, and thus tends not to end as gracefully as a class. My class, ENVS 142, Writing Natural History, is over the moment the registrar posts the grades. But closure is not so easy for the expedition itself. To finish an expedition properly, ritual is required. Students have their own rituals, I suspect, and I have mine. My ritual takes place on water.

I slide my neoprene shorts over my knee, accidentally knocking the scab off a coral cut, one of my last souvenirs of this year's expedition. Environmentalists, especially when they're my age, should know better than to bump into coral; the shiny new scar serves as a reminder that my praxis can still stand improvement.

A dreary marine layer hangs thick overhead. Seas are gray, nothing sparkles. A loon calls as I slip my kayak into the water. Common loon. Its cartoonish voice sounds close by, but I've read somewhere that the loon's call travels farther than most waterbirds', making distance hard to judge. I first heard loons at the age of sixteen, on a canoe trip in Canadian wilderness. Since that time the loon's nervous giggle has been a sound I identify with "other" waters, not home waters.

Common loons, and sometimes even Pacific loons, visit San Francisco Bay in the winter months, especially when the herring spawn, but loons tend to be silent outside of breeding season. In the spring, they seem to vanish moments after they molt into their checkerboard nuptial plumage. They're usually gone by the time I return from Baja, but this one, the one I'm hearing, has waited for me to come home and seems to be calling me to come out and play. I'm hoping it's already in breeding plumage, wearing its checkerboard. That would be worth seeing.

My boat feels light and tippy, and I remember from previous years that it will take a good half hour to reestablish my bond with it. The hip and thigh pads snuggle me so perfectly that it feels more like I'm wearing the kayak than sitting in it, but for the first few minutes everything feels wrong; I've become accustomed to the weight and poor fit of a rental boat. I attempt to focus on the loon, which I'm no longer hearing, and I head for the far side of Richardson Bay.

I paddle past a western grebe, its throat graced by fresh white feathers, and I wonder why it hasn't migrated yet. Already in its summer plumage, the black cap gives it a natty, coifed look, almost jaunty. It will leave us soon, no doubt, and after this weekend the next time I see one of its cousins I will take this to be a sign of winter's approach here in Sausalito.

I paddle slowly, bracing gently when a ferry wake hits me abeam. We seldom have to deal with water misbehaving like this down in Baja; I miss the trustworthy blue of the Sea of Cortez. Although I see a harbor seal in the distance, I'm not seeing any loons.

It feels strange to paddle alone.

The moment I make it to the far side of Richardson Bay, a breeze pipes up, blowing westerly, directly from where I've just come. Have I failed to notice a tailwind all this time? I turn my bow into it instinctively, and I'm surprised that it's already strong enough to bend back the brim of my hat. Wind doesn't normally sneak up on me like this, and I scold myself for having been daydreaming, thinking about waters afar when I should be focusing on conditions around me. There's no guide here to notice things for me.

My kayak doesn't have a name, but you could call it "Warbler" for the sun-faded yellow in need of a good buff. It handles wind chop differently from my Baja boat, *Opsrey*. "Warbler" slices through the steeper chop, happy to allow green water over the bow, since that's what spray skirts are for. *Opsrey*, back in the week-ago past, insisted on hobbyhorsing over every little wave. An expeditionary boat, *Opsrey* was designed to carry a load, and I long ago noticed that it behaves better with extra weight in the bow, which is why I always insist on carrying the library in my boat.

I lean into my stroke, feeling like Superman, while "Warbler," built of lightweight polycarbonate, skips homeward, accelerating into the headwind is if it were merely air. I'm soaked within minutes, pleased that I decided to wear my winter anorak rather than the lighter spray jacket I almost wore. Wet but still dry, I'm finding it invigorating to paddle at my own pace, rather than having to worry about leaving any duckies behind. Each time I punch through another wave, the delight ratchets up another notch on the scale. 5.0, 5.1, 5.2 . . .

As the spray covers my glasses I suddenly realize why I didn't see any loons over on the far side of the bay—they probably knew this wind was coming. Loons hunt visually, paddling with eyes and bills below water; they were probably smart enough to stay on the windward side where they could still hunt because the water didn't have enough fetch to get choppy.

Outsmarted by a loon.

I return to the marina wet and happy, delighted to be home. The latest expedition is over for me now, now that I've figured out once again how to paddle alone. A year from now I'll be back on the island, packing *Opsrey* with field guides, a travel guitar, a black light for the scorpions, dive gear, my one-man tent, and a bag full of candles. I will groan when I take the first few strokes, at which point it will feel like I'm paddling a pickup truck. But my heart will be buoyant: the island still has lessons to teach.

# Bibliography

Aburto-Oropeza, Octavio, et al. "Mangroves in the Gulf of California Increase Fishery Yields." *Proceedings of the National Academy of Sciences of the United States of America* 105, no. 30 (July 2008): 10456–59.

Bayer, Range D. "Social Differences in Defecation Behavior of Great Blue Herons (*Ardea herodias*)." *Auk* 97, no. 4 (October 1980): 900–901.

Beebe, William. *Zaca Venture*. New York: Harcourt, Brace, 1938.

Boyd, Brian, and Robert Michael Pyle, eds. *Nabokov's Butterflies: Unpublished and Uncollected Writings*. Boston: Beacon Press, 2000.

Brower, David. "The Condor and a Sense of Place." In *The Condor Question: Captive or Forever Free?* edited by D. Phillips and H. Nash, 265–78. San Francisco: Friends of the Earth, 1981.

Dillard, Annie. *Pilgrim at Tinker Creek*. New York: Harpers, 1974.

Ducre, Norberto. "Descripción de la California." Translated by Homer Aschmann. In *The Natural and Human History of Baja California*, 25–46. Los Angeles: Dowson's Book Shop, 1966.

Eisen, Gustav A. "Explorations in the Cape Region of Baja California in 1894, with References to Former Expeditions of the California Academy of Sciences." *Proceedings of the California Academy of Sciences,* 2nd ser., 5 (1895–96): 733–55.

Fleischner, Thomas L. "Natural History and the Deep Roots of Resource Management." *Natural Resources Journal* 45, no. 1 (Winter 2005): 1–13.

Fleischner, Thomas L. "Our Deepest Affinity." In *Nature, Love, Medicine: Essays in Wildness and Wellness*, edited by Thomas L. Fleischner, 3–15. Salt Lake City: Torrey House Press, 2017.

Gotshall, Daniel W. *Sea of Cortez Marine Animals: A Guide to the Common Fishes and Invertebrates; Baja California to Panama*. Monterey, CA: Sea Challengers, 1998.

Iovino, Serenella, and Serpil Oppermann, eds. *Material Ecocriticism*. Bloomington: Indiana University Press, 2014.

Jamie, Kathleen. *Findings: Essays on the Natural and Unnatural World*. New York: Sort of Books, 2005.

Janovy, John. *Vermilion Sea: A Naturalist's Journey in Baja California*. Boston: Houghton Mifflin, 1992.

Krutch, Joseph Wood. *The Forgotten Peninsula: A Naturalist in Baja California*. New York: William Sloane Associates, 1961.

Lindsay, George Edmund. "Sea of Cortez Expedition of the California Academy of Sciences, June 20–July 4, 1964." *California Academy of Sciences* 30, no. 11 (1964): 211–42.

Linnaeus, Carl. *Systema Naturae per Regna Tria Naturae, Secundum Classes, Ordines, Genera, Species, cum Characteribus, Differentiis, Synonymis, Locis*. Stockholm: Laurentius Salvius, 1758.

Mace, Michael. *California Condor North American Studbook*. San Diego: San Diego Zoo Global Institute for Wildlife Research, 2014.

McCracken, Gary F., and Mary K. Gustin. "Nursing Behavior in Mexican Free-tailed Bat Maternal Colonies." *Ethology* 89, no. 4 (January 1991): 305–21.

Meloy, Ellen. *Eating Stone: Imagination and the Loss of the Wild*. New York: Pantheon, 2005.

Nabokov, Vladimir. "On Discovering a Butterfly." 1942. In *Nabokov's Butterflies: Unpublished and Uncollected Writings*, edited and annotated by Brian Boyd and Robert Michael Pyle, 273–74. Boston: Beacon Press, 2000.

Nelson, Edward W. "Lower California and Its Natural Resources." *Natural Academy of Sciences First Memoir* 16 (1922).

Nichols, John. "The Holiness of Water." In *Dancing on the Stone: Selected Essays*, 15–23. Albuquerque: University of New Mexico Press, 2000.

North, Arthur Walbridge. *Camp and Camino in Lower California: A Record of the Adventures of the Author while Exploring Peninsular California, Mexico*. New York: Baker & Taylor, 1910.

Percy, Walker. "The Loss of the Creature." In *The Message in the Bottle: How Queer Man Is, How Queer Language Is, and What One Has to Do with the Other*, 46–63. New York: Farrar, Straus and Giroux, 1975.

Romano-Lax, Andromeda. *Searching for Steinbeck's Sea of Cortez: A Makeshift Expedition along Baja's Desert Coast*. Seattle: Sasquatch Books, 2002.

Scott, Kirsty. "In the Nature of Things." *The Guardian*, June 17, 2005, https://www.theguardian.com/books/2005/jun/18/featuresreviews.guardianreview15.

Steinbeck, John. *The Log from the Sea of Cortez: The Narrative Portion of the Book, Sea of Cortez (1941), by John Steinbeck and E. F. Ricketts*. New York: Viking Press, 1951.

Steinbeck, John, and E. F. Ricketts. *Sea of Cortez: A Leisurely Journal of Travel and Research*. New York: Viking Press, 1941.

Swift, Jonathan. *Gulliver's Travels into Several Remote Regions of the World*. 1726. Reprint, Boston: D. C. Heath, 1900.

Thoreau, Henry David. *Letters to a Spiritual Seeker*. Edited by Bradley P. Dean. New York: Norton, 2006.

Townsend, Charles Haskins. "Voyage of the 'Albatross' to the Gulf of California in 1911." *Bulletin of the American Museum of Natural History* 35 (1916): 399–476.

Wallace, Michael P., M. Clark, J. Vargas, and M. C. Porras. "Release of Puppet-Reared California Condors in Baja California: An Evaluation of a Modified Rearing Technique." In *California Condors in the 21st Century*, edited by A. Mee and L. S. Hall, 227–42. Cambridge, MA: Nuttall Ornithological Club; Washington, DC: American Ornithologists' Union, 2007.

White, Gilbert. *The Natural History and Antiquities of Selborne.* 1789. Reprint, London: White, Cochrane, 1813.

Williams, Terry Tempest. *Refuge: An Unnatural History of Family and Place.* New York: Pantheon, 1991.

Wilson, Edward O. *Naturalist.* Washington, DC: Island Press, 1994.

Zwinger, Ann. *A Desert Country near the Sea: A Natural History of the Cape Region of Baja California.* New York: Harper and Row, 1983.